100 BEST CAREERS

IN

ENTERTAINMENT

Shelly Field

MACMILLAN • USA

This book is dedicated to my parents,
Ed and Selma,
and my sisters, Jessica and Debbie,
who showed me that with love, support, and encouragement
anything and everything is possible.

First Edition

Macmillan General Reference
A Prentice Hall Macmillan Company
15 Columbus Circle
New York, NY 10023

An Arco Book

MACMILLAN is a registered trademark of Macmillan, Inc.
ARCO is a registered trademark of Prentice-Hall, Inc.

Library of Congress Cataloging-in-Publication Data
Field, Shelly
   100 best careers in entertainment / Shelly Field.—1st ed.
      p.   cm.
   At head of title: ARCO.
   "An Arco book."
   ISBN 0-02-860017-7
   1. Performing arts—Vocational guidance. 2. Broadcasting—
   Vocational guidance. [1. Performing arts—Vocational guidance.
   2. Vocational guidance.] I. Title.   II. Title: One hundred best
   careers in entertainment.   III. Title: ARCO 100 best careers in
   entertainment.
PN1580.F59   1995
792'.02'9373—dc20   94-36715
                                                                  CIP
                                                                   AC

Manufactured in the United States of America

10 9 8 7 6 5 4 3 2 1

CONTENTS

· · · · · · · · · · · ·

CHAPTER 3: CAREERS IN RADIO

CHAPTER 4: CAREERS IN TELEVISION, FILM, AND VIDEO

PREFACE

· · · · · · · · · · ·

This is a comprehensive guide to 100 of the best careers in the entertainment industry. It is a valuable resource for those planning careers, those just entering the job market, and those hoping to change careers.

Thousands of people aspire to work in the entertainment industry but have no idea how to get in. They dream of the glamor and excitement, but have no concept of what the job opportunities are, where to find them, the training that is required, or the skills and talents that are needed. *100 Best Careers in Entertainment* is the single essential source for learning about job opportunities in this field and for tips on breaking in.

This book was written to help anyone prepare for an interesting, exciting, glamorous, and/or well-paying career in the entertainment industry. The 100 careers discussed in this book encompass a multitude of interests and fields.

The entertainment industry offers vast opportunities for a wide range of people with a variety of skills. Many of the skills are transferable from other industries and professions. For example, an electrician who understands the intricacies of circuitry can often transfer skills to a theater stage or to a television or movie studio. The fund-raising and development director of a health-care agency may transfer skills to a similar job in an opera, orchestra, or ballet company. A publicist promoting a company or product may transfer his or her talents to promoting an entertainer or entertainment event.

There are many opportunities in the field of entertainment. People with a variety of skills and talents both on the front line and behind the scenes are required. You do not have to be Neil Simon to enjoy a career in theater; Whitney Houston to have a satisfying career in music; Mikhail Baryshnikov to become a dancer; or David Letterman to work in television. The key to finding a job in the part of the industry you are interested in is to determine your skills and talents and develop them. Once you have grabbed the first rung, you can climb the career ladder to success.

Information Sources

Information for this book was obtained through interviews, questionnaires, and a wide variety of books, magazines, newsletters, television and radio programs, and other sources. Some information came from personal experience working in the industry. Other data were obtained from various facets of the performing arts and entertainment industries.

Among the people interviewed were men and women working in all aspects of the entertainment field, including music, theater, television, film, video, radio, and dance. Individuals in the business, administrative, and support end of the business as well as those in the spotlight were interviewed. Employment agencies were contacted, as well as schools, personnel offices, placement offices, union/trade associations, ballets, orchestras, theater groups, operas, record company executives, radio and television personnel, personal managers, booking agents, musicians, singers, actors, actresses, casting directors, dancers, publicists, theater, club, and venue owners and employees, producers, and directors—to name a few.

100 Best Careers in Entertainment is divided into 10 general sections: Careers in the Business End of the Industry; Careers in Performing and Writing; Careers in Radio; Careers in Television, Film, and Video; Careers in Recording and the Record Business; Careers in Halls, Arenas, Clubs, and Other Venues; Careers in Theater; Careers in Orchestras, Opera, and Ballet; Careers on the Road; and Miscellaneous Careers in the Entertainment Industry. Within each section are descriptions of a wealth of individual jobs.

There are two parts to each job classification. The first part offers job facts in an overview chart; the second presents descriptive information in a narrative text.

The text details the job description and responsibilities; employment opportunities; earnings; advancement opportunities; education and training; experience and qualifications; organizations that offer additional information; and tips for obtaining the specific job.

Names, addresses, and phone numbers of trade associations, organizations, and unions are listed in the appendices to provide resources for further information. Names and addresses of industry trade publications, as well as television and cable stations, are also included.

By reading this book, you are taking the first step towards finding a career in the entertainment industry and preparing for it. Whether you choose a career in performing or one behind the scenes, your job can be exciting, rewarding, and satisfying. A career in entertainment is waiting for you—you just have to go after it!

Shelly Field

ACKNOWLEDGMENTS

· ·

I thank every individual, company, agency, association, organization, and union who provided information, assistance, and encouragement for this book.

First and foremost, I acknowledge with appreciation my editor, Linda Bernbach, for providing the original impetus for this book and support and guidance throughout its creation, development, and writing. I gratefully acknowledge the assistance of Ed and Selma Field for their ongoing support in this project.

Others whose help was invaluable include Academy of Country Music; Actors' Equity Association; Alliance of Resident Theaters of New York; American Federation of Musicans; American Guild of Musical Artists; American Guild of Variety Artists; American Society of Composers and Publishers; American Society of Music Copyists; American Symphony Orchestra League; Arista Records; Barbara Ashworth, Beauty School Of Middletown; Association of Theatrical Press Agents and Managers; John Balme, Director, Lake George Opera Festival; Allan Barrish; Jan Behr, associate business agent, Local 162 IATSE; Eugene Blabey, WVOS Radio; Fredda Briant, Business Representative, Theatrical Wardrobe Union; Broadcast Music, Inc.; Mary Cawley; Lilyan Chauvin, president, Organization of Professional Acting Coaches and Teachers; Sandra Clark, Karen Cobham, Broadway Unit Coordinator of Makeup Artists and Hairstylists; Janice Cohen; Dr. Jessica L. Cohen; Lorraine Cohen; Norman Cohen; Kathleen Conry, Director/Actress; Jan Cornelius: Crawford Memorial Library Staff; Meike Cryan; Daniel Dayton; W. Lynne Dayton; The Dramatists Guild; Scott Edwards; Ernest Evans; Sara Feldberg; Field Associates, Ltd.; Deborah K. Field, Esq.; Finkelstein Memorial Library Staff; Forestburg Playhouse; John Gatto; Sheila Gatto; Margo George, Model Management; Gina Giambattista, Administrator, University/Resident Theatre Association, Inc.; Sally Gifft, Assistant Business Representative, United Scenic Artists; Tina Gilbert; George Glantzis; Kaytee Glantzis; Sam Goldych, Monticello Central Schools High School Librarian; Gail Haberle; Herman Memorial Library Staff; Paul Holmes, stage manager; Hudson Valley Philharmonic; International Alliance of Theatrical Stage Employees; International Association of Auditorium Managers; International Brotherhood of Electrical Workers; Jimmy "Handyman" Jones; K-LITE Radio; Dr. John C. Koch, Sullivan Country Performing Arts Council; John Lawler; League Of Resident Theaters; Ann J. Ledley, Business Representative, Actors' Equity Association; Bob Leone; Liberty Central School; Liberty Public Library Staff; Terry Lowe; Ginger Maher; Len Mandile; Ernie Martinelli; Robert Masters, Esq.; Judy McCoy; Phillip Mestman; Rima Mestman; Metropolitan Opera; Beverly Michaels, Esq.; Martin Michaels, Esq.;

Jason Milligan; Monticello Central High School Guidance Department; Monticello Central School High School Library Staff; Monticello Central School Middle School Library Staff; Sharon Morris; Music Business Institute; Music Educators Conference; Florence Naistadt; National Association of Broadcast Employees and Technicians; National Association of Broadcasters; National Association of Music Merchants; National Association of Schools of Dance; National Association of Schools of Music; National Association of Schools of Theatre; National Dance Association; National Music Publishers Association; Chris Nelson; Earl Nesmith; New Dramatists; Jim Newton; New York State Employment Service; Organization of Professional Acting Coaches and Teachers; Karen Pizzuto, Communications Director, IATSE; Debra Pless; Rob Pless; Anita Portas, IATSE; Public Relations Society Of America; Harvey Rachlin; Ramapo Catskill Library System; Doug Richards; John Riegler; Gary Roth, BMI; Jim Ryan, business representative, United Scenic Artists; Craig Sandquist, Producer, Forestburg Playhouse; Richard Schaefer, lighting designer; Nelson Sheeley, freelance director; Jeffrey Sherwin, Esq.; Smith Employment Agency; Society of Stage Directors and Choreographers; Laura Solomon; The Songwriters Guild; Debbie Springfield; Fred Steinman; Matthew E. Strong; Sullivan County Community College; Sullivan County Performing Arts Council; The Teenagers; Thrall Library Staff; Marie Tremper; Leo S. Ullman, Esq.; United Scenic Artists; United States Department of Labor; University Resident Theatre Association; Brenda Walker; Lisa Weiss, dancer; Dr. Diana Worby; Rachael Worby; Johnny World; WTZA-Television; WSUL Radio; WVOS Radio; and George Wurzbach.

In addition, because there is such a great mystique surrounding the entertainment business, much of the material was provided by sources who wish to remain anonymous. My thanks to them all the same.

INTRODUCTION
· · · · · · · · · · · · · · · ·

The entertainment industry is a multibillion-dollar business. There are thousands of people working in the industry and there is room for thousands more. One of them could be you.

Careers in entertainment fall into two distinct fields: the performers and the people who provide back-up, encouragement, and support for them.

The tremendous audiovisual advances that expose entertainers to growing numbers of people worldwide create an increasing demand for entertainment of all types. There are exciting opportunities for new personalities in the fields of film, radio, video, television, music, and the stage.

Nearly every house and every vehicle has the capability of receiving the images, sounds, and/or voices of entertainers. Satellites in the sky permit sounds and visuals to travel instantly from one end of the United States to the other, as well as from one country to another. This incredible communications network requires a tremendous number of support personnel of every conceivable kind. Trained technicians with a variety of skills will be increasingly demanded by the world of entertainment.

The entertainment industry, probably more than any other, depends heavily on support people. These individuals have a tremendous impact even though they are not generally in the spotlight or on center stage.

Most prominent to the public are the entertainers, singers, dancers, actors, musicians, and others whose live or recorded performances delight the public. However, whether you choose to work in the spotlight or in the background, your job can be a satisfying and rewarding career experience and can help many thousands enjoy the pleasures of entertainment.

Within each section of this book you will find information to acquaint you with job possibilities in the entertainment industry. Each entry is organized as follows:

1. Job Description and Responsibilities

Every effort has been made to give well-rounded job descriptions. As no two companies are identically structured, no two jobs will be precisely the same.

Keep in mind also that job titles for specific work may vary from company to company throughout the industry. The duties and responsibilities of these jobs are the same; only the names are different.

2. Employment Opportunities

This section discusses various employment opportunities and/or settings for jobs in each area.

3. Earnings

Salary ranges for the job titles in the book are as accurate as possible. Earnings for a job depend on the size, location, and prestige of a company, as well as the experience, education, training, and responsibilities of the individual. In many instances, especially with entertainers, earnings depend to a great extent on the popularity of and demand for the individual.

4. Advancement Opportunities

A variety of options for career advancement have been included. However, there are no hard and fast rules for climbing to the top of your career in the entertainment industry. While work performance is important, advancement is based on experience, education, and attitude. Advancement in this industry is also based on popularity, being in the right place at the right time, and drive and determination.

5. Education and Training

Because the best qualified people are the most likely to be hired, this section presents recommended educational and training requirements for each job area. These requirements may include attendance at technical and vocational schools, conservatories, colleges and universities or on-the-job training, apprenticeships, private study, etc.

6. Experience and Qualifications

This section discusses helpful or required experience, qualifications, and skills.

7. For Additional Information

This section lists trade associations, organizations, and unions that offer career assistance, advice, or information. Many also provide scholarships, fellowships, seminars, and other beneficial programs. Addresses and phone numbers are located in the last section of the book in the Appendix.

8. Tips

This section contains ideas on how to get a job, gain entry into the areas you are interested in, prepare yourself, or become more successful in a current position.

This book will help you prepare for a career you will enjoy and find rewarding for years to come. Don't get discouraged. Keep knocking on doors, sending out resumes, and applying for jobs until you get the job you want. Then use your drive and determination to become the best you can be.

Persevere. The people who don't make it in the entertainment industry are the ones who gave up too quickly. If they had waited one more day, they might have attained the career they worked so hard for. Don't give up and you too can have the glitter, glamor, and gold you have been dreaming of. Good luck!

CHAPTER 1

. . . .

Careers in the Business End
of the Industry

While entertainers generally thrive on performing, many do not have the time, patience, inclination, and/or training to accomplish the myriad of business and backup details needed to assure overall success.

In most instances entertainers depend on a range of management people trained and skilled in various aspects of business to handle their affairs. Individuals working in the business end of the industry may be salaried, earn a fee or percentage off the top, or have various other compensation arrangements.

Some of the people that successful entertainers may have surrounding them to handle their business details include personal managers, business managers, professional managers, press agents/publicists, promoters, booking agents, tour coordinators, tour managers, road managers, attorneys, fan club directors, and more.

Space restrictions limit discussing all possible opportunities. Jobs covered in this section are:

Personal Manager	Booking Agent
Concert Promoter	Press Agent/Publicist
Business Manager	

Individuals interested in business careers in entertainment should also review entries in other sections of this book, including "Careers in Recording and the Record Business"; "Careers in Halls, Arenas, Clubs, and other Venues"; "Careers in Theater"; "Careers in Orchestras, Opera, and Ballet"; and "Careers on the Road." All have related opportunities.

1

PERSONAL MANAGER

Job Description: Represent performer; oversee and guide every aspect of performer's career.

Earnings: Impossible to determine due to nature of the job; 10 percent–50 percent of client's earnings.

Recommended Education and Training: No educational requirement; a college background is useful; courses, seminars, and workshops in business and entertainment industry will be helpful.

Skills and Personality Traits: Aggressiveness; strong communications skills; ability to negotiate; ability to appreciate raw talent; ability to work under pressure.

Experience and Qualifications: Experience in any facet of the entertainment business is valuable.

Job Description and Responsibilities

There are many talented people in this world. Often the difference between success and failure in an entertainer's life is the individual's personal manager. A personal manager represents talent in the entertainment industry by overseeing all aspects of a client's career. He or she is responsible for advising clients on all business and creative decisions in an attempt to help artists rise to the top of their field.

Personal managers are also responsible for locating the best support personnel to surround their artists. These people may include booking agents, business managers, accountants, attorneys, press agents, promoters, record companies, and coaches, among others.

A personal manager may represent one or more clients in any phase of the entertainment industry. After a personal manager and an artist discuss and agree on the terms that will be offered to both parties, a personal management contract will be signed. It will specify the responsibilities of each. Usually the contract signed between the manager and client runs for a specified number of years with an option clause that can be picked up by one of the parties.

In some cases, a manager may put up money to finance a client whom he or she believes in strongly. In other instances the individual might find a financial backer to finance the client's career until it gets off the ground.

Depending on the type of client involved, managers may search out television or film roles, engagements, recording contracts, etc. They will also be responsible for negotiating deals and contracts for their clients.

Long hours are spent dealing with the client as well as with others on the client's behalf. The two parties will also meet on a regular basis to discuss problems and to develop methods of advancing the client's career, public image, and new projects.

Personal managers are directly responsible to their clients. Sometimes the client will heed the advice of the manager and at other times he or she will not. A career as a personal manager can be very fulfilling and rewarding, especially when a manager takes raw talent and builds a client's career into success and stardom.

Employment Opportunities

Almost anyone can become a personal manager by locating talent, signing a contract, and guiding a client's career. Fortunately for these individuals there are thousands of people who want to be entertainers and are looking for someone to oversee their career. While not everyone can be a successful manager, individuals who can spot raw talent and then develop a plan to promote it will thrive. Managers may work with clients in any facet of the entertainment business, including:

- Singers
- Musicians
- Recording groups
- Magicians
- Sports figures
- Movie and television stars
- Actors/Actresses
- Speakers
- Comedians
- Models
- Radio personalities

Earnings

It is impossible to determine the potential earnings for personal managers due to the nature of the job. Factors affecting income include the number of clients on the manager's roster as well as the prestige and success of each client.

Personal managers receive their fee in the form of a percentage off the top of their client's earnings. This percentage varies with each client and manager and is negotiated before a contract is signed. The percentage can range from 10 percent to 50 percent with an average rate of 15 percent to 20 percent.

Managers representing a client or clients who are successful will usually enjoy financial success as well. Managers working with top movie or television stars, sports personalities, or recording groups can earn $1 million or more annually.

Advancement Opportunities

There are a number of ways to advance as a personal manager. One method is to locate and sign a client or clients who have already achieved stardom. In order to do this, however, the manager must have already established a proven track record.

Another way is for the manager to start with a relatively unknown client and guide his/her career to a higher level of success and/or stardom.

Education and Training

While there is no educational requirement to become a personal manager, a college background is useful. Majors and/or courses that will be helpful include journalism, business, law, communications, marketing, and public relations. There are also courses and majors available in colleges throughout the country in music merchandising, performing arts management, and the music and sports businesses that can be of value.

Seminars and workshops offered through trade associations and unions are also available.

Experience and Qualifications

No matter what field personal managers represent, they should have a broad knowledge of all aspects of the entertainment industry. Personal managers who start at the local level often learn as they go. Others obtain experience through internships or apprenticeships.

Contacts within the industry are vital. If individuals do not have these contacts, they must have the ability to cultivate them. Personal managers should be positive, aggressive, and creative individuals with an ability to negotiate. The ability to recognize and develop raw talent is essential to success in this field.

For Additional Information: The Conference of Personal Managers (CPM) is an organization that sets the standards for conduct in this field. Other associations and organizations that may provide additional information include the American Federation of Musicians (AFM) and Actors' Equity.

TIPS

- Try to find an apprenticeship or internship with a personal manager, management company, booking agency, television or radio station, theater group, etc. This will be helpful in learning the ropes and making contacts.
- Consider working in a management company as a secretary, administrative assistant, or similar position to learn as much as you can about the industry.
- A lot of talented new artists place advertisements in the trades or in the classified sections of newspapers seeking management. While some artists are seeking financial backing, others may be looking for someone to help guide their careers.
- Attend talent shows, showcases, and other venues that might have new performers looking for guidance.

- Locate books and articles on entertainers and sports figures who have attained stardom and success. The more you learn about their struggles, the more you will know how to plan other people's career paths.
- It is often easier to break into the management end of the entertainment business if you do so on a local level. There are thousands of singers, dancers, musicians, comics, etc., who need guidance and support from someone capable and willing to help them.

CONCERT PROMOTER

Job Description: Produce individual concerts and/or entire tours; provide or raise funds financing and promoting a production.

Earnings: Impossible to determine due to nature of the job.

Recommended Education and Training: No formal education or training required; seminars and workshops on all facets of music business, publicity, and promotion useful.

Skills and Personality Traits: Communications skills; business skills; aggressiveness; self-motivation; enthusiasm.

Experience and Qualifications: Knowledge and background in music business; ability to take financial risk; experience working with a promoter helpful.

Job Description and Responsibilities

Concert promoters present talent in various venues. It is the first job of a concert promoter to provide or raise the funds necessary for financing the production. If the promoter does not have sufficient money to properly produce a show, partners and/or investors may be brought in to help back the project, sharing expenses and potential profits.

Promoters are ultimately responsible for the total production of an individual concert or an entire tour. Among the myriad areas of responsibility are selecting, negotiating, and contracting for performers including stars, back-up artists, musicians, etc.; selecting the geographic location(s), and specific venue(s) for the performances; scheduling the number of performances and show times; establishing a budget; and advertising and publicizing the shows in order to sell tickets.

Promoters may handle all of these tasks on their own or may retain outside consultants such as publicists, public relations firms, and ticket selling agents. Individuals may also work in conjunction with the performer's record company, agent, publicist, and manager in order to develop public attention before the concert and maximize the income potential of the event.

In many instances, promoters have publicists arrange press conferences so that the media will know about a concert or tour and tout it to their readers, viewers, and/or listeners. In other cases, press kits, news releases, photographs, CDs, and free tickets will be provided to the media prior to the concert to gain their attention.

The promoter must make sure that all contractual obligations are fulfilled. Most acts, for example, must be paid a percentage of the monies owed to them immediately upon signing a contract. The balance must usually be paid at the performance. Many performers also have contract riders that stipulate "extras" that the promoter must provide. These can include anything from soft drinks in the dressing room to fully catered meals, limo transportation to and from concerts, or first-class travel and accommodations.

The promoter is responsible for hiring support personnel when necessary, including people to unload and move equipment, security guards, lighting and sound technicians, ushers, stage managers, and others. The promoter must also be sure that all union requirements are adhered to.

Promoting is a very intriguing business. While there are a great number of people who were not successful in this profession, others have made great fortunes.

Employment Opportunities

Although technically, almost anyone in a position to take a financial risk can become a promoter, in reality, it is a difficult field to break into with superstar acts. Many agents and managers of top groups and single artists are afraid to work with a new promoter. Certain arenas and stadiums are also under contractual agreement with promoters who have already proven themselves.

There are, however, many new acts and/or smaller venues that are willing to take a chance with a new promoter. This is probably the best way to enter the field. Options for breaking into this field include:

- Small halls
- Clubs
- Colleges/Universities
- Local venues
- New and up-and-coming acts
- Promotion companies

Earnings

Promotion is a risky business. Individuals may make money, lose money, or break even. Profits are earned through ticket sales and, in some cases, through the merchandising of promotional items such as T-shirts, CDs, cassettes, and posters. In order to make a profit, of course, the promoter must bring in more revenue than what was spent. The potential range of earnings is tremendous. Top promoters who are successful in the music industry earn $1 million or more annually.

Advancement Opportunities

There are a number of methods of advancement for concert promoters. Individuals can promote the shows of more prestigious acts or promote more prestigious venues. Promoters can also advance their careers by signing a promotion contract with a new up-and-coming act that hits it big.

Education and Training

While there is no formal educational requirement needed to become a promoter, a business background is usually beneficial. Those interested in pursuing a college education might consider a school with a major in business or communications. Degrees in the music business or in music merchandising are also now offered in a number of schools. These are especially useful because of opportunities to make contacts and to network.

Seminars and workshops in promotion, publicity, and all facets of the music business are also helpful.

Experience and Qualifications

Experience working with another promoter would be ideal. However, barring that, a knowledge of and background in various facets of the music industry are required. No promotion is a guaranteed success. Therefore promoters should be in a position to take a financial risk. The more contacts in the industry that promoters have, the better off they will usually be.

Successful promoters are typically enthusiastic, creative individuals with a great deal of stamina.

For Additional Information: Additional information may be provided by the Country Music Association (CMA), the Gospel Music Association (GMA), and The National Academy of Recording Arts and Sciences (NARAS).

TIPS

- One of the best ways to break into promotion is to become an assistant to an established promoter. If there is no position open as an assistant, take any opening available. Work hard, keep your eyes and ears open, and learn as you go.
- Get experience by volunteering to promote an event for a not-for-profit organization, school, church, or community group. They put the money up for the show and you handle the promotion.
- Colleges normally have student committees that work on booking and promoting concerts and other activities. Get on that committee and learn the ropes.

• Search out an apprenticeship or internship with a promotion company. Once a promotion company has trained you, it is likely to hire you.
• Consider beginning your career with a show that requires only a small outlay of cash. You won't make a lot of money, but you won't lose a lot either and you'll gain needed experience.

BUSINESS MANAGER

Job Description: Manage financial and business affairs of entertainers; seek out and secure endorsements and sponsorships.

Earnings: $15,000–$500,000+

Recommended Education and Training: Minimum of bachelor's degree in business administration or accounting; MBA may be preferred.

Skills and Personality Traits: Accounting skills; aggressiveness; negotiation skills; communications skills; business sense.

Experience and Qualifications: Experience as accountant, stockbroker, financial advisor, or assistant to business manager helpful; comprehensive knowledge of tax laws and investments; contacts or dealings in entertainment industry.

Job Description and Responsibilities

Business managers working in the entertainment world handle the financial affairs of entertainers. They may also advise people in other fields outside of the entertainment industry. In some cases, the business manager may be retained to handle the business affairs of an entire act instead of an individual entertainer. Responsibilities and duties can vary greatly depending on the specific client.

The main functions of the business manager are to oversee the finances of an entertainer and optimize the individual's earning power. In this capacity, the business manager may perform a number of duties.

Business managers often act as financial advisors, counseling their clients on good investments, tax issues, and legal matters. He or she is expected to summarize a client's investments, properties, business dealings, and financial status and to provide financial statements to the client.

Business managers are responsible for keeping abreast of the financial arrangements between the entertainer and the companies with which he or she does business. These include record and merchandising companies, book publishers, ticket agencies, and more. Managers may also request audits of these companies, as well as hire CPAs to handle the fiscal research. Business managers must be available to their clients or their clients' representatives to discuss financial status, investments, and any problems that may arise.

Other functions of business managers include keeping track of all bills incurred by the entertainer, checking them for accuracy, and issuing payment. These may include personal as well as business-related bills. The manager may be expected to ensure that the entertainer is paid on time and as otherwise contracted. It is the responsibility of the business manager to find ways to save the entertainer money, as well as to find programs and processes that can make money.

The individual may be responsible for setting up a payroll system and paying personnel employed by the entertainer, including opening acts, musicians, vocalists, road crews, and secretaries. Similarly, the business manager will make sure that consultants, such as public relations firms, press agents, attorneys, accountants, etc., are properly paid.

The business manager may negotiate on behalf of the entertainer with agents, record companies, motion picture studios, television producers, concert halls, merchandising firms, publishing companies, and the like. Business managers are directly responsible to their client.

Endorsements can be extremely lucrative to an entertainer. In many cases, business managers in the entertainment industry are expected to seek out and negotiate these endorsement and/or sponsorship possibilities.

Employment Opportunities

Business managers, handling all aspects of the entertainment industry as well as other fields, can service one or more clients. Individuals aspiring to become business managers in the entertainment industry will have an easier time entering the field if they live in areas where there are a great number of entertainers. Depending on the specific area of entertainment the business manager is seeking clients in, good geographic possibilities include:

- New York, NY
- Los Angeles, CA
- Beverly Hills, CA
- Hollywood, CA
- Nashville, TN
- Branson, MO
- Las Vegas, NV

Earnings

The annual income of business managers varies greatly from person to person. An individual may earn only $15,000 a year or may make $500,000 or more.

Variables include the skills, expertise, aggressiveness, levels of responsibility, and reputation of the business manager. Other factors include the method used to charge fees and the prestige and earnings of the client. Since business managers usually handle more than one client, the number of clients represented is also an important factor in earning potential.

Business managers charge clients a fee. Individuals may charge the client a flat fee on a retainer basis, an hourly fee, or a percentage of a client's total gross income. The most common charging method used in the entertainment industry is a portion of the client's income with percentages ranging from 3 percent to 10 percent.

Advancement Opportunities

Advancement for business managers in the entertainment industry is indicated by a larger and/or more prestigious client list. As individuals' earnings are usually dependent on a percentage of a client's gross income, the more money a client makes, the more the business manager can earn.

Education and Training

While there is no formal educational requirement to become a business manager, a minimum of a four-year degree is recommended with majors in accounting, finance, or business administration. A graduate degree in one of these fields will be helpful in honing skills.

Continuing education in the form of seminars, workshops, and classes in tax laws, tax shelters, investments, etc., will be useful. Seminars in all aspects of the entertainment industry will also help a business manager to be cognizant of the specific business needs of entertainers, as well as assist in building a contact network.

Experience and Qualifications

Experience requirements vary in this line of work. As in other aspects of the entertainment industry, there is no single clear-cut way to enter this field.

Some business managers started out as accountants, stockbrokers, or financial advisors. Others worked as business managers with clients in fields that were not entertainment-oriented. Some individuals were involved in the business end of the entertainment industry in some other capacity.

All successful business managers with clients in the entertainment world possess an innate business sense, excellent negotiation skills, and contacts in the entertainment business. The ability to seek out and secure endorsements for clients is a qualification that will make one business manager stand out from others in the field.

Individuals must have a thorough knowledge of all types of investments and a comprehensive understanding of tax laws.

For Additional Information: There are no organizations dealing specifically with business managers in the entertainment industry. However, there are trade associations and organizations that can provide additional general information to those interested in the financial field. These include the National Society of Public Accountants (NSPA), the National Association of Accountants (NAA), and the American Institute of Certified Public Accountants (AICPA).

TIPS

- Contacts are extremely important in obtaining clients. Network with people in the entertainment field. Join entertainment-oriented trade associations and organizations. Tell others in the industry what you do.
- Word-of-mouth advertising is always effective. The word of one happy client will put the business manager on the road to success.
- Break into the entertainment industry by starting with lesser-known acts. This will provide you with a chance to prove yourself while they are proving themselves.
- Consider advertising in the trades.
- Seek out a position with a business manager as an administrative assistant.
- Become as qualified as possible. Take seminars on business management, tax shelters, investments, etc. These seminars do not have to be specific to the entertainment industry. However, you might also look for seminars, classes, and workshops in a variety of aspects of the entertainment business. These will be helpful in cultivating contacts and learning about all facets of the entertainment industry.

BOOKING AGENT

Job Description: Secure work for entertainers and performing artists; negotiate contracts; sign new talent.

Earnings: $15,000–$1 million-plus

Recommended Education and Training: College background or degree helpful.

Skills and Personality Traits: Sales skills; marketing skills; persuasiveness; organization skills; negotiation skills; aggressiveness.

Experience and Qualifications: Experience working in some facet of entertainment or the performing arts.

Job Description and Responsibilities

Booking agents are the individuals who assist entertainers and performing artists in finding jobs. These agents may represent a variety of different types of entertainers, or may specialize in a particular type of performer. For example, some agents solely represent classical musicians, singers, and dancers. Others may represent recording groups, dance troupes, comedians, singers, and speakers. Booking agents usually represent more than one client. Clients can be represented exclusively or nonexclusively.

Agents working in an agency are assigned clients. These individuals are responsible for obtaining engagements or jobs for their clients. This may be accomplished by seeking locations for the entertainer to be booked. Agents may routinely mail literature and photographs about agency clients to promoters, clubs, halls, theaters, and other venues.

In some situations, promoters and venue owners may seek out the booking agent to engage certain performers and entertainers. This occurs a great deal when the agent represents well-known and popular clients.

Agents spend a good part of their day talking on the phone to venue managers, owners, talent buyers, and promoters as well as with their clients or their management. Topics of phone conversations include looking for possible venues, securing engagements, and negotiating contracts.

It is the responsibility of agents to negotiate fees for their client's performances, engagements, and in some cases, commercial endorsements. Sometimes agents negotiate for lesser fees because an appearance may provide special exposure. In other situations, the client may have another appearance scheduled in the area. Agents may also negotiate for accommodations, transportation, instrumental augmentation, or other expenses.

Agents are expected to prepare and send copies of contracts to the promoter or talent buyer. These contracts must include all pertinent information including the date, location, and negotiated price. Negotiated extras such as transportation, food, accommodations, etc., will be listed in the rider to the contract.

Artists will be paid a percentage of their fee when the contract is signed. Agents are responsible for collecting money due from the promoter or talent buyer, taking the agency fee, and paying the act.

Another responsibility of booking agents may be to locate and sign new talent. Agents often attend showcases, concerts, recitals, and other performances to investigate new acts. They may also review audio- and videotapes of potential clients seeking representation.

Employment Opportunities

Booking agents can be self-employed or may work for a booking agency. Individuals may work for theatrical agencies that primarily handle actors and actresses, or for general talent agencies that handle a multitude of different clients in the performing arts.

While small cities may host one or more agencies, the greatest number of opportunities are located in large, culturally active cities. The major booking agencies can be found in:

- Los Angeles
- New York

Earnings

Booking agents' compensation is determined in a number of ways. Generally, individuals are paid on a commission basis, earning a percentage off the top of the fee that an entertainer is paid for performances. Commissions can range from 10 percent to 25 percent of a client's gross earnings. Depending on the type of contract that has been negotiated, agents may receive a commission on personal appearances and engagements as well as from recordings, commercial endorsements, books, etc.

Individuals working for an agency may receive a salary plus a percentage of the money that they generate. Earnings are dependent on the number of clients an agent handles as well as the client's popularity, fees, demand, and prestige. Other factors include the experience and levels of responsibility of the agent.

Individuals just beginning their careers or those working with lesser-known clients may only earn $15,000 to $25,000 annually. Those working with well-known clients and superstars can earn between $150,000 and $1 million-plus each year.

Advancement Opportunities

There are a number of methods of advancement for booking agents. Individuals may be assigned more prestigious clients by the agency they are working with or may find a similar position in a larger and more active agency. Some agents start booking up-and-coming clients who zoom to the top. This results in increased earnings. Other ways aggressive agents climb the career ladder are by building a roster of popular clients and by striking out on their own and beginning their own booking agency.

Education and Training

Educational requirements vary from agency to agency. Some may only expect their agents to hold a high school diploma. Other agencies prefer or require their agents to have a college background or diploma. Courses and seminars in all facets of entertainment, performing arts, contracts, contract law, business, and selling will be advantageous.

Experience and Qualifications

Experience working in the entertainment industry and performing arts is helpful. Any experience booking talent would also be beneficial. This may be acquired in a number of ways, including working on college activities committees, with arts councils, or as an intern, as well as booking local talent into clubs.

To be successful, booking agents should be aggressive, persuasive individuals with excellent sales and marketing skills. Strong negotiating skills are imperative. Agents should have good communications skills and an excellent phone manner. An understanding of the fundamentals of contracts is a great asset.

For Additional Information: Individuals interested in learning more about careers as booking agents can obtain additional information by contacting the American Federation of Musicians (AFM), the Screen Actors Guild (SAG), the American Guild of Musical Artists (AGMA), Actors' Equity, and the American Federation of Television and Radio Artists (AFTRA).

TIPS

- Internships are an excellent method of learning the skills and techniques necessary to becoming a booking agent. They are also a good way to get your foot in the door and make contacts.
- Many larger booking agencies have training programs designed to teach young, aggressive newcomers the trade. Send these agencies your resume with a short cover letter inquiring about opportunities.
- Agencies often promote from within. Look for positions as administrative assistants, secretaries, receptionists, or even mail room clerks to get your foot in the door.
- Offer to work with your local arts council booking talent for their events.
- Consider booking talent on a small scale for local clubs and acts.

PRESS AGENT/PUBLICIST
· ·

Job Description: Develop and implement publicity campaigns to help entertainers, musicians, and other performing artists get their names and projects better known.

Earnings: $15,000–$150,000+

Recommended Education and Training: Bachelor's degree in communications, public relations, journalism, marketing, English, advertising, liberal arts, or related subjects.

Skills and Personality Traits: Verbal and written communications skills; persuasiveness; creativity; aggressiveness.

Experience and Qualifications: Experience working in publicity, public relations, journalism, etc., is helpful.

Job Description and Responsibilities

The main function of press agents or publicists working in the entertainment industry is to help make the public and the media more aware of the name and/or project of an entertainer or entertainment event. This effort is accomplished by developing and implementing a publicity campaign designed to grab the attention of the media and public.

Press agents work with all types of entertainers and entertainment events. These include performing artists, movie stars, actors, actresses, television stars, disc jockeys, radio commentators, models, comedians, singers, musicians, magicians, sports figures, theatrical productions and reviews, television shows, sports events, concerts, and so forth.

Each entertainer/event wants to be put in the spotlight. Press agents must be creative in developing campaigns that place their clients and projects in the public eye. Publicists achieve exposure for their clients in a number of ways. Methods of exposure depend largely upon the degree of fame a client already has.

Clients who are already well-known will often be sought after by interviewers, editors, journalists, talent coordinators, reporters, etc. Press agents in these situations must be selective in determining the opportunities that will be most effective in obtaining the type of exposure the client requires.

Press agents working with lesser-known clients must explore methods to get the media interested. Often, they write press releases for the media. In order to grab the media's attention, press agents must develop a "hook" that draws attention to their release over the others. Press agents are expected to develop, prepare, and distribute press or media kits for editors, journalists, television and radio producers, talent coordinators, and others. Press kits may contain photographs, biographies, reviews, feature stories, articles, press releases, audio- and/or video-tapes, etc., featuring the client and their project(s).

Another method of garnering attention is for the press agent to arrange interviews between the entertainer and print and broadcast editors and reporters. Hopefully, these people will then write favorable feature stories and articles. The press agent will also try to schedule interviews and appearances on news, variety, and television and radio talk shows. Press agents must continually come up with unique angles to peak the interest of the media. Sometimes the press agent uses paid advertising to augment publicity efforts.

Press agents are well-known for creating hype. This method of promotion saturates the market with a barrage of publicity used to promote clients and projects. Hype often generates a unique type of notoriety in the entertainment business.

Other functions of press agents include scheduling and arranging press conferences on behalf of their clients, creating media interest in their clients, and shielding clients from media when exposure may be harmful.

A great deal of the working life of press agents is spent on the phone talking about their clients to people in positions to help to promote them. Other portions of the day are spent writing press releases, developing press kits, and designing, developing, and implementing campaigns.

As in many other areas in the entertainment business, this is not a nine-to-five job. The business and social lives of a press agent often intermingle. Most press agents attend a great many press parties, dinners, luncheons, and other social events to promote their clients and to attract new ones. Much of this is done after normal working hours.

It is gratifying for a press agent to see a client rise to the top.

Employment Opportunities

Press agents may work full-time or part-time. They may be employed on staff or freelance as independents. Individuals who freelance must find their own clients.

Employment opportunities exist throughout the country. Most opportunities will be located in large, culturally active cities with a great number of entertainers and entertainment events.

Employment opportunities and/or clients for press agents include:

- Singers, musicians, or musical groups
- Dancers
- Recording artists
- Publicity firms
- Public relations companies
- Radio stations or specific shows
- Television shows or stations
- Motion pictures
- Record companies
- Theatrical companies
- Performing arts complexes
- Sports figures
- Sports arenas
- Entertainment complexes
- Personalities
- Magicians
- Comedians

Earnings

Earnings for press agents can range from approximately $15,000 to $150,000 or more annually. Earnings are affected by whether the agent is self-employed or on staff, as well as on the individual's experience, responsibilities, qualifications, and professional reputation. Other variables include the type, number, prestige, and popularity of clients.

Publicists who belong to the Publicists Guild and who work for a studio, agency, or television station that has a contract with the guild will have their minimum earnings set by that union. Minimum weekly salaries range from approximately $1,100 to $1,300.

Advancement Opportunities

There are a number of different advancement opportunities for press agents depending on the path they want to take. Individuals can locate a more prestigious company or employer within the entertainment industry. Press agents can also advance by being assigned more prestigious clients.

Many individuals advance their careers by striking out on their own as independent freelance press agents. Such people must usually have some experience and a proven track record to be successful in this endeavor.

Another method of career advancement occurs when a press agent works with an unknown client who then makes it big. This can happen when a recording group's tune climbs the charts, a smash television pilot turns its cast into stars, or any similar event that may happen in the world of entertainment.

Education and Training

Most companies that hire press agents require them to hold a bachelor's degree. Good majors include public relations, communications, marketing, advertising, English, journalism, and liberal arts.

Seminars, courses, and workshops in all facets of publicity, promotion, writing, business, marketing, and the entertainment industry will be useful in honing skills and making important contacts.

Experience and Qualifications

Experience requirements vary from job to job. Some individuals find entry-level positions working as assistants to other press agents. Most jobs as full-fledged press agents require some sort of experience in publicity, public relations, journalism, or related areas. This can be acquired through internships, jobs as print or broadcast journalists, or positions in publicity or public relations that are unrelated to the entertainment field.

Press agents must have a thorough understanding of the entertainment industry. Contacts—or at least the ability to make them—are essential.

Successful press agents should be creative, persuasive, aggressive individuals with the ability to work well under pressure. Excellent written and verbal communications skills are imperative.

For Additional Information: Individuals aspiring to become press agents in the entertainment industry can obtain additional information about careers in the field by contacting the Association of Theatrical Press Agents and Managers (ATPAM), the Public Relations Society of America (PRSA), the National Entertainment Journalists Association (NEJA), and the Publicists Guild (PG).

TIPS

- Consider breaking into the field on a small scale. Offer to develop and implement a publicity campaign for a local music act, singer, television or radio station, etc. This will give you good hands-on experience as well as help you make useful contacts.
- Volunteer to do the publicity for your local community theater.

- Look in the classified section of the newspaper under such headings as "Press Agent," "Publicist," "Entertainment Publicity," "Music Publicist," or "Entertainment."
- Look for an internship in the field. Contact large entertainment-oriented public relations and publicity firms, record companies, and television stations and inquire about internship programs. Companies often hire after an internship has ended.
- Get experience writing for a local newspaper. Although it would be preferable to write entertainment-oriented articles, reviews, and interviews, any kind of writing experience will help.
- Join trade associations and attend their meetings. These are especially useful for making professional contacts.
- Take courses, seminars, and workshops in publicity, entertainment, writing, and the like.
- Send your resume with writing samples to record companies, entertainment-oriented public relations companies, film companies, and radio and television stations. Indicate your interest in working in entertainment publicity and inquire about openings.

CHAPTER 2

· · · · · · · · · · · ·

Careers in Performing and Writing

Every person has a different way of expressing creativity, and in the world of entertainment, creative expression has many outlets. Some individuals sing, play a musical instrument, act, dance, or make people laugh. Others use the written word and musical notes to create songs, scripts, and stories. Many utilize several of these forms of creative expression.

Our society values the expression of creativity in all its forms. Who is to say that making people laugh is more or less important than making people think? Who can make the decision that composing a song requires more or less talent than singing it?

Teamwork can often enhance creativity and maximize talents. It takes a writer to develop and produce the lines spoken by actors and actresses. Similarly, choreographers prepare the path for dancers. Songwriters pen the words and/or music for singers.

There are intriguing career opportunities in the performing arts for those aspiring to be entertainers, just as there are interesting options open to creative people with wordsmithing talents.

Each career, whether in performing or writing, requires varying degrees of training, study, experience, and expertise. A ballet dancer, opera singer, or conductor may take years of concentrated study to reach the pinnacle of their career goals. A comedian with a natural talent for comedy may simply require honing of appearance and/or presentation skills.

Careers in performing and writing have a good deal in common. In order to be successful, both types of careers require persistence on the part of the individual and a strong commitment to the craft.

Space restrictions limit discussing possible opportunities. Careers covered in this section are:

Singer	Soap Opera Actor/Actress
Background Singer	Dancer
Opera Singer	Ballet Dancer
Chorus Singer—Theater	Choreographer
Recording Group or Artist	Clown
Show Group	Comedian
Dance Band	Model
Conductor	Songwriter
Section Member—Orchestra	Playwright
Studio Musician	Screenwriter/Scriptwriter
Actor/Actress	

Individuals interested in careers in performing and writing should also review entries in other sections of this book, including "Careers in Radio"; "Careers in Television, Film, and Video"; and "Miscellaneous Careers in the Entertainment Industry." All provide related opportunities.

SINGER

. . . .

Job Description: Sing either live and/or on recordings for public entertainment.

Earnings: Impossible to determine due to nature of the job.

Recommended Education and Training: No formal educational requirement; private voice lessons may be helpful.

Skills and Personality Traits: Good singing voice; flexible vocal style; charisma; ability to read music.

Experience and Qualifications: Experience singing in public helpful.

Job Description and Responsibilities

Professional singers perform either live or on recordings. Individuals may sing a variety of styles of music including classical, folk, jazz, country, blues, opera, theatrical, and rock-and-roll. In addition to singing, individuals may utilize other methods of entertainment including dancing, playing instruments, acting, or telling jokes.

Singers may perform as soloists or together with other individuals in groups. They may perform as lead singers, background vocalists, chorus singers, etc.

Individuals may sing in clubs, concert halls, theaters, on cruise ships, or on records. Some stay on their home turf and entertain locally. Others tour regionally, nationally, or throughout the world.

Professional singers working as soloists are usually expected to put together shows with a complete repertoire of songs. Even if a singer has a hit tune, he or she must develop an act. The performance can include original tunes, standards, or popular songs in one or more styles. Many singers develop elaborate shows with scenery, props, and costumes. These shows usually require musicians as well as background singers.

Some singers are also recording artists. These people record tunes that are either classics, originals, or remakes of older songs. Many recording artists also are expected to tour, performing tunes from their albums to promote sales.

Fame, fortune, and/or public acceptance signal success in this field.

Employment Opportunities

As with all types of singers and entertainers, the more flexible and versatile the individual is, the more employment opportunities will become available. Unless singers are very well-known, they usually must either audition in person for jobs or provide audition or demo tapes.

Agents and managers may be helpful when searching for work or attempting to obtain a recording contract.

Some lucky and talented singers become top touring concert acts or recording artists. Major recording capitals include New York City, Los Angeles, and Nashville.

Many singers have lucrative and successful careers performing in a variety of other settings. Depending on their styles, talents, and aspirations, singers can often find employment in:

- Nightclubs
- Dinner theaters
- Hotel lounges
- Concert halls
- Musical theatrical productions
- Broadway musicals
- Operas
- Studio sessions (musical recording, radio jingles, television commercials)
- Cruise ships

Earnings

It is impossible to determine the earnings for singers due to the nature of the job. Some individuals earn a minimal amount throughout the year while others make hundreds of thousands of dollars. Compensation depends on the type and amount of work the individual does as well as the singer's reputation and popularity.

Singers who have recorded chart-topping hits can earn a million dollars or more from recordings, royalties, and live shows. Those performing in local clubs can start off working for the "door" (a portion or the full amount of the show's admission price). Earnings can go up dramatically as singers become more popular.

In some situations, singers have their minimum earnings set by unions, including the American Federation of Television and Radio Artists (AFTRA) or the American Guild of Musical Artists (AGMA). In other situations, singers may negotiate earnings on their own with club owners, agents, managers, and recording companies, or they may have a personal manager or booking agent perform these tasks.

Advancement Opportunities

Advancement opportunities for singers depend on individual career positions at particular times. To a great majority of singers, the ultimate advancement is becoming a top recording artist. However, advancement can mean finding more consistent work or locating more prestigious jobs.

Education and Training

With the exception of opera singers, no formal education is required to become a singer. Opera singers, discussed separately in another section, are usually required to have years of formal vocal training.

Many aspiring singers, as well as those currently working, feel that private classes are helpful. Some singers are self-taught. There are others who have attended conservatories or universities with music programs.

Experience and Qualifications

Experience requirements vary from job to job. Some experience singing in public usually helps the individual to feel more comfortable when performing. Experience can be acquired in many settings including nonprofessional singing in school, church, or community productions.

A good singing voice is necessary for prolonged success in this field. Charisma is helpful, especially when performing live. Talent, luck, perseverance, and being in the right place at the right time are all necessary to build a successful career.

For Additional Information: Additional information for individuals interested in pursuing a career in this area can be obtained by contacting the American Federation of Television and Radio Artists (AFTRA) and the American Guild of Musical Artists (AGMA).

TIPS

- Make a demo tape to showcase your talents. Leave copies with recording studios, producers, engineers, etc.
- Have professional business cards printed advertising your vocation. Be sure to include your phone number. Give the cards to everyone you know. Leave them in every place that might offer a possibility of employment. You might consider printing your cards on an oddly colored stock. While this will probably be more expensive, people will more likely remember the cards and your name.
- Your phone is one of your most important business tools. It should be covered at all times and be answered professionally, whether you answer it yourself or you use a phone service or an answering machine. Check your messages often, and always call people back immediately.
- Join the union locals and visit frequently. Union secretaries and other personnel usually know about openings. Leave your business card.
- Consider getting experience as a background singer. Opportunities are often available in the recording studio or as back-up for solo singers.
- Take advantage of every opportunity to perform. This will help you hone your craft, give you valuable experience, and put you in the public eye.
- Read both the national and local trades. Possibilities for jobs and openings are often discussed, listed, or advertised.
- You might also place a small ad in a newspaper, entertainment magazine, or trade to advertise yourself. This will help make people aware of your availability.
- Consider finding an agent to help you obtain auditions and jobs.
- Always show up for auditions, performances, and recording sessions. Make sure you are on time. Competition in this field is fierce. Develop a reputation for being reliable and dependable.
- Contact cruise lines to find out about requirements for performing on their ships.
- You should also contact hotel chains and resorts. Most have opportunities for entertainers. Send your resume and a demo tape with a short cover letter.
- If you are interested in recording, try to find original tunes or new versions of old tunes to put on your demo. Be persistent in sending out demo tapes. If you have the talent, one will eventually find its way to someone who will give you a chance.
- Consider arranging a showcase for yourself. Prepare the best show you can and invite agents, managers, record company A & R people, the media, etc., to your show.
- Take part in amateur competitions, talent showcases, and the like to obtain exposure and experience.

BACKGROUND SINGER

Job Description: Back up the singing of other vocalists and musicians during live performances and/or on recordings.

Earnings: Impossible to determine due to nature of the job.

Recommended Education and Training: No formal educational requirement; private voice training may be helpful.

Skills and Personality Traits: Good singing voice; flexible vocal style and range; ability to harmonize; ability to sight read; dependability.

Experience and Qualifications: Experience singing in vocal groups.

Job Description and Responsibilities

Background singers provide background vocals for other singers and musicians in both live performances and on recordings. They perform in a wide array of settings on either a full-time or freelance basis.

Background singers perform at concerts with entertainers including solo artists, bands, club acts, floor shows, and nightclub groups. Individuals may become members of a chorus or may accompany solo performers in theatrical productions. They may also sing jingles for radio or television commercials or work in the recording studio as session singers for recording acts.

The responsibilities of background singers vary depending on the type of work required. Those working with lounge acts, show groups, and popular entertainers will be expected to tour with the act and sing background at all the shows. In order to do this effectively, the singer must learn the entertainer's complete repertoire and attend rehearsals so that vocals blend and harmonize. Background singers working in theatrical productions will have similar duties.

Most background singers aspire to work in the recording studio doing the background vocals for recording acts, jingles, and television commercials. While they usually receive a small amount of (if any) public recognition for this type of employment, the financial rewards often outweigh the anonymity. In order to obtain work in studios, background singers must develop a reputation for not only having a great voice, but also having the ability to sing in a variety of styles.

Background singers working on commercial recordings or on jingles for television or radio are expected to walk into a studio, quickly go over the music, and be able to record without any errors. In this type of situation, background singers will often have to harmonize with other people whom they have never sung with before. Improvisation is often necessary. The individual must have the ability to pick up on what the producer has in mind and carry it out. Those who can will be called upon for additional jobs when they become available.

Employment Opportunities

Versatility is imperative in this type of work. Individuals must have the ability to sing in a variety of styles. There will be more and more opportunities for the background singers who demonstrate their versatility and flexibility.

These singers provide the background vocals in nightclub acts, floor show groups, and musical productions. They might sing background vocals for a local bar band or a top touring act. Other opportunities for background singers include musical theatrical productions such as operas, Broadway plays, summer stock, regional theater productions, and road company productions.

Background vocalists are needed for studio sessions for musical recordings, radio jingles, and television commercials. TV variety shows often have bands or orchestras that require background vocalists, as do films with a musical flavor. Jobs in recording are obtained through contractors and producers in the recording field. While recording studios are located throughout the country, more opportunities will be available in major recording capitals, including:

- New York City
- Los Angeles
- Nashville

Earnings

Earnings for background singers will depend on the type and amount of work the individual performs. Other factors include the reputation and popularity of the vocalist.

Successful background vocalists who do a great deal of studio work can earn $150,000 or more annually. Individuals singing with local night club bands may only earn $35 to $75 per night while working sporadically. Those performing with popular entertainers might have weekly earnings of $1,000 to $1,500.

Financial security for many background vocalists will come as a result of a steady stream of jobs in studios for recordings, jingles, and commercials. Individuals working as vocalists in recording studios, television shows, films, or certain theatrical situations will have their minimum earnings set by unions. The American Federation of Television and Radio Artists (AFTRA) sets minimum earnings for singers performing at recording sessions, radio jingles, or television commercials. The Screen Actors Guild (SAG) negotiates minimum earnings for those working on television commercials. The American Guild of Musical Artists (AGMA) or Equity does the same for background vocalists performing in theatrical jobs.

Factors affecting minimum fees vary depending on the situation. For example, minimum fees for vocalists making recordings are determined by how long the finished product will be; the day and time of the recording session; the length of time the vocalist is in the studio; and the number of other vocalists singing on the recording.

Advancement Opportunities

There are a number of paths for advancement for background singers. Some locate more prestigious acts to work with. A background singer may, for example, find a position singing with a popular entertainer. This will result in increased earnings and a more secure income.

Individuals with a good vocal range and a flexible singing style who live in the right geographic area can advance by obtaining steady work for recording sessions and jingles.

Many background singers try to advance their careers by becoming soloists or major recording artists.

Education and Training

There is no formal educational requirement necessary to become a background singer. Some background singers are self-taught. Others have attended conservatories or universities with music programs. Many individuals also take private classes or have vocal coaches.

Experience and Qualifications

Background singers usually have sung in some capacity before obtaining a job in this field. Some individuals have performed in school or community choruses, church choirs, or school or community musical productions.

Background singers should have a good singing voice, flexible vocal style, good range, and the ability to harmonize. While it is not always imperative for all jobs, the ability to sight read is helpful.

For Additional Information: Additional information regarding background singers and minimum fees can be obtained by contacting the American Federation of Television and Radio Artists (AFTRA), the Screen Actors Guild (SAG), Actors' Equity, and the American Guild of Musical Artists (AGMA).

TIPS

- Have professional business cards printed advertising your vocation. Do not forget to have your phone number on the card. Distribute them as widely as possible. Try to design your cards in such a way that they will stand out from the rest.
- Make sure your phone—one of your most important business tools—is answered professionally and covered at all times. It doesn't matter if you take calls yourself or if you use a phone service or an answering machine. Remember to check your messages often and to call people back immediately.
- Join the union locals and visit them often. Union secretaries and other personnel

are usually knowledgeable about job openings. Be sure to leave your business card.

- Similarly, visit and hang around various recording studios. The more people see you, the greater the chance that they will remember to call you for work. Become friendly with the receptionists, secretaries, producers, engineers, etc. These people know when there are going to be recording sessions and can provide valuable assistance in finding jobs. Leave your card with a phone number where you can be reached.
- Make contacts. Join local organizations and trade associations. Get to know contractors and producers.
- Read both the national and local trades. Possibilities for job openings are often discussed, listed, and/or advertised.
- Local newspapers and entertainment magazines may advertise openings for background vocalists. Look in the classified section under headings such as "Vocalist," "Background Singer," "Music," or "Recording."
- You can also advertise yourself by placing a small ad in a newspaper, entertainment magazine, or trade. This process can make people aware that you are available for work.
- Consider hiring an agent to help you obtain auditions and jobs.
- Always show up on time for auditions, performances, and recording sessions. There is fierce competition in this field, and a reputation for being reliable and dependable will be a strong asset.
- Make a demo tape to showcase your talents. Leave copies with recording studios, producers, engineers, and the like.

OPERA SINGER
. . . .

Job Description: Singing in operas.

Earnings: $10,000–$150,000+

Recommended Education and Training: Degree from a music conservatory, college, or university.

Skills and Personality Traits: Excellent vocal skills; acting ability; extraordinary voice; multilingual fluency.

Experience and Qualifications: Experience singing classical music; familiarity with operatic music.

Job Description and Responsibilities

Opera singers sing classical music in theatrical productions set to music. These musical productions are called operas. Operas, like plays, are stories which come to life through words, costuming, scenery, and lighting. In operas, the words are sung instead of spoken. The story or script is called the libretto. The actors in this case are singers who must also act. As in other theatrical productions, there are different types of roles opera singers can obtain. These include roles as principal singers, feature or support singers, and chorus singers.

Most individuals start their careers in apprenticeship programs. It takes years of hard work and training to become a full-fledged opera singer.

Opera singers must audition constantly. They will do so in order to participate in apprenticeship programs, enter conservatories and universities, and eventually to obtain jobs.

Responsibilities of a professional opera singer include rehearsing and training privately, attending show rehearsals, becoming familiar with the specific operas, learning the staging of parts, having costume fittings, and determining hair and makeup for performances. In addition to singing, individuals must have the ability to act in order to interpret the story of the opera. In cases where operas are performed in other languages, the singer must either be fluent in the other language or be able to learn the part in that particular language.

Employment Opportunities

Opera singers generally retain managers or agents to help them find employment. These people are usually located in agencies specializing in clients involved with classical music. Other individuals may learn about openings in trade papers or through unions.

While New York City is the opera capital of the United States, opportunities for opera singers can be located in any culturally active city in this country or worldwide that hosts an opera company.

Depending on experience, vocal skills, and reputation, opera singers can find work as:

- Chorus singers
- Soloists
- Lead singers

Earnings

Professional opera singers can earn between $10,000 and $150,000 or more annually, depending on a number of variables. These include the size, budget, prestige, and geographic location of the specific opera company as well as the reputation, role, and experience of the singer. Individuals also may earn royalties from recordings.

Opera singers are either paid by the performance or on a weekly basis. Those working in unionized halls will have minimum earnings set by the American Guild of Musical Artists (AGMA). Minimum earnings are based on the type of role an individual is singing, the number of performances, and the number of rehearsals required.

Widely experienced opera singers who are in demand can earn $150,000 or more annually. In contrast, individuals starting their careers in apprenticeship programs will have earnings of $200 to $350 weekly. As additional experience is obtained in young singer programs, weekly earnings can increase to a range between $450 and $650.

Advancement Opportunities

Opera singers need drive, determination, talent, and luck to advance their careers. Individuals can climb the career ladder by being awarded a solo part or lead in an opera. They may also find employment with more prestigious opera companies.

Education and Training

Opera singers are trained in classical singing. Training can be attained in music conservatories or in colleges or universities with classical music departments.

Most opera singers also attend classes with private vocal coaches to augment their training.

Experience and Qualifications

It takes years of practice to become an opera singer. Individuals must obtain experience singing classical music through internships and apprenticeships as well as summer workshops and other special programs. These programs are often sponsored throughout the country by opera companies as well as by music conservatories, colleges, and universities.

In order to be successful in this field, aspiring opera singers must be extremely dedicated to their vocation. They must practice for many hours, day after day. It takes a great deal of stamina and perseverance.

For Additional Information: Individuals interested in becoming opera singers can obtain additional information by contacting Opera America (OA), the Central Opera Service (COS), Metropolitan Opera Association (MOA), the National Opera Association (NOA), and the American Guild of Musical Artists (AGMA).

TIPS

• Learn from others. Attend every live opera you have the opportunity to see. You might watch performances on public and cable television. Videotapes of operatic performances are also available in local video stores and libraries.

- Get experience wherever you can. Join your community or school opera companies and participate in their operatic productions.
- Get the best education and training possible. Take advantage of every opportunity to take classes with private coaches and teachers. Colleges, universities, and music conservatories that offer majors in classical music training also often provide opportunities to perform that might not be available elsewhere.
- Get your foot in the door by participating in internships and apprenticeship programs as well as summer workshops and young singer programs. Contact opera companies throughout the country to obtain information on various programs.
- Many companies also offer grants and competitions that will provide valuable experience and exposure.
- Most classical music agencies are located in New York City. Send your resume with a short cover letter to agencies telling them you are looking for representation. Before you sign any contract, make sure it is reviewed by an attorney who is knowledgeable about the music industry.
- Read the trades to find out about openings.
- The union may also be knowledgeable about current openings.

CHORUS SINGER—THEATER

Job Description: Sing, dance, and/or act in chorus of theatrical productions.

Earnings: $250–$1,500+ per week.

Recommended Education and Training: Vocal training through private study, coaches, or conservatories helpful.

Skills and Personality Traits: Good vocal range; ability to harmonize; ability to read music; acting skills; dancing skills.

Experience and Qualifications: Experience singing in musical productions.

Job Description and Responsibilities

Musical theater productions consist of featured or lead singers and chorus singers. While featured singers portray the main characters in a production, chorus singers stay in the background to provide harmony and fill out the show scene.

Chorus singers are often called upon not only to sing, but to act and/or dance in productions. Many chorus singers are aspiring actors and actresses who happen to be able to sing as well. In some cases, the individual's acting or dancing skills are what land him or her the job. As there may be hundreds of others auditioning for the same roles, the more talents the individual displays, the better the chances of being hired.

Chorus singers audition for producers or casting directors to obtain jobs. There are a number of ways individuals can find out about this process. Auditions are advertised and listed in the industry trade papers. Some may learn about the job opportunity through word of mouth. Individuals may also have agents or managers obtain auditions for them.

When going to auditions, chorus singers must bring sheet music with them. In this way, they are able to perform songs they are familiar with and have practiced. Most productions usually provide an accompanist. However, singers may occasionally bring their own accompanist. In smaller productions, auditioning singers may be instructed to bring a cassette tape of accompanying music.

When going to auditions, individuals must also bring professional photographs called 8 × 10 glossies and a resume listing credits, experience, education, and training. These are left with the producer and/or casting director.

Auditioning is a difficult process. There are often many people trying out for the same position. Chorus singers must be thick-skinned and have the ability to deal with rejection. After an audition, the singer may get the job, be turned down, or be called back to audition a second or third time for the same part.

Once chorus singers are hired they must attend production rehearsals, and there's a great deal of rehearsing they must do on their own. After receiving a copy of the script and music, they must learn the words, parts, and music. Other responsibilities include getting fitted for costumes and having their hair and makeup styled.

Chorus singers are expected to be at every production performance. Depending on the show schedule, individuals may work in the afternoon at matinees, in the evening, or on weekends.

Employment Opportunities

Employment opportunities for chorus singers in theatrical productions can be located throughout the country. The greatest number of opportunities will be found in large, culturally active areas. Musical productions may utilize 15 or more chorus singers. Employment settings include choruses in:

- Broadway productions
- Off-Broadway productions
- Road company productions
- Dinner theater productions
- Cabaret theater productions
- Regional theater productions
- Stock productions
- Operatic productions

Earnings

Annual compensations for chorus singers in theater are difficult to determine. Earnings are determined, to a great extent, by the amount of work the individual obtains and the type of productions. Other factors include the talent and responsibilities of the singer.

Individuals working in many situations will have their minimum earnings negotiated and set by the union. In most unionized theaters, the union handling chorus singers is Actors' Equity. Weekly earnings can range from $250 to $1,500 or more. Those working in small productions in nonunionized theaters will earn the least. Individuals working as chorus singers in Broadway musicals can earn a minimum weekly salary of approximately $950. Some chorus singers can negotiate weekly earnings of $1,500 or more.

Advancement Opportunities

There are a number of advancement opportunities for chorus singers. The most common way to move up is to find similar positions in more prestigious productions. Other advancement opportunities include working as a solo or background singer in other media including television, concerts, or recordings.

Most chorus singers aspire to become featured singers. Many also strive to become actors or actresses in their own right.

Education and Training

While there are no formal educational requirements to become a chorus singer in the theater, training is helpful. This can be acquired through private study, vocal coaches, and attending music conservatories. Workshops and classes in acting and dancing are also valuable.

Experience and Qualifications

Chorus singers should have experience performing in musical productions and in other public situations. This can be accomplished through participation in school and community productions, talent shows, summer stock, etc.

A good vocal range, the ability to harmonize, and proficiency in singing various styles of music are imperative to a career in this field. The ability to read music is also necessary. Acting and dancing skills add to a chorus singer's marketability.

For Additional Information: Those interested in learning more about chorus singing for theatrical productions should contact the American Guild of Musical Artists (AGMA) and Actors' Equity Association (Equity).

TIPS

- Get as much experience as possible singing, dancing, and acting. Participate in school, community, and other amateur productions.
- Contact Equity to get lists of resident, stock, and dinner theaters throughout the country. These will provide you with a good source of names and addresses to write to concerning auditions for upcoming productions.
- Check with the AGMA and Equity to see if you meet membership requirements. Join if you can.
- People working in the union offices generally know of auditions, openings, and the like. Visit often. It is a good way to get leads and make contacts.
- Read the industry trades. You will learn about new productions, classes, workshops, auditions, etc.
- Make sure you have professional photographs taken in a variety of poses. At least one should be a "head" shot. Your photos should have your name printed on them as well as a contact phone number. The number may be yours or that of your manager or agent.
- Take private singing lessons from a variety of professionals. This will help you learn different styles and techniques.
- Take acting and dancing classes to increase your marketability.
- Consider an agent. Good agents will help you locate auditions and jobs. Check out the credentials and reputation of an agent before signing any contracts.

RECORDING GROUP OR ARTIST

Job Description: Record songs for singles and albums.

Earnings: Impossible to determine due to nature of the job.

Recommended Education and Training: No formal educational requirement.

Skills and Personality Traits: Vocal or musical proficiency; stage presence; charisma.

Experience and Qualifications: Experience playing music or singing.

Job Description and Responsibilities

Most musicians and singers aspire to record a song and have it become a hit. While with current technology, almost anyone can record a song, the trick is to hit the charts. Recording groups or artists record their music professionally. They may record any type of music, including pop, country, rock, folk, jazz, R & B, rap, and classical.

Groups or individuals seeking to work in the recording field take a number of different paths to get there. Some begin as dance bands, bar bands, or show groups. Others write songs and make demos. No matter how they choose to start, aspiring recording artists must obtain a recording contract.

Once this is done, the artists need to decide on the right song or songs to record. In some cases, the artist or group will write their own tunes. In others, artists work with management, music publishers, or a label's A & R people to find suitable material.

Studio time is expensive. Before going into the recording studio, artists must learn the songs they will be recording. Once in the studio, engineers, arrangers, studio musicians, and background vocalists all work with the recording artists to produce the record.

When the record is completed, the recording artist or group will work with the various departments at the record company developing and implementing strategies to make the record a hit. Publicity, press kits, and copies of the record are sent to the media. The recording artists will be required to make promotional appearances, be interviewed by the media, and appear on television talk, variety, and news shows. Recording artists are also expected to perform at concerts scheduled to promote the record.

Having a hit record is the ultimate goal for most musical artists. However, in order to remain successful in this industry, recording artists must continually find and record hits.

Employment Opportunities

Today, in addition to the major record labels, there are also a great number of independent record labels. Some find that it is easier to break in by working with an independent label. While it is difficult to become a top recording group or artist, it is not an impossible dream. Many who fail may have just given up too soon. Major recording capitals include:

- New York City
- Los Angeles
- Nashville

Earnings

Due to the nature of the job, it is impossible to determine the earnings of recording artists. Recording groups and artists can earn hundreds of thousands of dollars. There are some very successful and popular artists who earn millions of dollars. Earnings for recording artists and groups come from a number of sources including the sale of records, concert tours, public appearances, and merchandising.

Record companies usually recoup their expenses from the record's profits. If the record cost a great deal to produce, the artist will not see a large amount of profits even if the song is a hit.

Factors affecting earnings include the popularity of the artist or group and the specific record, as well as the type of recording contract. Individuals who write the songs they record earn extra money each time the song is performed or a record is sold.

Advancement Opportunities

Advancement opportunities for recording artists depend on their position in the industry. After making a record, the next rung on the career ladder is getting it on the charts, to be followed by moving the record up the charts and then into the top 10 list. Having a number one record on the charts is a major achievement. Recording artists continue to advance their careers by recording and selling additional hit records. Most recording artists strive for gold and platinum record awards. These are given for selling millions of recordings.

Another form of career advancement for recording artists is being nominated for and winning a Grammy award, which is given by National Academy of Recording Arts and Sciences.

Education and Training

Recording artists are not required to have any specialized educational background. Many individuals have undergone musical or vocal training at private study schools, colleges, or conservatories.

Experience and Qualifications

Most successful recording artists have had some type of experience playing music and/or singing either professionally or on an amateur level. Many groups started out playing in bars, nightclubs, or for private parties. Other artists had prior experience writing music or lyrics.

Recording artists must be proficient in playing one or more musical instruments and/or singing. A basic understanding of the music and recording industry is helpful.

For Additional Information: Associations and organizations that can provide additional information regarding this career include the American Federation of Musicians (AFM), the National Academy of Recording Arts and Sciences (NARAS), the Country Music Association (CMA), and the Gospel Music Association (GMA).

TIPS

- A demo recording is required and should be sent to prospective record labels. While the demo need not be expensive, make it as professionally as possible. Try to use original material.

- Make sure your name (or group's name), address, and phone number are on each demo. Also include the title and writer of each song. Use labels with neatly typed or computer generated information.
- Do not record more than three or four songs on a demo.
- Never send your demos to record companies without inquiring about their interest. Call or write and ask for a specific person's name to send the demo to instead of just using a title like "A & R Director." Remember to send return postage if you want your material back.
- Wait approximately four weeks before contacting the company to inquire about your demo.
- Many successful recording artists begin their careers as session musicians. Consider this path to obtain some exposure.
- Don't give up. If you believe your act has talent, persevere. You will eventually obtain a contract.
- Consider finding an independent label, where it is usually a great deal easier to obtain a contract.
- Never sign a recording contract without first hiring an attorney who understands the music industry to look it over.
- Participate in competitions that offer exposure to recording industry professionals.

SHOW GROUP

Job Description: Perform shows in night clubs, concert halls, hotel lounges, cruise ships, and more.

Earnings: $250–$10,000+ per appearance.

Recommended Education and Training: No formal educational requirements.

Skills and Personality Traits: Musical and/or vocal skills; stage presence; charisma.

Experience and Qualifications: Performing experience.

Job Description and Responsibilities

Show groups work in a variety of settings, putting on entertaining shows for patrons. These groups consist of a combination of musicians, singers, dancers, comedians, and/or other performing artists. They may have four, ten, or more members, depending on the specific group.

Show groups may be expected to perform one or more sets during the engagement, and may also be required to play dance sets during the course of the evening. Dance sets consist of popular tunes, classics, and/or oldies for patrons to dance to.

Show sets are developed and put together to entertain a seated audience. A show consists of a combination of music, songs, jokes, skits, dancers, sound and/or special effects, and light shows. Music can include popular songs, oldies, classics, or original tunes. Group members usually wear some type of costume or costumes during shows.

While there are some show groups that put on simple performances, popular and successful show groups develop elaborate productions with a great deal of pizzazz. Exciting finales, especially, leave people wanting to come back for more.

Show groups may be booked into a club or venue for two weeks or a month at a time. They then move on to another gig or job. If the club manager or owner likes a show and patrons regularly return, groups are usually booked back again in the near future. It is a common occurrence for show groups to build up followings in specific areas where they perform consistently.

In order to continue getting booked, show group members must be extremely professional. The group must always arrive for their sets on time and put on the best show possible.

Groups in this profession must travel extensively. Job opportunities will be located almost anywhere. Some show groups tour within a certain local area. Others travel throughout the country "living out of a suitcase." Depending on the specific job, accommodations and lodging may be part of the package. Many show groups attain a certain amount of stardom within the areas where they perform.

Employment Opportunities

There are many opportunities throughout the country to locate employment. Lesser-known acts should start looking for work in smaller venues. Once an act builds up a following, employment opportunities become much easier.

There are a couple ways to find jobs in this area. Some groups book themselves. Others seek the help of one or more booking agents to handle the task of finding jobs.

Show groups can work in a number of settings. These include:

- Nightclubs
- Hotel lounges
- Bars
- Concert halls
- Cruise ships
- Opening act for touring artist or group
- Convention centers
- Private parties and functions

Earnings

There is a tremendous range of earnings for show groups. Those just starting out may earn only $250 for a show. As they obtain more experience and exposure, develop more extensive shows, and build larger followings, earnings go up dramatically. There are many show groups throughout the country earning $10,000 or more per show.

Advancement Opportunities

Show groups can advance their careers by building large followings. Once that occurs, groups can obtain a greater number of bookings or work in larger, more prestigious venues. Some show groups find steady work and increased earnings in large hotels and casinos in Las Vegas, Reno, and Atlantic City.

There are also show groups that aspire to become major recording groups. While this is difficult, it can be done.

Education and Training

There are no formal educational requirements for becoming a member of a show group. Members may have gone through music, vocal, or other performing arts training in high school, college, private classes, or they may be self-taught.

Experience and Qualifications

Members of show groups usually need some type of prior performing experience. Many individuals previously worked as musicians or singers in dance, lounge, or bar bands. Others worked on-stage in varying capacities.

In order to become successful in this field, members of show groups must have a great deal of charisma and stage presence. Individuals need the ability to either play an instrument, sing, dance, or perform in some other manner. Because the stage show is initially such an important part of the excitement and allure of these groups, one or more members must have the talent and ability to develop a show. Or this task may also be handled by other professionals in the field.

For Additional Information: Additional information regarding careers in this area can be obtained by contacting the American Federation of Musicians (AFM).

TIPS

- Get experience and exposure by volunteering to put on a show for a community or not-for-profit function.
- Jobs may be advertised in the newspaper classified section. Look under headings such as "Entertainers," "Show Groups," "Floor Show Band," "Entertainment," and "Nightclubs."
- Join the union. They often know about openings before other people. Go to union meetings and hang around their offices. This is a good way to meet

people, make contacts, and network. The union newsletter may also list or advertise jobs.

- Have professional photos taken of your group appearing as they will on stage. Print the group's name as well as the name and phone number of your agent or manager on the bottom of the photo. If you do not have an agent or manager, make sure that you print a phone number where either someone will always answer the phone or there is an answering machine.
- Be professional. Show up on time for interviews and auditions with managers, agents, club managers, owners, and the like.
- Develop a brochure or flyer about the group that you can send to club owners, managers, agents, etc. Make sure it is professional and neat. Creating it doesn't necessarily have to cost a fortune. You might consider quick printing as an alternative to regular printing.
- Get recommendations from club owners and managers where you have worked. These, along with a list of clubs and venues where you have appeared, can be used for other mailings and can be given to prospective club owners, managers, and agents.
- If you have the capability, you might consider making a short video of your performance. This is a useful tool to send or give to people who may be interested in booking your act.
- Get booking commitments in writing. Contracts are used in the entertainment business. They do not have to be elaborate; they should include dates, times, monies, number of shows, and any other pertinent information. The contract must be signed by both parties to be binding. You might want a qualified lawyer to look at your first couple of contracts.

DANCE BAND

Job Description: Provide music for dancing and/or listening in venues or at functions.

Earnings: $100–$1,500+ per engagement.

Recommended Education and Training: No formal educational requirements.

Skills and Personality Traits: Proficiency playing one or more instruments and/or singing; ability to read music; stage presence.

Experience and Qualifications: Experience playing an instrument and/or singing, formally or informally.

Job Description and Responsibilities

The main responsibility of dance bands is to provide dance music for patrons of clubs or guests at parties. Dance bands consist of musicians and vocalists. In many cases, one or more of the musicians double as vocalists. Musicians may include guitarists, pianists, organists, synthesizer players, drummers, and horn and bass players.

Dance bands usually specialize in one or two varieties of music such as pop, country, rock, top 40, jazz, dance, etc. They may play only "covers," but may also augment shows with original material. They are employed to play a specific number of sets or shows per performance. Sets are usually 30 minutes to one hour in length. Bands customarily take breaks in between sets.

In addition to performing, dance bands must also rehearse regularly. During these periods, band members will hone their sound as well as work on new material to add to their playlist. In this way, the band will not have to continually repeat the same set. Music is continually changing. It is imperative for the dance band to know all the current tunes in their specific genre of music as well as in a host of others.

Bands usually decide ahead of time what songs will be played in a set and in what order. Many dance bands also take written or verbal requests from the audience. Some bands have specific parts of the show during which they take requests, while others take them throughout the set.

Quite often, the first professional job for many individuals who want to work in the music business is with a dance band. Most usually start out by supplementing the income from a day job with work in a band. Individuals may join a band that is seeking a member who can play a specific instrument or sing in a particular style. Other people form their own bands with talented friends, acquaintances, and colleagues.

Employment Opportunities

Dance bands find employment opportunities throughout the country. Groups may book themselves or retain agents to handle this task. Possible employment settings include:

- Night clubs
- Bars
- Lounges
- Cruise ships
- Hotels
- Schools, colleges, and universities
- Private parties and functions

Earnings

Earnings for dance bands have a broad range. Variables include the popularity of the act as well as their location, experience, and professional reputation. Some bands are paid by the performance. Others may be compensated by the week.

Bands may earn from $100 to $1,500 or more per engagement. Those working in unionized settings will have their base pay negotiated and set by the American Federation of Musicians (AFM) union.

Advancement Opportunities

Advancement opportunities for dance bands vary. Groups may build large followings, which result in repeated bookings and increased fees. Other bands may develop a show and become show groups. Most dance bands aspire to play original material and become major recording acts.

Education and Training

There is no formal educational requirement for members of dance bands. Many members of bands, however, have had formal or informal musical or vocal training. This training may be acquired through private study or school, or may be self-taught.

Experience and Qualifications

Experience requirements for dance band members vary from group to group. Some bands that are just starting out have no professional experience. While some individuals may have played in school bands or sung in choruses or choirs, others might only have played or sung informally.

The individual members of the group must have the capacity to work together. All should have the ability to play one or more instruments or sing fairly well. The ability to read music is helpful but not always required. A strong stage presence is needed for success.

For Additional Information: The American Federation of Musicians (AFM) can provide additional information on this career.

TIPS

- Consider putting together an attractive brochure or flyer about your band. The brochure can be given or mailed to club owners, agents, or other potential talent seekers.
- Jobs are often advertised in the local newspaper in the classified section. Look under headings such as ''Band Wanted,'' ''Music,'' ''Entertainment,'' and ''Clubs.''
- You may also consider placing a small ad in the local or regional paper indicating your band's availability. Always make sure that you list a phone number where people can reach you at any time if they are interested.

- Have business cards printed with your band's name and specialty. Give them to everybody. It will be a worthwhile investment. When people need a band, they will remember your availability.
- Put business cards and flyers up on bulletin boards in stores, schools, malls, churches, etc. Remember, everyone is a potential client!
- Be professional. Get to auditions and jobs on time. Do what you are supposed to do and build a professional reputation.
- Get every job commitment in writing. Standard contracts are available in most stationery stores. If someone else gives you a contract, read it thoroughly or have an attorney look it over. Make sure names, dates, places, times, number of sets, and terms of payment are specified. Do not leave any lines blank. Both parties must sign a contract in order for it to be valid.
- Have professional photos taken of the band as they will appear on stage. Remember to print the group's name, representative, and phone number on the photo so that prospective customers can call you for jobs.
- Consider volunteering to play for a school or community event. You will gain valuable exposure that could lead to jobs.
- Remember to rehearse before a job, not during it.
- The greater the range of music your band can play, the more marketable it will be.

CONDUCTOR

Job Description: Conduct orchestra; prepare orchestra for performances.

Earnings: $13,000–$265,000+

Recommended Education and Training: Training in conducting and music.

Skills and Personality Traits: Communications skills; ability to play piano; ability to sight read.

Experience and Qualifications: Hands-on experience as a conductor required; internships or positions as assistant conductors are useful; comprehensive knowledge of symphonic repertoire.

Job Description and Responsibilities

The conductor of an orchestra is responsible for the orchestra's musical operation. In this top musical position, the individual is expected to prepare the orchestra for performances.

Each conductor has his or her own personal style of conducting. That is why the same orchestral score can sound completely different when performed by various orchestras and led by different conductors. A really talented and charismatic conductor is remembered long after a performance. These individuals are often asked to make appearances as guest conductors with other orchestras.

The conductor has a considerable number of duties. Long before the first concert, as the orchestra's music director, he or she must plan and design the entire musical season. This includes selecting the orchestra's repertoire and determining how each score will be played. The conductor must also plan special shows and decide when and if guest conductors, artists, and soloists will be needed.

The conductor is expected to be present during auditions for section members and section leaders. Many hours are spent at rehearsals preparing for each performance. He or she must be present during each rehearsal and performance of the orchestra, and must also go on tour with the orchestra when appearances in other cities or countries are scheduled.

Other responsibilities of a conductor include being available for both public and private appearances at functions, fund-raising events, or affairs designed to help develop the orchestra's image.

Off-season, many conductors lead a special concert series or teach at seminars, symposiums, and workshops.

Employment Opportunities

Individuals obtain jobs as conductors by auditioning. The field is very limited, so it is extremely difficult to get a job. Experienced and successful conductors may retain agents and/or personal managers to assist in their quest for a satisfactory position.

Positions often exist on a part-time basis in smaller orchestras. These openings are useful because they offer an opportunity to obtain experience and recognition.

Depending on their experience and reputation, conductors may work with orchestras of various types, sizes, budgets, and prestige. These include:

- Major orchestras
- Regional orchestras
- Metropolitan orchestras
- Urban orchestras
- Community orchestras
- Orchestras for theatrical performances
- Orchestras for opera companies
- Orchestras for ballet companies

Earnings

There is a tremendous salary range for conductors depending on the type of orchestra, its budget, and its prestige as well as the responsibilities, experience, and reputation of the conductor. Earnings can start at approximately $13,000 and go up to over $200,000. Salaries for conductors are negotiated with the board of directors of the orchestra.

Successful conductors working with major orchestras can earn $265,000 or more annually. Individuals may also augment their salaries with royalties from recordings and teaching.

Conductors working with regional or urban orchestras may have earnings ranging from $13,000 to $70,000-plus. Those working in smaller community orchestras may be paid on either a full- or per-service basis. They generally earn between $50 and $400 per service.

Advancement Opportunities

Since the conductor of an orchestra holds the top musical position, there can be no advancement within that specific organization. Advancement opportunities come when the individual locates a position as a conductor with a larger or more prestigious orchestra.

Conductors may advance their careers by moving from a community to an urban orchestra; urban to metropolitan; metropolitan to regional; and regional to major orchestra.

Education and Training

The best training grounds for aspiring conductors are summer seminars and work-shops led by successful and well-known people in the field. These programs help individuals to develop their own unique style of conducting.

Training in conducting is necessary, whether through college, conservatory, private study, seminars, or workshops. Musical training is also required.

While a degree is not usually required, it is recommended for a number of reasons. Schools usually provide opportunities that individuals are not normally exposed to. For example, many conservatories and schools offer assistant programs where students are offered an opportunity to conduct.

Experience and Qualifications

Most conductors have worked for many years as musicians while studying to be a conductor. Experience is imperative in this job and may be obtained in a number of ways. Individuals can often find opportunities to conduct for youth orchestras at schools, college orchestras, small community orchestras, or chamber ensembles. Other experience can be obtained through internships and special summer programs.

Conductors must be able to play the piano and at least one other instrument. The ability to sight read is mandatory. The most compelling qualification a conductor must have is the ability to communicate musical thoughts both verbally and through body movements.

For Additional Information: Additional information about a career in conducting can be obtained by contacting the American Symphony Orchestra League (ASOL). Individuals might also write to the American Federation of Musicians (AFM) and the American Guild of Musical Artists (AGMA).

TIPS

- Positions may be advertised in the newspaper classified or display section. Check under headings such as ''Conductor,'' ''Assistant Conductor,'' ''Orchestra Music Director,'' ''Symphony,'' ''Orchestra,'' and ''Music.'' These openings are usually advertised prior to the beginning of a season.
- Other jobs may be listed in arts council publications, trade journals, union newsletters, and classical music publications. You might want to check the ASOL newsletter as well as the AFM publication, *The International Musician.*
- Consider an internship in conducting. These may be offered by orchestras, universities, conservatories, or trade associations.
- Get as much experience as possible. Offer to conduct your community orchestra or the local school's youth orchestra.
- Look for seminars and workshops in conducting that are associated with renowned conductors.
- Try to find a mentor. It is always helpful to have someone you respect take you under his or her wing and help you realize your aspirations.

SECTION MEMBER—ORCHESTRA

Job Description: Play an instrument in an orchestra.

Earnings: $300–$1,750+ per week.

Recommended Education and Training: Comprehensive musical training required.

Skills and Personality Traits: Excellent musician; dedication to music; ability to perform in front of audience; ability to deal with rejection.

Experience and Qualifications: Experience playing in orchestral settings.

Job Description and Responsibilities

The musicians who play in an orchestra are called section members. The number of section members in an orchestra and the instruments they play vary depending on the specific orchestra and its size and budget.

Section members must audition in order to get a job in an orchestra. Individuals may audition a number of times before they get a position. They may have their first audition in front of the section leaders for their instrument group. If they make it past this audition, they will be asked to come back to play in front of the concertmaster or concertmistress, conductor, personnel director, and possibly, the orchestra manager.

Every orchestra does not play the same type of music or the same scores. As part of an orchestra, the section member must become totally familiar with that orchestra's repertoire and have the ability to play the music perfectly before the rehearsal. The individual must spend a great many hours practicing the instrument and the specific music.

The purpose of orchestra rehearsals is not to hone the skills of the individual section members, but to draw together the performances of all the members so that the music is played in perfect unison and harmony.

Section members are required to attend all rehearsals and performances. As orchestras frequently tour, it is mandatory for section members to travel. Since all travel expenses are paid, this is an added perk for members, especially when the orchestra tours in different countries.

Employment Opportunities

There are many different types of orchestras in which section members may be employed. Classifications are based on the orchestra's annual budget. These include major, metropolitan, urban, and community orchestras.

In addition to playing in symphony orchestras, section members might perform in a variety of other orchestral settings including:

- Orchestras for ballets
- Orchestras for modern dance performances
- Orchestras for musical theater productions

Earnings

There are a large number of variables that can affect the salaries of section members. These include the classification, size, budget, geographic location, and type of orchestra that the section member is playing with. Annual earnings for individuals working in nonsymphonic orchestras depend on the number of weeks per year that a company is in session or that a production runs.

As with other jobs in the entertainment field, earnings are also affected by the section member's reputation, talent and proficiency on his or her instrument, experience, and seniority.

Section members who work in unionized orchestras have their minimum salaries negotiated by the local affiliation of the American Federation of Music (AFM). Section members working in major orchestras can earn between $500 and $1,750 or more per week. Individuals working in smaller and less prestigious orchestras can expect to earn between $300 and $700-plus per week.

Those who work in small or urban orchestras are often paid on a per-service basis. This means they are paid each time they rehearse or perform with the orchestra.

Other income for section members can include monies from recording sessions and travel expenses when the orchestra is on tour.

Advancement Opportunities

There are a couple of options section members can choose in order to advance their careers. Individuals can locate similar positions in larger and more prestigious orchestras. Another option is to advance to the position of section leader.

Education and Training

Extensive, comprehensive music training and study is necessary in order to become a section member of an orchestra. Training may be procured through private study, or through a more formal education at music conservatories, colleges, and/or universities.

Experience and Qualifications

Section members are required to have experience in orchestral settings. This can be obtained by playing in college and community orchestras and/or musical productions.

Section musicians must spend a great deal of time practicing their instruments and rehearsing the repertoire in order to excel and be a cut above the rest.

For Additional Information: Aspiring section members may obtain additional information about a career in music by contacting the American Symphony Orchestra League (ASOL), the National Orchestral Association (NOA), and the American Federation of Musicians (AFM).

TIPS

- Get as much experience as possible in orchestral settings. Offer to play in community and school orchestras as well as any type of production requiring music.
- Contact the American Symphony Orchestra League, the National Orchestral Association, colleges, conservatories, universities, orchestras, ballets, and opera companies to learn about summer programs that may be available for section members.

- Openings may be advertised in trade newsletters and journals.
- Occasionally, opportunities may be advertised in the newspaper classified or display section. Check under such headings as "Music," "Orchestra," "Symphony," "Section Member," or "Musician."
- Become involved with the National Orchestral Association and the American Symphony Orchestra League. These organizations provide guidance and support as well as offer internship, apprenticeship, and fellowship programs.
- Audition whenever possible. For many, auditions can be a difficult and nerve-racking experience. The more you audition, the more comfortable you will be with your next experience.

STUDIO MUSICIAN

Job Description: Back up music and/or singing of artists on recordings.

Earnings: $300–$100,000+

Recommended Education and Training: Training in one or more instruments through private study, classes, conservatories, college, or self-study.

Skills and Personality Traits: Musical proficiency playing one or more instruments; ability to sight read; versatility; reliable.

Experience and Qualifications: Experience playing an instrument.

Job Description and Responsibilities

The main function of a studio musician is to accompany and back up an artist or group with one or more instruments during recording sessions. Studio musicians are used on virtually every type of recording from pop and rock to opera and Broadway musicals.

One of the major ways that studio musicians obtain jobs is through contractors. Contractors are called when extra musicians are required for a recording session. They may be contacted by the performing artists themselves, the artists' management companies, recording studios, producers, or record label staff members. Contractors then hire the appropriate studio musicians.

Studio musicians may also be requested directly by the artist or group doing the recording session or by the management company. Recording studios, record label staff members, and producers may also recommend studio musicians.

Studio time is very expensive. Studio musicians are always expected to show up on time. In some situations, the musician is given music to learn before the session. In others, the musician does not see the music until the day of the recording. Individuals must be able to play the music in the manner and style requested without a great deal of rehearsal. Therefore, sight reading is imperative.

On the negative side, studio musicians are not in the limelight. In many situations they do not receive credit on recordings. As a rule, they must play the music given to them without improvising and without expressing personal creativity. On the positive side, successful studio musicians can have very lucrative careers. In addition, since there are no regular hours, individuals have the opportunity to explore other options in their free time.

Employment Opportunities

In order to be successful, studio musicians must be extremely talented and aggressive. The more instruments they can play, the more employable and marketable they will be. Individuals who are dependable, reliable, easy to get along with, and versatile will be called back by contractors and requested by recording artists, producers, and the like.

Studio musicians may be needed for musical recordings as well as for background music for commercials, television shows, and films.

Although opportunities are located throughout the country, the greatest number of employment opportunities will be in culturally active cities hosting a large number of recording studios. These cities include:

- New York
- Los Angeles
- Nashville

Earnings

It is difficult to determine earnings for studio musicians. Earnings depend on the amount and type of work individuals do as well as on their experience and reputation. Studio musicians who play more than one instrument on a recording will be paid more.

Minimum fees for studio musicians are negotiated and set by the American Federation of Musicians (AFM). The base scale for a three-hour call is approximately $300. Studio musicians who are in demand or who have built a good reputation can negotiate higher rates. There are many studio musicians who earn in excess of $100,000 annually.

Advancement Opportunities

Being in greater demand results in increased earnings for studio musicians. Many individuals advance their careers by striking out on their own to become recording artists or performers.

Education and Training

There is no one way to train to become a studio musician. Some individuals are self-taught on one or more instruments. Others are trained through private lessons or attendance at conservatories, universities, and colleges.

Experience and Qualifications

Studio musicians must have experience not only playing their instruments, but playing in different musical situations. This is usually obtained by playing in school bands or orchestras and in local music groups. Many studio musicians also are performing musicians and work with musical acts as sidemen (or women).

Studio musicians must be excellent at their craft, and the ability to sight read is a significant edge.

For Additional Information: People aspiring to work as studio musicians can obtain additional career information by contacting the American Federation of Musicians (AFM), the National Academy of Recording Arts and Sciences (NARAS), the Country Music Association (CMA), and the Gospel Music Association (GMA).

TIPS

- While your talent may get you the job, you may occasionally need to promote yourself to get noticed.
- Have professional business cards printed advertising your specialty. Make sure you have your phone number on the card. Leave them in every place and with every person that might possibly have need of your services. Think of a design for your cards that will make them stand out (e.g., an oddly colored stock). While this will probably be more expensive, people will more likely remember the card.
- Your phone is one of your most important business tools. It should be answered professionally and covered at all times. Whether someone answers the phone or you use a phone service or answering machine, check your messages often and call people back immediately.
- Join the union locals and visit frequently. Union secretaries and other personnel usually know about openings. Leave your business card with them.
- Visit and hang around various recording studios. The more people see you, the greater the chance they will remember to call you for work. Become friendly with the receptionists, secretaries, producers, engineers, etc. These people know when there are going to be recording sessions. They can provide valuable assistance in finding jobs. Leave your card with a phone number where you can be reached.
- Make contacts. Join local organizations and trade associations. Get to know contractors and producers.

- Read both the national and local trade publications. Possibilities for jobs and openings are often discussed, listed, and/or advertised.
- Local newspapers and entertainment magazines may advertise openings for studio musicians. Look in the classified or display section under headings such as "Studio Musician," "Session Musician," "Backup Musician," "Music," or "Recording."
- You might also place a small ad in a newspaper, entertainment magazine, or trade to advertise yourself. This might help make people aware that you are available.
- Consider finding an agent to help you obtain auditions and jobs.
- Always show up for auditions, performances, and recording sessions. Make sure you are on time. A reputation for being reliable and dependable will give you an edge in this highly competitive field.
- Make a demo tape to showcase your talents. Leave copies with contractors, recording studios, producers, engineers, etc.
- Consider working with a performing artist or group as a back-up musician. It will provide good experience and help to make additional important contacts.
- Continue taking classes and workshops whenever you can find them. They will help you hone your playing skills and might teach you new techniques.

ACTOR/ACTRESS

Job Description: Perform in theatrical productions, television shows, films, commercials, etc.; learn lines and/or body movements; attend rehearsals.

Earnings: Impossible to determine due to nature of the business.

Recommended Education and Training: No formal educational requirement; courses, workshops, and seminars in acting, theater arts, film, or television may be useful in honing skills.

Skills and Personality Traits: Acting skills; good memory.

Experience and Qualifications: Experience acting in school or community productions.

Job Description and Responsibilities

Actors and actresses perform in dramatic and comedic roles in television, films, video, and theatrical productions as well as in television commercials. They may play supporting or featured roles. The success or failure of many TV shows, movies, and plays is often based, to a great extent, on the acting abilities of the cast.

While individuals may begin their careers in any medium, most actors and actresses start out performing in school productions and/or community theater. From there they may go in any number of directions. Some individuals stay in theater throughout their entire career. Others dream of starring in a weekly television series or on the big screen and work toward those goals. Many find a constant stream of work appearing in television commercials. No matter what medium an individual selects, the difficult part is usually finding work.

Actors and actresses audition or try out for parts. Auditions may be obtained in a number of ways. Many actors and actresses have agents who set up auditions for them. Other people read about auditions in the industry trades. Auditions are also obtained through contacts within the business.

For many, auditioning is a difficult procedure. Individuals may try out for many parts before finally landing a role. At auditions, individuals are usually asked to read part of a script so that the director, producer, and/or casting director can see and hear if they are right for the role. Actors and actresses usually leave a professional resume listing their achievements, acting experience, and other skills in the performing arts. One or more 8 × 10 glossy photographs should accompany the resume. Individuals may be called back to audition a second or third time until the director or producer makes a final decision.

Once actors and actresses get roles, they are required to learn the lines and attend rehearsals. Rehearsal time will vary with the project. Rehearsals for theatrical productions are usually longer than those for television and film parts. Those working on daily soap operas might only rehearse a couple of hours before filming. Those in weekly shows may rehearse the show all week before taping. Theatrical productions can have a few weeks or more of rehearsal.

Actors and actresses have opportunities to bring stories to life either on film, television, or stage. It is an exciting life in which an appearance in one film, commercial, television show, or theatrical production can dramatically affect one's life and career.

There is no one way to become successful in this industry. Many actors and actresses move from theater to television to films to commercials and back again. Others start in commercials and land roles in film or television shows. The dream of most actors and actresses is to reach a degree of fame in one or more mediums.

Employment Opportunities

There are tens of thousands of people aspiring to become actors or actresses. While many of these are unemployed in the field, others stay busy acting in dinner theaters, summer stock, regional theaters, and films. The largest number of opportunities for acting in television, films, and commercials is found in New York City and Los Angeles. Those seeking employment in theater can find more opportunities in these and other large, culturally active cities. Actors and actresses can work in a number of employment situations, including:

- Television shows
- Cable shows
- Theater (regional, summer stock, dinner theater, Broadway, off-Broadway, off-off-Broadway)

- Touring troupes
- Motion pictures
- Educational films
- Music videos
- Commercials

Earnings

It is impossible to determine the earnings of actors and actresses due to the nature of the business. Most actors and actresses work and are paid on a per-project or day-to-day basis. Individuals working in many situations have minimum earnings negotiated and set by unions. These include the Screen Actors Guild (SAG), Screen Extras Guild (SEG), Actors' Equity Association (AEA, or Equity), The American Guild of Variety Artists (AGVA), the American Guild of Musical Artists (AGMA), and the American Federation of Television and Radio Actors (AFTRA).

Factors determining earnings include whether the individual is working in television, films, commercials, or theater. Earnings are also dependent on the prestige and popularity of the production or project as well as on that of the actor or actress.

It is important to note that unions set minimum earnings, although many feature stars in television, films, theater, and commercials receive a great deal more. In addition to being compensated for acting in a production, many individuals are paid royalties or residuals every time a program, commercial, or film is shown. This can be especially lucrative when television shows go into syndication.

There are some actors and actresses who barely earn enough to make ends meet. These individuals usually hold down other jobs to pay their expenses. There are other actors and actresses working in television, film, and commercials who earn millions of dollars annually.

Advancement Opportunities

One of the interesting factors in becoming an actor or actress is that stardom can come at any time. Many individuals spend years trying to gain some notoriety in the field, while others become "overnight" successes. Advancement opportunities are endless. Depending on the medium in which individuals work, they can become major film stars, regulars on television shows, stars in Broadway plays, or be called constantly to appear in commercials.

Education and Training

There are no formal educational requirements for becoming an actor or actress. Many individuals attend college and major in theater arts, television, or film. Others have degrees in totally unrelated fields.

Most actors and actresses find that workshops, seminars, and classes in acting are useful in honing skills and learning new techniques. A good majority continue taking classes throughout their careers to improve their craft.

Experience and Qualifications

Experience requirements vary from job to job in the acting profession. Some directors feel more comfortable with experienced people. Others are willing to work with newcomers.

Experience is obtained through participation in school and community productions as well as in summer stock and dinner theaters. Many actors and actresses acquire experience in workshops, classes, and seminars or through bit parts in television and movies.

Actors and actresses must be extremely confident people with articulate, clear speaking voices. There is no particular physical trait that can guarantee success in this area. A good memory is essential in learning and remembering lines. Individuals must also have the talent to portray roles effectively.

For Additional Information: Aspiring actors and actresses can obtain additional information about a career in this field by contacting the Actors' Equity Association (AEA), the Screen Actors Guild (SAG), the American Federation of Television and Radio Arts (AFTRA), the American Guild of Variety Artists (AGVA), and the American Guild of Musical Artists (AGMA).

TIPS

- Prepare a professional resume listing your experience in acting and other performing arts.
- Have professional 8 × 10 glossy photographs taken to go along with your resume.
- While experience is not always required, acting experience will make you feel more comfortable and confident. Participate in school productions, community theater, summer stock, etc.
- Look for acting workshops, seminars, courses, and the like. These will help you hone skills, offer valuable experiential opportunities, and assist you in making important contacts.
- Read the industry trades. You will learn about openings, auditions, workshops, and classes as well as keep up on industry news.
- Until you have established yourself, take advantage of every opportunity to work.
- Consider an agent. This individual will help you find work and locate auditions and casting calls. Before you sign with an agent, check out his or her credentials. You should also have an entertainment industry attorney look over any contract.

SOAP OPERA ACTOR/ACTRESS

Job Description: Act on daytime soap operas; portray specific characters.

Earnings: $100+ per day: extras with no lines, 30-minute soap; $250+ per episode: extra with 5 lines or less, one-hour soap; $600+ per episode: principal player with 6 lines or more, one-hour soap; $100,000+ annually: featured actors and actresses.

Recommended Education and Training: Classes, seminars, and workshops in acting, theater, film, and television.

Skills and Personality Traits: Acting skills; clear speaking voice; good memory; perseverance.

Experience and Qualifications: Acting experience.

Job Description and Responsibilities

Soap opera actors and actresses portray characters in ongoing story lines on daytime television. Individuals can work in featured roles, supporting roles, as principals, or as nonspeaking extras.

A soap opera features one or more main families, each with its own characters. Actors or actresses playing featured roles portray these characters and are the stars of the show. The characters are the people around whom the stories revolve.

Soaps also have additional characters who are tied in some way to the main families; their lives and stories often intertwine. The people who play these roles are the supporting cast.

There are a number of different types of extras working on soaps. Atmosphere players or people who fill out the cast are the individuals who have no lines and are shown in a scene. They might be filmed eating in a coffee shop or restaurant, dancing at a club, waiting in line at a movie, walking through a department store or hospital, etc.

Other extras referred to as "under-fives" may speak five lines or less per show. An under-five may play the role of, e.g., a waitress asking for an order or a nurse asking about medication.

Other extras called "day players" have more than five lines per episode. Extras often end up landing recurring roles. Many featured actors and actresses began in soaps as extras.

Generally, there are at least three different story lines occuring simultaneously on a soap. Since each story may involve different characters, all of the characters may not appear on camera daily.

Soap opera stars go into the studio early in the morning and often work late into the night. Once at the studio, they must rehearse scenes in preparation for the day's shoot. During this time any changes in the script or blocking will be handled.

Before the actual taping, soap stars must spend time with makeup artists, hairstylists, costume designers, and dressers to perfect the look of the character they portray.

After taping, the soap actor or actress must go home and learn the next day's lines. Some of the most talented people in television work in daytime television. For most dramatic television programs, individuals prepare one show a week. Soap opera actors and actresses must prepare five shows per week.

In order to better portray their characters, individuals may talk to professionals and others who have gone through life experiences similar to stories on the soap. Soap opera actors and actresses may also be expected to go on remotes—live broadcasts originating outside the studio—to other parts of the country or the world.

Soap stars often juggle their daytime careers with appearances in theater, clubs, or other entertainment venues as well as make personal appearances for fans.

Employment Opportunities

Soap operas are taped in New York City and Los Angeles. Popular soap operas include:

- *One Life To Live* (ABC)
- *Loving* (ABC)
- *All My Children* (ABC)
- *General Hospital* (ABC)
- *Days of Our Lives* (NBC)
- *Another World* (NBC)
- *The Young and The Restless* (CBS)
- *Bold and The Beautiful* (CBS)
- *As The World Turns* (CBS)
- *Guiding Light* (CBS)

Earnings

Minimum earnings for soap opera actors and actresses are negotiated and set by the American Federation of Television and Radio Artists (AFTRA) union. Earnings are based on the type of role being played and the length of the soap opera. Principal players (those with six lines or more) earn a minimum of $600 per show for an hour-long soap. Extras with no speaking lines start out at $100 per day for a 30-minute soap. Individuals speaking five lines or less earn a minimum of $250 per episode for an hour-long show. Featured actors and actresses can earn over $100,000 annually.

Advancement Opportunities

Individuals working as extras with no lines on soaps can advance their careers by landing speaking roles. Actors and actresses already hired for speaking parts can often climb the career ladder by obtaining recurring roles. The ultimate advancement for those in this field is landing a featured role on a popular soap.

Education and Training

There are no formal educational requirements to work as an actor or actress on a soap opera. Many successful soap stars have attended college and taken majors in theater arts, television, film, or in totally unrelated fields.

Classes, workshops, and seminars in acting are helpful for most actors and actresses in perfecting their crafts and learning new techniques. There are also a number of schools offering classes for extras taught by professionals in the field. These include the Collier School, the Video Associates School, and the Weist Baron School, all located in New York City.

Experience and Qualifications

All acting and performing arts experience is helpful to aspiring soap stars. This can be obtained by participating in school and community productions, summer stock, dinner theater, etc. Ambitious actors and actresses can acquire television experience on soaps by starting as extras.

Often at the beginning, the actor's or actress's appearance is more important than their acting ability—especially if the individual is working as an atmosphere player. Their look must fit the role. As individuals begin to land speaking parts, acting ability becomes increasingly important.

For Additional Information: Individuals aspiring to work on soaps can obtain additional career information by contacting AFTRA, Actors' Equity Association (AEA), and the casting office of any of the soaps listed.

TIPS

- Soap operas are taped in New York City and Los Angeles. In order to work on soaps, you must live near one of these areas.
- Have professional photographs taken. Take a number of different poses. Soap opera casting directors often look for real people, not glamorous stars, to appear as extras.
- Get as much acting experience as possible, whether it be in school or community productions, summer stock, dinner theaters, and so forth.
- Develop a professional resume listing your training, experience, and credits in acting and the other performing arts.
- Make sure you also incorporate in your resume jobs you have held in other fields. Knowledge of other fields may make you appear more qualified for a role.
- Include hobbies and special skills such as singing, playing instruments, doing stand-up comedy, horse riding, decorating cakes, wrestling, boxing, skating, dancing,

skiing, sketching, painting, etc. You can never tell when a casting director is looking for somebody with a special skill that you just happen to have.

- In some situations, clothing is not provided for extras. Your resume might include a section on special clothing that you own, such as a closet full of gowns, tuxedos, costumes, etc.
- Soap opera stars often begin their careers as extras.
- Send your resume and photograph to the casting directors of all of the soaps. The names of the casting directors are usually listed in the credits after the show.
- Some soaps have phone hot lines for extras to call and leave messages regarding their availability. Call the shows directly to get their phone numbers.
- Look for acting workshops, seminars, courses, etc. These will help you hone skills, offer valuable experiential opportunities, and assist you in making important contacts.
- Read the industry trades. They contain information about openings, auditions, workshops, and classes, as well as the latest industry news.
- Look for an agent to help you find work and to locate auditions and casting calls. Before you sign with an agent, check out his or her credentials and have an entertainment industry attorney look over any contract.
- Until you have become established, take advantage of every opportunity to work, no matter how small the part. These roles will help you get your foot in the door, give you exposure and credits, and help you make contacts.

DANCER

Job Description: Express ideas, tell stories, and entertain through the use of body movement.

Earnings: $25–$10,000+ per appearance.

Recommended Education and Training: Dance training acquired through classes, private lessons, school, workshops, etc.

Skills and Personality Traits: Dance skills; creativity; gracefulness.

Experience and Qualifications: Experience requirements vary.

Job Description and Responsibilities

Professional dancers perform a vast array of dance styles including ballet, classical, ethnic, jazz, folk, and modern dance. The common thread among dancers, no matter what their style, is the ability to express ideas and tell stories through the use of body movement.

Dancers in all facets of entertainment must stay in excellent physical shape and health. In order to do this, most dancers lead very physically, mentally, and nutritionally disciplined lifestyles.

Dancers usually get jobs by auditioning. One can read about auditions or casting calls in the trades and local newspapers, or hear about open auditions through word of mouth. Some dancers retain agents and/or managers to help them find auditions and work.

When dancers go to auditions they usually bring a resume or background sheet. This lists their accomplishments and jobs in dance and other performing arts, in addition to their education, training, and special skills (such as singing or choreography). The resume should include the individual's name, address, and phone number as well as the name and phone number of an agent or manager if one is involved. Dancers are also usually asked to bring professional 8 × 10 glossy photographs. These items are left with the people holding the auditions.

Auditions are stressful for most performers. There can be hundreds, even thousands of people auditioning for a small number of positions. There is often a great deal of rejection in this career. Those who handle rejection positively and continue auditioning usually end up getting a job.

Professional dancers are required to attend rehearsals to learn steps and routines as well as perform. Rehearsal times vary depending on the specific type of production. Dancers working in television may be required to learn new steps and routines on a weekly basis. Those dancing in troupes, companies, theatrical productions, musicals, etc., may perform the same routines consistently.

Professional dancers constantly strive to become more proficient by improving techniques, styles, and performances.

Employment Opportunities

While professional dancers can find employment throughout the country, the greatest number of opportunities will be located in culturally active cities. There are a multitude of employment settings for professional dancers depending on the areas they wish to pursue. These include:

- Dance troupes
- Ballet companies
- Modern dance companies
- Music videos
- Touring musical artists and groups

- Theatrical productions (musicals, comedies, dramas, etc.)
- Television variety shows
- Motion pictures and films
- Cruise ships
- Stage shows

Earnings

Earnings for professional dancers are extremely difficult to determine due to the nature of the career. Factors affecting earnings include the experience, expertise, qualifications, professional reputation, and popularity of the dancer. Other variables include the type and number of annual performances.

Those working in unionized situations will have minimum earnings negotiated by one of the unions. Depending on the type of job the dancer is involved in, unions include the Actors' Equity Association (AEA), the American Guild of Musical Artists (AGMA), the American Federation of Television and Radio Artists (AFTRA), the Screen Actors Guild (SAG), and the Screen Extras Guild (SEG).

Dancers may be paid by the performance, project, day, or week. There are some individuals who receive approximately $25 per show. Very successful dancers may earn $10,000 or more per performance.

Advancement Opportunities

Advancement opportunities for dancers are based on talent, being at the right place at the right time, and perseverance. Dancers can climb the career ladder by locating similar positions with more prestigious companies or in better productions. Some individuals also advance their careers by becoming choreographers.

Education and Training

Educational and training requirements vary depending on the type of dancing an individual is interested in pursuing. The greatest amount of intensive training is required for ballet dancers. However, the majority of successful professional dancers take lessons and classes throughout their careers.

Training can be obtained in a number of ways. Individuals may attend a college offering a degree in dance. Dancers also can take classes and private lessons as well as attend summer programs and workshops.

Experience and Qualifications

Experience requirements vary depending on the specific job. In many situations, the dancer's audition is what counts, not what the individual has accomplished previously. In other instances, in order to get an audition, dancers must have varying degrees of experience.

Dancers must be physically fit and healthy to withstand the physical demands of training and the job. Successful dancers usually are creative and graceful individuals.

Professional dancers must be able to watch a choreographer and learn steps and routines quickly. It is also imperative that dancers have the ability to feel the music and be able to use their bodies as they move to the sound, music, and rhythm.

For Additional Information: Aspiring dancers can obtain additional information by contacting the American Dance Guild (ADG).

TIPS

- Obtain experience by volunteering to teach a specific style of dance class to children in your local community center.
- Perform at every opportunity, whether it be in school plays, talent shows, community theater productions, etc.
- Develop and write a professional resume listing your accomplishments in the performing arts. You should also have professional photographs taken to give out at auditions with your resume.
- Consider sending your resume and photographs with a short cover letter to professional dance companies, dance troupes, stage show producers, and the like.
- Look for summer programs and internships to learn new skills and techniques and to make important contacts.
- Many of the trades advertise or list openings and auditions.
- Consider finding a booking agent to represent and negotiate for you and help you find jobs.
- Study the work of others by attending musicals, plays, ballets, stage shows, and other live performing arts productions utilizing dance. You can also watch dancers perform on television, in videos, and in motion pictures.
- Training is extremely helpful in this profession. Take as many classes, workshops, and lessons as you can afford. Try to find classes offered by different instructors, teachers, and dancers. This will help you hone skills as well as learn new styles and techniques from a variety of professionals.
- Learn as much as you can about dance styles, techniques, and steps. In addition to taking classes, study books on dance and choreography.

BALLET DANCER
. . . .

Job Description: Perform and dance in ballets and recitals.

Earnings: $250–$10,000+ a week.

Recommended Education and Training: Ballet training through private lessons, ballet schools, and ballet company training programs.

Skills and Personality Traits: Excellent dancing skills; gracefulness; dedication; physical fitness.

Experience and Qualifications: Experience dancing in front of audience necessary.

Job Description and Responsibilities

Ballet dancers are highly trained individuals who perform in productions using dance movements and music to tell a story. A ballet dancer's life is filled with classes, workshops, rehearsals, and performances. Even after they become part of a company, the training does not stop. It continues as long as the dancer has a professional career.

Music for ballet productions may either be prerecorded or performed live by an orchestra. The music determines the types of steps dancers use. These steps are combined, developed, and put together by a choreographer so that the movements interpret the story. Most ballets also use elaborate scenery and lighting to further convey the story's allure and mood.

Ballet dancers wear specially designed costumes which give them freedom of movement while dancing. The costumes help the dancers communicate the events occuring on stage during a show. Makeup and hairstyles help create the enchantment. Depending on the production and the type of dancing required, individuals also wear either ballet slippers or toe shoes.

Individuals interested in careers as ballet dancers will have to audition to become part of a company. Ballet companies at times hold auditions for new dancers. Those hired will have a number of responsibilities.

Dancers are expected to attend every rehearsal set by the company. During these times, they will learn their parts and practice, coordinating them with other dancers in the production. Dancers are also being fitted for costumes during this time period as well as having makeup and hairstyles created and developed.

Dancers perform in every production. If the company goes on tour, dancers are expected to go on the road and to continue to fulfill their duties.

Employment Opportunities

Ballet dancers audition to become members of ballet companies. Individuals may seek these auditions on their own or have agents handle the task. They may work in national, international, or regional ballet companies. Culturally active cities throughout the country and the world that host one or more ballet companies offer opportunities for talented, determined dancers. Some of these cities include:

- New York City
- London
- Miami
- Boston
- Houston

- New Orleans
- Dallas
- Washington, D.C.
- Seattle
- Pittsburgh

Earnings

Earnings of ballet dancers range greatly depending on their reputation and experience as well as the type of parts they perform. Other variables include the size, budget, and prestige of the specific ballet company the dancer is working with.

Ballet dancers may be paid by the week or by the performance. Those working in unionized settings will have their minimum earnings negotiated and set by the American Guild of Musical Artists (AGMA). Minimum weekly earnings in these situations start at approximately $500. Solo and principal dancers have higher minimum earnings, and dancers who are in demand can command much higher earnings. Those working in nonunionized settings will have minimum weekly earnings starting at $250.

Advancement Opportunities

Ballet dancers can advance their careers in a number of ways. Individuals may audition for and obtain a position with a more prestigious ballet company or may become a lead or principal dancer in a ballet production.

Education and Training

Extensive training in the art of ballet is necessary to become a successful ballet dancer. Most decided on a career in dance when they were fairly young and began taking lessons at that time. The best continue with their training throughout their careers.

Ballet training can be obtained by taking private lessons, attending ballet schools, and going through extensive training programs with ballet companies.

Experience and Qualifications

Ballet dancers obtain experience dancing in front of audiences in amateur and school recitals. A tremendous dedication is required to succeed in this field. Dancers must practice, train, and rehearse continually. They need to be exceptionally talented dancers who are graceful as well as creative in their movements.

For Additional Information: Individuals interested in a career in ballet dancing can obtain additional information by contacting the American Dance Guild (ADG), the Ballet Theater Foundation (BTF), and the American Guild of Musical Artists (AGMA).

TIPS

- Dance whenever you have the opportunity. Take part in community and school productions.
- Training is everything in this field. Get the best training you can.
- Try to supplement regular training with classes and workshops given by a variety of teachers. You will learn a variety of styles and techniques.
- Expect to have limited free time. Training, classes, rehearsals, and practice are necessary to succeed.
- Contact ballet companies throughout the country to locate summer workshops and programs. These will be useful in obtaining extra training and experience.
- Internships, apprenticeships, and other training programs will also be valuable in obtaining experience. These may be located through ballet companies.
- Read the trades such as *Backstage* and *Variety*. Many ballet companies advertise openings or auditions in these papers.
- Contact ballet companies yourself to find out when they will be holding auditions and what the requirements are.
- Don't give up. Talent, drive, determination, and perseverance can help you succeed in this field.

CHOREOGRAPHER

Job Description: Develop dance routines for dance, theatrical, movie, television, and musical productions; teach movements to dancers.

Earnings: Impossible to determine due to nature of the job.

Recommended Education and Training: No formal choreography training necessary; training as a dancer necessary.

Skills and Personality Traits: Conceptual ability; technical dance expertise; ability to teach others; creativity.

Experience and Qualifications: Experience as a dancer required.

Job Description and Responsibilities

Choreographers are responsible for creating dance routines seen in television shows and in ballet, theatrical, and musical productions and more. The main functions of a choreographer are to create and compose dance movements that are visually pleasing and that have the ability to interpret a story, feeling, or emotion.

In most situations, the choreographer will have a degree of input in the recommendation of dancers used for a project. When auditioning dancers, the choreographer may first illustrate routines for individual dancers or groups and then have them repeat the routine. In this fashion, the choreographer can determine which dancers will be best suited for a specific project.

Depending on the type of production being choreographed, the choreographer will have varied responsibilities. He or she will meet and work closely with production or show directors, producers, music directors, stage managers, costume designers, etc., in an effort to review ideas and other input.

After determining the desired basic concept, the choreographer will develop dances and movements to convey it. This is a creative process. Some accomplish this with actual dancers. Others work out routines on paper. Very creative choreographers can often achieve this goal by working out routines in their mind. After developing the routine they have to try them out with actual dancers to make sure that they work within the allotted time frame and the chosen music.

Choreographers must then teach dancers the steps, making changes where necessary and rehearsing until the routines have been perfected. In some instances, choreographers oversee the entire process, while in others assistants take charge of various tasks.

Unless the choreographer has a long-term contract, once a production is choreographed he or she usually moves on to another project. While professional dancers may have to stop working as they grow older or when injuries occur, established choreographers can enjoy a long professional life. For many, seeing dancers complete creative dance routines that they have developed is a fulfilling and rewarding experience.

Employment Opportunities

Individuals may have the easiest time breaking in to this line of work in small regional theaters or ballet companies. Some who are interested in this type of work put together their own dance troupes and work in places such as Las Vegas, Reno, or Atlantic City. Others find work with music management firms, record companies, television shows, and the like. Choreographers often augment their earnings by teaching. Other options for employment include:

- Theatrical productions
- Ballet companies
- Musical stage shows
- Music videos
- Music groups
- Musical/dance reviews

Earnings

Top choreographers can earn $500,000-plus annually. However, this is not the norm for most choreographers. Earnings can vary tremendously depending on the skills, expertise, experience, and responsibilities of the individual as well as the prestige and type of production choreographed. Many choreographers receive a small fee or get no fee at all in order to obtain experience. Some work through a contract negotiated by the Society for Stage Directors and Choreographers (SSDC). This organization sets the minimum weekly salary for choreographers.

Advancement Opportunities

Advancement in this field is achieved by obtaining a larger number of more prestigious projects to choreograph, such as segments for television shows, films, Broadway shows, popular videos, etc. Advancement in this area, like other parts of the entertainment industry, revolves around luck, contacts, and being in the right place at the right time.

Education and Training

Most choreographers train to be dancers. This can be accomplished through formal or informal study with teachers and other professional dancers. Those interested in obtaining a formal education might seek a degree in dance and/or theater.

Experience and Qualifications

It is imperative that choreographers be good teachers, get along well with others, and have the ability to communicate their ideas. One should be creative and have a technical knowledge of dance and music.

Most choreographers start their careers as dancers in any number of fields including theater, ballet, films, television, and music. Many find that they are more interested in the creative end of dance than in the actual performance.

For Additional Information: Contact the Society of Stage Directors and Choreographers (SSDC) for additional information on choreographers.

TIPS

- In order to obtain experience, volunteer to choreograph shows for local community theater groups, school, college, and university shows, and any other productions you hear about.
- Take as many classes and workshops as possible with a wide array of teachers. In this way you will learn from people who have a variety of ideas. You will also begin making important contacts.
- Network in any way you can. Join organizations, associations, and unions that can help you meet people in the field.
- Find a mentor who will not only take you under his or her wing, but will also teach you about the industry.
- Try to find an internship or apprenticeship with a dance troupe, organization, or theater group.

- Seek out opportunities to see other people's work. Attend ballets, theatrical productions, musicals, and plays. Watch variety and award shows on television and view movies that contain choreographed pieces. The more you see, the more ideas you will get.
- Read books and articles on dancers and choreographers. Study other people's techniques and expertise.
- Positions for choreographers are often advertised in the trades. Local projects may be listed in arts council newsletters or advertised in the classified section under the headings of "Choreographer," "Theater," "Music," or "Dance."

CLOWN

. . . .

Job Description: Entertain and perform for audiences in comical costume and makeup.

Earnings: $250–$1,500+ per week in circuses; $50–$250 per performance for private parties and events.

Recommended Education and Training: Classes or workshops in clowning or clown college.

Skills and Personality Traits: Ability to make people laugh; makeup skills; comic timing; mime skills; coordination; imagination.

Experience and Qualifications: Experience performing in front of people helpful, but not required.

Job Description and Responsibilities

Clowns are performers who entertain people with humorous interpretations through body movements, facial expressions, and gestures. Clowns can entertain in circuses or may perform at parties or other events.

Individuals usually have personalized makeup and costumes which identify and distinguish them from all other clowns. Makeup and costuming can make the individual look sad or happy, and help the clown mold his or her routine.

Clowning around can include numerous activities such as performing mime, magic, or slapstick comedy. Some clowns entertain with skits while others do balloon tricks or juggle. Clowns may also have specialized skills allowing them to ride a unicycle, walk on stilts, or walk on high wires. Some also include animals in their act.

Clowns working in circuses travel month after month as the circus moves around the country. Those who are successful have the satisfaction of knowing they make the people who see them happy. Young children are usually enthralled while adults are often brought back to their childhoods.

Employment Opportunities

Clowns can perform in a number of different situations. There are many circuses that travel throughout the country. The best known is the Ringling Brothers and Barnum & Bailey Circus. Individuals may work full-time as circus clowns or may perform freelance for:

- Private parties for adults or children
- Trade shows
- Hospitals
- Mall or shopping center entertainment
- Fairs

Earnings

Earnings for clowns performing in circuses range from approximately $250 to $1,500 or more per week. In many situations, expenses for food and travel are taken out of those earnings. Clowns who freelance may receive $50 to $250-plus per performance. Variables include the professional reputation and geographic location of the individual.

Advancement Opportunities

Clowns can advance their careers by locating positions in larger, more prestigious circuses. Advancement opportunities for individuals who freelance include obtaining more bookings and receiving increased fees.

Education and Training

There are a number of options for training to become a clown. Many local Shriners clubs offer classes in clowning throughout the country. The same is true of community colleges. Clowning classes and workshops teach individuals techniques such as how to apply makeup, design and make a costume, and how to dress and act. Classes also show students how to ''clown around.'' Activities might include mime, balloon tricks, juggling, throwing pies, squirting seltzer, and performing skits.

The Ringling Brothers and Barnum & Bailey Circus also conducts the only recognized Clown College in the world. The school, taught by professional clowns, teaches individuals the craft of clowning. After completing Clown College, clowns may also receive additional training from master clowns for a number of years while they are working in a circus.

Experience and Qualifications

Many clowns begin their careers by donating their time at children's hospitals and other not-for-profit organizations. They obtain experience that money cannot buy making children laugh in institutions that offer little to smile about. Others acquire experience in schools or performing at parties.

Individuals aspiring to become clowns should be friendly, sensitive people who look at life in a positive manner. Clowns should have the ability to make people laugh. Comic timing is essential. Coordination is helpful when juggling, riding unicycles, walking on stilts, etc. However, every clown does not perform these activities.

For Additional Information: Those interested in becoming clowns can obtain additional information by contacting the Ringling Brothers and Barnum & Bailey Clown College, local Shriners groups, or the personnel manager or director of traveling circuses throughout the country.

TIPS

- Begin developing business for parties as a freelance clown by designing and printing business cards with your name, phone number, and specialty. Give the cards to everyone you know. Put them on bulletin boards in supermarkets, shopping centers, party shops, etc.
- You might also want to place a small advertisement in the local newspaper announcing your availability for parties, functions, and other entertainment events.
- Perform at talent shows, reviews, and the like. All experience will be worthwhile. The exposure will also be helpful.
- If you want to dedicate your life to becoming a professional clown, apply to the Ringling Brothers and Barnum & Bailey Clown College.
- Volunteer to perform in hospitals. It will be good exposure and experience for you and will do something positive for children who need something to laugh at.

COMEDIAN

....

Job Description: Attempt to make an audience laugh by telling jokes, stories, etc.

Earnings: Impossible to determine due to the nature of the job.

Recommended Education and Training: No formal educational requirements.

Skills and Personality Traits: Ability to perform in front of audience; ability to see things in a humorous light.

Experience and Qualifications: Experience performing in front of audience.

Job Description and Responsibilities

Comedians amuse audiences by performing monologues or skits, telling jokes, singing songs, and using body movements or facial contortions in an attempt to make audiences laugh.

Stand-up comedians may work alone or in pairs. Those who work in pairs usually have one individual who acts as the "straight man" (or woman) who talks about things in a serious fashion. The other individual feeds off the other's lines in a humorous way. Comedians may also work in comedy troupes performing skits.

Comedians work in a wide array of entertainment venues and situations including in nightclubs, theaters, halls, arenas, on television and radio, and as performers for private parties.

Individuals just starting out in the field usually must "pay their dues" performing in comedy clubs and talent showcases for little or no money. Successful comedians often go back to the comedy clubs to polish their skills and perfect their act.

After an audience hears a joke or monologue more than a couple of times, it stops being funny and instead becomes predictable. Comedians must continually work on their acts. Some write their own material that evolves from personal experiences. Others use the services of one or more comedy writers. Performance length can vary from five or six minutes at talent showcases to 45 minutes to an hour as a headliner.

Even the most successful comedians have bad nights where their timing is off or the audience does not respond as they should. Comedians must be able to deal with rejection. Everyone will not always think they are funny.

Success is based on a multitude of factors including talent, ambition, determination, drive, professional contacts, and being in the right place at the right time.

Employment Opportunities

Talented individuals will find employment throughout the country. Comedians who are not well-known will usually have to audition for club owners, managers, promoters, and agents. This can be done live or with videotapes. Many agents, club owners, promoters, and managers frequently go to comedy clubs seeking out new talent.

While many people just starting out in their career try to get jobs themselves, most comedians eventually seek out agents. Comedians can work in a variety of situations. They can be the stars themselves or may open for other acts including singers, recording artists, musicians, and even other comedians. Employment opportunities include:

- Comedy clubs
- Nightclubs
- Cruise ships
- Hotels
- Lounges
- Halls
- Television

Earnings

Earnings for comedians can and do vary tremendously. Individuals can earn between $100 and $25,000 or more per show. Factors affecting earnings include the experience, professional reputation, and popularity of the individual as well as the specific venue of the performance.

Those just starting out may perform just for the experience and exposure. Others may perform for "the door." This means that the individual receives a portion or the full amount of the admission price paid by people who came to the show.

Advancement Opportunities

It is much easier for comedians to advance their careers now than it was 10 years ago. Today, comedy clubs are springing up throughout the country. Almost every city has at least one if not more. There are also a large number of opportunities to appear on television, whether it be on local, network, independent, or cable station shows.

There are a number of different paths comedians can take for career advancement. They may perform in more prestigious venues or get booked on television talk and variety shows. Another means of career advancement is becoming more successful and sought out. This results in commanding and receiving higher fees.

Some comedians stop working stand-up and instead go on to perform in situation comedies or films. Performers who have successfully accomplished this include Bill Cosby, Sinbad, Jerry Seinfeld, Roseanne, Eddie Murphy, and Robin Williams. Other comedians such as Joan Rivers, Jay Leno, Chevy Chase, and

Jenny Jones have gone on to host television talk shows. The sky is the limit as far as advancement opportunities for comedians.

Education and Training

Comedians come from all walks of life. Some hold bachelor's or graduate degrees. Others have not even graduated from high school. There are no formal educational requirements.

Seminars, workshops, and courses in comedy performance and writing are helpful. These may be offered through colleges, universities, and schools either for credit or noncredit classes.

Many feel that the best training is on-the-job experience performing at comedy clubs and talent showcases.

Experience and Qualifications

Comedians usually start out performing in talent showcases, comedy clubs, or similar venues to gain exposure, experience, and to work on an act. There are a great many comedians who believe their careers really started in school as the class clown.

Being funny is of course important. The ability to see life and daily occurrences in a humorous manner is imperative. In order to be successful, it is mandatory that comedians must have the ability to share these thoughts and feelings verbally in front of an audience and to be comfortable doing so.

For Additional Information: Aspiring comedians may contact the Association of Entertainment (AE) or the National Mime Association (NMA) to learn more about careers in this field. Additional information can be obtained from the American Guild of Variety Artists (AGVA), The Hollywood Comedy Club (HCC), and the American Federation of Television and Radio Artists (AFTRA).

TIPS

- Take classes and workshops in performing and writing comedy.
- There are a great number of comedy "competitions" throughout the country. These are often sponsored by television stations, comedy clubs, and/or corporate sponsors. Try to get involved with these programs. They are excellent ways to obtain exposure.
- Offer to emcee any type of entertainment event you can find. Consider local talent and variety shows, telethons, charity dinners, luncheons, etc.
- Don't forget to take part in local talent and variety shows yourself.
- Perform as often as you can to hone your skills, obtain experience and exposure, and perfect your act.

- A great deal of the success in this field is based not only on talent, but drive, determination, ambition, and perseverance. Do not give up. Believe in yourself!
- Go to clubs and watch other comedians perform to see what makes their acts successful.
- You will also learn a great deal by watching comedians perform on television. Check out their style, techniques, timing, and content.
- Do not try to get a paying job in comedy until you and your act are ready.
- Locate all the nightclubs and comedy clubs in your area and find out the requirements for performing. Many have amateur or "open mike" nights as well as talent showcases where new entertainers can try out material and hone their acts.
- Consider talking to local bands, singers, and other musical acts about opening for them.
- When you are ready, contact agents who specialize in booking comedy acts.

MODEL

Job Description: Pose for photographs; appear in advertisements and/or commercials; model clothing or accessories.

Earnings: Starts at $8 per hour and may go up to $2 million or more annually.

Recommended Education and Training: Modeling school.

Skills and Personality Traits: Poise, well-groomed; physically fit; physical stamina; attractive; photogenic.

Experience and Qualifications: Experience and qualifications vary for different types of modeling.

Job Description and Responsibilities

Models may work in a number of different situations. Some pose for photographs, artwork, advertisements, or commercials. Others appear on the covers or inside pages of virtually any type of magazine, catalog, or newspaper. Some model clothing and accessories or demonstrate a vast array of items at trade shows.

There are a number of different types of models. They include artist's models, stroll models, product promotional models, fashion models, print models, showroom models, runway models, and fit models.

Artist's models are used in commercial art and college situations. The main function of an artist's model is to pose for artists either one-on-one or in front of a group. This is a particularly grueling type of modeling for most people.

Individuals must sit, stand, or pose in one position for extended lengths of time. During this period the artists will sketch, draw, or paint their image of the model. Individuals must sometimes model nude in this line of work.

Stroll modeling entails walking through department stores, boutiques, restaurants, tea rooms, etc., showing clothing and accessories to potential buyers. They may often stop to chat with customers to tell them about the product or its costs.

Individuals doing product promotional modeling go to trade shows and demonstrate products to people in the trade and to other potential customers. In order to be effective, these models are fully familiarized with the product they are demonstrating prior to their modeling assignment.

Showroom models display the fashions of clothing manufacturers or designers. This is one of the least glamorous positions in modeling. However, it is the type of modeling that often leads to bigger and better things. Many individuals who demonstrate talent are often chosen to work as runway models in fashion shows.

Fit models stand perfectly still while designers place fabric on them and cut and drape the fabric to develop clothing designs.

Print models are the individuals seen in pictures used in catalogs and fashion magazines. The model's allure and appearance is used to enhance the appeal of a product and hopefully, make it sell better. This is the most glamorous type of modeling; these individuals have the opportunity to become well-known. Print models often lead exciting, glamorous lives.

Responsibilities and duties depend on the type of model and on the specific assignment she or he was hired for. No matter what kind of modeling the individual performs, the main function of each is to pose for some specific purpose.

The first step models usually must take is finding a modeling agency to represent them. In return, they pay the agency a fee off the top of their earnings. Models need to compile a portfolio of professional photographs of themselves in different poses, situations, etc. These are then shown to potential employers or agencies to demonstrate the individual's photogenic qualities.

Once models find an agency willing to represent them, a contract is usually signed. The agency may arrange for different photographs to be taken. When the agency is called, they will send models on interviews. Other jobs are obtained strictly from photographs. Major agencies often represent models who are sought by prestigious magazines and companies.

Sometimes photo shoots take place in a studio. In other situations, the model may be whisked off to a faraway, exotic location. A shoot may take a few hours or all-day. Some shoots may last a number of days, depending on how extensive the advertising campaign or project is.

Employment Opportunities

Modeling opportunities are available for women, men, and children. While there are a number of opportunities for models to work on-staff at clothing manufacturers, designers, department stores, or boutiques, most models freelance. Some pursue other career goals or school while working part-time in modeling. Others are lucky enough to have sufficient bookings to work solely in modeling.

In order to obtain bookings, most models sign with a modeling agency and often a management company. There are many fine agencies, management companies, and managers located throughout the country and in Europe. Major agencies in this country are located in New York City. The major modeling agencies include:

- Click
- Ford
- Elite
- Willhelmina

Earnings

Earnings for models can vary greatly depending on a number of factors. These include the experience, responsibilities, reputation, and popularity of the individual as well as the actual type of modeling.

Artist's models may earn between $50 and $300-plus per session. Product promotional models may earn between $8 and $15 per hour. Fit models are paid approximately $125 per hour.

While print models have the most glamorous type of job, it does not always pay well. Many famous cover models receive only a token payment such as $100 per cover. The reason for this is that appearing on a cover often opens doors with corporations. After appearing on a cover, a model may sign a deal with a large cosmetic or clothing company as well as with other national or international corporations. This does pay well. Successful print models or those appearing on television commercials may earn $500,000 or more per year. Superstar models working in these situations often earn $2 million or more annually.

Department store models usually receive between $8 and $15 per hour. Runway models may earn between $50 and $100 per show. In New York City, individuals can earn $100 or more per show. Runway models who are in demand and recognizable as celebrities earn $1,000 per show.

Advancement Opportunities

Advancement opportunities for models depend on the current level of the individual's career. For some, advancement might mean more bookings resulting in steadier work. To others it might mean modeling in more prestigious fashion shows. Some models work in television appearing in commercials or modeling on television shopping networks and so on.

Most models strive to grace the covers of fashion magazines. This often will push their career to new heights. Covers mean recognition in modeling. That often results in an individual's being picked up by major cosmetic, clothing, or other companies to represent their products. The high point of modeling is to become a superstar model like Christie Brinkley or Isabella Rosellini.

Education and Training

While there are no formal educational requirements, some sort of training will be beneficial. There are many modeling schools located throughout the country. These schools teach the skills and techniques of modeling, walking, standing, dressing, makeup application, and more. They often provide a basic understanding of the industry and offer tips on finding jobs and agents. Many managers and agents feel that those who go through modeling schools have more self-confidence and flair than those who do not.

Experience and Qualifications

As experience is acquired, models become confident and more sure of themselves. Models should be well-groomed individuals with a great deal of physical stamina. Although it may not look difficult to stand in one position for hours on end or to walk up and down a runway, it is not easy.

Models come in all sizes, shapes, and ages. There is no one look or physical appearance that insures success. While for many years the only type of woman acceptable for this position was tall and thin, things have changed. Large-sized and petite models are often sought for certain assignments, as are older women.

Certain modeling assignments do require individuals to meet certain specific qualifications. Strolling floor models, or example, need to be attractive and a perfect size as well as have a pleasant personality. Fit models need to be a perfect size.

Product promotional models have no height requirements but need to be personable and good-looking. They must also be familiar with the product. Female print models must be five-foot-nine or taller. Most male print models must be exactly six feet tall. Those who are one or two inches over must have a terrific look in order to be considered. Runway models need a flair about them and the ability to move gracefully on the runway. Most must also be a perfect size with a height requirement of at least five-foot-nine. An exception would be runway models for petite lines of clothing.

For Additional Information: Individuals interested in pursuing a career in modeling can obtain additional information by contacting modeling agencies, managers, or schools. Other information may be available from the Modeling Association of America International (MAAI), the World Modeling Association (WMA), or the International Talent and Models Association (ITMA). These organizations sponsor annual conventions where schools and managers bring their modeling talent to the attention of agency people.

TIPS

- Look for a reputable school of modeling. You will learn the basic skills and requirements needed for the profession. It will also give you the confidence and flair that others who have not attended school may not have.

- Many schools also have placement services or act as agencies or management firms, sending individuals out on modeling assignments.
- Take any additional classes you can in grooming, fashion, makeup application, color coordination, walking, etc.
- No matter what type of modeling you work at, you must look healthy and fit. Eat right, drink plenty of fluids, get enough sleep, and exercise.
- There may be opportunities advertised in the newspaper classified section. Look under headings such as "Model," "Children's Model," "Artist's Model," and "Fashion Shows."
- If you are interested in working as an artist's model, contact art schools in your area.

SONGWRITER

· ·

Job Description: Compose lyrics and/or music for songs.

Earnings: Impossible to determine due to nature of the job.

Recommended Education and Training: No formal educational requirements; workshops, seminars, and classes in songwriting useful; music training through self-teaching, private study, conservatories, colleges, or universities may be helpful.

Skills and Personality Traits: Creativity; musical talent; understanding of music theory.

Experience and Qualifications: Experience writing music, lyrics, or poetry helpful.

Job Description and Responsibilities

Songwriters are responsible for writing the lyrics and/or music of a song. These individuals are also called composers, writers, or lyricists.

Songwriters may sit at a desk everyday for a certain number of hours attempting to write a song or may only try to write when they have an inspiration, an idea, or a feeling. Some can sit down and write a song about any subject.

While many songwriters work alone, others collaborate. Songs are created in a number of ways. Many writers create the words first and then compose the music. Others do the reverse. Some handle both tasks almost simultaneously.

For those aspiring to be a commercial songwriter, writing a song is only the tip of the iceberg. After completing a song, one must find a way to market it. To begin marketing a song, the songwriter must first make sure the tune is protected so others cannot say they wrote the song after they hear it. The most common way of protecting music is to apply for and obtain a copyright on the piece. This is accomplished through the federal government which will supply forms and copyrighting instructions.

Once a copyright has been obtained, the songwriter must attempt to locate someone who is interested in recording or using the song. To do this, the individual will usually make a demo showcasing the song or songs. While the demo should be as professional as possible, it does not have to be elaborately prepared. Up to three songs should be recorded on a clean tape. Labels should indicate the song titles, times, writer(s), and a contact phone number and address. Some also include lyrics and music.

After copies are made, the songwriter must send or deliver the demos and any other pertinent information to music publishers, recording acts, producers, A & R people, and management companies. Since many companies do not accept unsolicited material, it is a good idea to send a query letter asking for permission to send tapes before sending or delivering demos. If the songwriter wants the tapes back, self-addressed stamped envelopes or packages should also be included.

If a publisher, recording artist, or A & R person shows interest in a tune, the songwriter has a number of options. The individual can sell the song outright or just sell the rights to use it. A contract will be offered spelling out the terms of the agreement. Most successful songwriters seek the advice of attorneys who are familiar with the music industry to review these contracts and to protect the songwriter.

One of the reasons that songwriting is so attractive is that a song can turn into a hit at any time. There are many people who have written tunes, made deals with publishers, and then a couple of years later, have had major recording artists record their songs and turn them into major hits.

Employment Opportunities

While almost anyone who wants to can eventually write a song, not everyone can become a successful songwriter. Individuals can write the best song of the century, but unless they find someone to publish and record it, they will not experience any type of commercial success. Some songwriters write hundreds of songs in their lifetime and never sell a song. Others produce hit after hit.

One of the great things about this career is that it can be done on either a full-time or part-time basis. Some songwriters are also musicians, singers, or performers who want to write their own songs.

Songwriters can work by themselves or with collaborators. They write tunes for artists to sing in concerts or to record. Others may write songs for radio or television jingles, or music for plays, films, or television shows.

There are also employment opportunities on staff in a number of settings. These include working for:

- Record companies
- Recording artists
- Producers

Earnings

It is impossible to determine earnings of songwriters due to the nature of the job. Some write songs and never sell or publish them. Others may write a song that turns into a monster hit.

Factors affecting earnings include the number of songs the songwriter has had published and/or sold; the number of times each song is played, performed, or used; and the popularity of each song. Earnings will also depend on the specific type of agreement made for each tune. As noted previously, some individuals sell songs outright while others only sell the rights to use songs. Songwriters may receive writers' royalties and/or publishers' royalties. Earnings also depend on the number of collaborators who have written the tune as well as the method used for splitting the monies received.

One of the most exciting things about being a songwriter is that once a song is published, individuals may receive royalties for the rest of their lives. Financial success can occur at almost any time.

As songwriters generally receive a percentage of monies every time a song is performed, played, or used, they can earn a great deal of money. Very successful people in this field can and do earn over a million dollars annually. Depending on the success of the tune or tunes, earnings can continue indefinitely. This is especially true when artists record remakes of old hits.

Advancement Opportunities

The goal of most commercial songwriters is to write songs that turn into mega-hits and then become standards. This can occur one or more times during a songwriter's career.

Education and Training

There are no formal educational requirements for songwriters. Many individuals attend workshops, seminars, and classes in songwriting. Others read books on the subject.

Some songwriters may also obtain useful music training through self-learning, private study, conservatories, colleges, or universities.

Experience and Qualifications

Experience writing lyrics, music, and poetry is often useful in honing skills. While there is a fair amount of talent required for success in this field, there is also a great deal of luck required. It is necessary for songwriters to persevere and keep trying in order to get the attention of music publishers, recording acts, A & R people, etc. Many hits were not accepted on the first attempt to sell them.

A knowledge of the workings of the music industry is useful in marketing tunes. Musical talent and an understanding of music theory is helpful, but not always necessary.

For Additional Information: There are a number of associations and organizations that can provide additional information to aspiring songwriters. These include the American Society of Composers, Authors, and Publishers (ASCAP); Broadcast Music, Inc. (BMI); SESAC; The Songwriters Guild (SG); the Nashville Songwriters Association International (NSAI); the Country Music Association (CMA); the Gospel Music Association (GMA); and the National Academy of Recording Arts and Sciences (NARAS).

TIPS

- Look for songwriting workshops and seminars. These offer inspiration, advice, and tips. They are also a good place to make contacts.
- Go to the library and the bookstore to find books on songwriting. They can be another good source of inspiration, advice, and tips for honing skills in this field.
- Write as much as you can. It helps develop the craft of songwriting.
- Make sure you protect your songs! While copyrighting is the only real protection, some individuals suggest another method. Place the words and music of your song into an envelope, seal it, address it to yourself, and send it via certified registered mail. Do not open the envelope when you get it. Instead, put it away in case you require any type of proof.
- Staff positions as songwriters may be located in recording capitals such as New York City, Los Angeles, and Nashville.
- Learn as much as you can about every aspect of the music business. This will make you more effective when you try to sell, publish, and market your songs.
- Get the opinions and advice of people who listen to music for a living. Many guilds and associations have workshops or experts who offer professional advice. Other sources include disc jockeys, music directors and local musical artists.
- Publishers are the ones who pay writers for their work, not the other way around. Make sure you do not get involved with people who ask you to pay to publish your own songs.
- If your songs are good, they will eventually make it. Don't give up. Have faith and persevere. If you give up, your songs will not stand a chance.

Some playwrights advance their careers by writing scripts for successful television shows or films.

Education and Training

There is no formal educational requirement necessary to become a playwright. Seminars and workshops in all facets of writing, including scriptwriting as well as stage, theater, and acting, will be helpful in honing skills.

While college will not guarantee success to a playwright, it is often useful. Colleges offering majors in theater, theater arts, scriptwriting, or acting often have programs where aspiring playwrights can have their plays worked on, further developed, and produced at the school. This offers playwrights opportunities and experiences others might not have.

Experience and Qualifications

The more writing experience a playwright can garner, the better. Writing skills and techniques need to be polished. While writing a script does utilize certain techniques, creativity is creativity—the more it is practiced, the better it becomes. Many successful playwrights also have written short stories, novels, or articles in magazines and newspapers.

Playwrights should have an excellent command of the English language and an ability to write dialogue. They need to be creative and exciting writers with the ability to bring stories to life.

For Additional Information: Learn more about a career as a playwright by contacting the Dramatist Guild (DG) and the New Dramatist.

TIPS

• Join the Dramatist Guild, the New Dramatist, and any other professional organizations you can locate. These groups provide professional and business guidance to their members as well as offer an array of other useful services. They also provide a number of internship programs.
• Take as many seminars, courses, and workshops as possible in writing and scriptwriting. These will give you the opportunity to learn a variety of methods, ideas, and writing techniques. They also force you into a position where you continue to write. Part of many workshops includes reviewing your work and offering ideas and suggestions to improve it.
• Enter playwrighting contests. These may be sponsored by organizations, local and national theater groups, colleges, universities, or play publishers.
• Attend every theater production you can. It doesn't matter if it is a play put on by a local theater group or school or a Broadway production. The more

exposure you have to a variety of theater productions, the more ideas you will generate and the better a writer you will become.
- Make contacts in the theatrical world. Start with your local theater group, summer stock, regional theaters, etc.
- It is imperative that you do not take rejection of your scripts personally. Keep writing. Perseverance is necessary for success.

SCREENWRITER/SCRIPTWRITER

Job Description: Develop and write scripts for television programs, film productions, and motion pictures.

Earnings: $13,000–$1 million-plus per script.

Recommended Education and Training: Courses, seminars, and workshops in script- and screenwriting.

Skills and Personality Traits: Writing skills; good command of the English language; creativity; imagination.

Experience and Qualifications: Writing experience helpful.

Job Description and Responsibilities

Script- and screenwriters are responsible for scripts used in television shows, films, and motion pictures. Individuals may be assigned scripts or may develop them on speculation. Depending on the situation, script- and screenwriters may develop an entire script or may work from an idea developed by another person.

Individuals writing for television may develop scripts for comedies, dramas, and made-for-television movies. Some scriptwriters also handle scripts for nonfiction programming such as documentaries and talk and variety shows. These types of scripts require different types of research and style. Screenwriters developing screenplays for motion pictures may craft scripts for a myriad of different types of films, from comedies to dramas to thrillers.

In order to write a script for television or film, writers must choose the subject and style. Sometimes, at this point, the individual will conduct research to determine the most effective way to tell a story or the type of characters that should be developed. The screen/scriptwriter must then draft a plot outline and develop a treatment describing the events of the story as they will happen in the script.

The scriptwriter may also be expected to meet with the producer and/or director as well as others in the production to make changes in the script. Scripts are usually never accepted as is. There are usually a great deal of changes and rewrites. In many situations, scripts are changed up to the moment of filming.

Individuals may write completely original scripts or may adapt stories of plays or books to television or motion pictures. Currently, there is also a trend to write scripts about real-life dramas. Scriptwriters may also prepare new or updated versions of movies or television programming.

Scriptwriters may work alone or collaborate with others. In some situations, such as writing for daytime soap operas, there is a head writer and a number of others who work under his or her direction. In these cases, the head writer may develop the ideas for scripts and then assign other writers the day-to-day tasks of dialogue.

One of the most exciting things about screen/scriptwriting is that the completed scripts for television or motion pictures can make such a great impact on the audience. Whether an individual writes a comedy that makes the audience laugh or a drama that makes people think, television and movies are a major force in entertainment today. Without a good script, even the best actors and actresses cannot pull off a production and make it successful.

Employment Opportunities

While scriptwriters and screenwriters can work anyplace, the best opportunities are in Los Angeles and New York City where the majority of television shows and motion pictures are produced. Individuals are usually hired or retained by the producer or director of a project.

Generally, television scriptwriters and screenwriters for films freelance. However, there are a limited number of staff positions available at studios, networks, and independent production companies. Writers for this medium can write scripts for:

- Motion pictures
- Television programs (dramas, sitcoms, soap operas, made-for-TV movies, etc.)
- Films

Earnings

Earnings for scriptwriters and screenwriters can range dramatically, depending on a number of variables. These include the specific film or television show as well as the experience, responsibilities, and reputation of the writer.

Individuals writing television scripts may have minimum earnings set by the Writers Guild of America (WGA). Minimum earnings negotiated by the WGA are determined by the length and type of the program along with various other factors. For example, an individual writing the script for a 30-minute sitcom can earn a minimum of approximately $13,000. Usually, much higher fees are negotiated for writers who have developed other successful scripts.

Screenwriters may also have minimum earnings negotiated and set by the WGA. Compensation is based on, among other things, the budget of the film. Minimum earnings for writing a screenplay range from $18,500 to $38,000. However, many screenwriters demand and receive much higher fees. It is not uncommon for screenwriters to receive $1 million or more for a script for a high-budget feature film.

Advancement Opportunities

Advancement opportunities for screenwriters and scriptwriters are endless. This is another of the careers where success can come at any time. Advancement in this field can mean selling a script for a television show or being asked to write the screenplay for an upcoming film. Writing the script of a feature film that turns into a box office hit usually means that the writer will have an easier time selling other scripts.

Many screenwriters advance their careers by becoming directors of films or television programs as well as working as writers.

Education and Training

While a college degree is not necessary to become a screen/scriptwriter, the educational background may provide helpful experience and training. Many individuals in this line of work have degrees in English, communications, theater arts, radio-television, film, liberal arts, or related fields.

Seminars, workshops, and classes in all forms of writing are useful in honing skills. Courses in playwriting, scriptwriting, and screenwriting will be beneficial for learning basic techniques.

Experience and Qualifications

Individuals in this career gain experience and perfect their craft by writing and rewriting. In general, the more the scriptwriter writes, the better the scripts will get.

Scriptwriters and screenwriters should be talented, creative, imaginative people with logical thought patterns. Good writing skills are essential, as is a command of the English language. Individuals must be dedicated to this profession, disciplined, and willing to persevere in order to succeed.

For Additional Information: Aspiring screenwriters and scriptwriters can obtain additional career information by contacting the WGA and the American Film Institute (AFI).

TIPS

- Write to the WGA to find out about membership requirements. Join as soon as you can. This union provides a great deal of professional guidance and support to its members.
- Get as much experience as possible writing scripts.
- Consider writing scripts for local community theaters or school groups. Techniques for writing are similar in theater, television, and film.
- Attend workshops, seminars, classes, and lectures revolving around the television and film industry.
- Join writers' groups and attend their meetings. In most of these groups, you can bring your work and have it critiqued. Many writers' groups also have periodic meetings in which known screen/scriptwriters lecture.
- Watch a variety of films and television programs to see how various scripts were developed.
- There are many books on the subject of screenwriting and scriptwriting. Read them to learn the basic techniques.
- Try to set aside some time each day to write. Work on a schedule. In that way, you will avoid becoming lax.
- Due to a variety of legal problems, most people in the position to buy a script will only look at the material if it is submitted by an agent. You therefore should try to find a literary agent who will represent you.
- *Never* pay an agent to represent you or to read your scripts. Agents are supposed to pay you after they sell your script, NOT the other way around.
- Contact the WGA to obtain a list of reputable agents.
- Generally, in order to find an agent who will consider representing you, you must send a script to be read. If you want it back with an answer, remember to send it with a self-addressed stamped envelope.

CHAPTER 3
. . . .

Careers in Radio

It is difficult in today's society not to be affected by radio. People might tune in to their favorite station to hear music, weather reports, news, or an interesting talk show. They may listen at home, in a car, or virtually anyplace else with portable headphones. In some instances, individuals do not even tune in personally, but hear programming in stores, shopping malls, businesses, and offices.

There are opportunities in a broad spectrum of radio careers in small, mid-sized, and major markets throughout the country. The radio industry requires an array of employees with various talents, skills, education, training, and experience. There are secretaries, accountants, computer operators, salespeople, receptionists, copywriters, community relations and promotional specialists, and public relations people, as well as music, program, news, and sports directors, reporters, disc jockeys, announcers, and talk show hosts.

Space restrictions limit discussing all possible opportunities. Careers covered in this section are:

Program Director—Radio
Music Director—Radio
Disc Jockey
Radio Talk Show Host
News Reporter—Radio
Promotion Director—Radio

Community Affairs Director—
  Radio
Traffic Manager—Radio
Advertising Salesperson—Radio
Advertising Copywriter—Radio/
  Television

Individuals interested in broadcasting careers in other media should also review entries in Chapter 4, "Careers In Television, Film, and Video."

PROGRAM DIRECTOR—RADIO

Job Description: Determining format and programming for radio station.

Earnings: $17,000–$100,000+

Recommended Education and Training: Requirements vary; college background or degree, or broadcast school training may be preferred.

Skills and Personality Traits: Communications skills; detail-oriented; supervisory skills; ability to make decisions.

Experience and Qualifications: Experience working for radio station necessary; knowledge of radio industry.

Job Description and Responsibilities

Radio stations offer a variety of formats and programming content. Some stations follow an "all talk" format. Others focus on country music, oldies, adult contemporary, or pop music. Many have a combination. Regardless of the format, each station must schedule programs, public information spots, and commercials. The person who handles the scheduling functions is the program director.

In this position, the program director has a multitude of responsibilities. The goal of a program director's efforts is to boost the ratings of a station. This can be accomplished in a number of ways.

At some stations, a format is already in place. At others, the individual may help determine the format with the station's general manager. This may occur when a station is sold to a new owner or when it is not doing well.

Radio stations earn their income through selling advertising, and advertising rates are determined by the number of people who listen to a station, so having a popular format is very important. The larger the listening audience, the higher the ratings, and the more a station can charge for its advertising.

When selecting a format, the program director will research the market, determine demographics, and get people's opinions on what they want to listen to on a radio station. The individual must have a complete knowledge and understanding of the community that the station serves.

After a format is chosen, the program director will be in charge of developing and scheduling specific programs within that format. In addition to commercial programming, the program director must also develop public service shows. He or she will assist the general manager in determining which disc jockeys or announcers should host what show and when each should air. The individual must also schedule news, weather, public service announcements, and advertisements.

If the format is music, in addition to scheduling, the program director is responsible for developing a segue or rotation schedule for music that is played.

An effective segue keeps an audience listening without becoming bored. Everything that is done by the program director is aimed at keeping current listeners tuned to the station as well as bringing in new listeners.

At many stations, the program director will also be the music director and will be expected to handle the responsibilities of that job. These include meeting with record promotion people, listening to new releases, and developing a playlist on a regular basis.

Other responsibilities and functions can include participating in special appearances and promotions of the station, hiring, training, supervising, and firing disc jockeys, and working closely with other departments to foster the image the station is attempting to project.

Employment Opportunities

Every station has a program director. At very small stations, the functions might be handled by the general manager or a disc jockey. Individuals may work for stations with a wide variety of formats including all talk, music, or a combination of both. Opportunities may also be located in commercial or public radio.

Employment settings can range from small, local radio stations, to networks, to those in major markets. Cities in which major market stations are located include:

- New York
- Los Angeles
- Chicago
- Atlanta
- Philadelphia
- Detroit
- Boston

Earnings

Program directors can have annual salaries ranging from approximately $17,000 to $100,000-plus. Determining factors in earnings include the size, location, and popularity of the specific station as well as the experience, reputation, and responsibilities of the program director.

Individuals with little experience or those working in smaller or tertiary markets will have earnings between $17,000 and $28,000. Those with more experience, or working for larger stations in secondary markets, can expect earnings ranging from $25,000 to $45,000. Program directors with a great deal of experience at large stations in major markets will earn between $40,000 and $90,000. Top earners at popular stations in major markets can earn up to $100,000 or more annually.

Advancement Opportunities

Program directors can advance their careers by locating similar positions at larger or more prestigious stations in secondary or major markets. This will result in higher earnings and increased responsibilities.

Program directors can also climb the career ladder through promotion to the position of station general manager.

Education and Training

As with many other jobs in entertainment, educational and training requirements vary. Some stations do not require anything except a high school diploma and a proven track record. Others require or prefer a college background or degree. A major or courses in communications, broadcasting, or journalism can't hurt and may be helpful in advancement. There are also programs in broadcasting available at vocational or trade schools.

Experience and Qualifications

Experience working for a radio station is usually necessary in order to become a program director. Many in radio begin honing their skills by working at college radio stations. Program directors as a rule begin as disc jockeys or announcers.

In order to be successful in programming, individuals must have a comprehensive knowledge of the type of audience the station is trying to reach. If the station format is music, program directors should be cognizant of music and music trends. Similarly, if the format is talk radio, the individual must have a thorough understanding of the market, events, and trends. Personal preferences and opinions cannot affect decision making regarding station programming. The ability to make informed decisions is mandatory.

For Additional Information: Associations and organizations that can provide additional information about a career in radio include the National Association of Broadcasters (NAB), The American Federation of Television and Radio Artists (AFTRA), the National Association of Broadcast Employees and Technicians (NABET), and the National Academy of Recording Arts and Sciences (NARAS).

TIPS

- Before attending any vocational or trade school, check into its reputation through your state's attorney general's office, the Department of Consumer Affairs, and/or the Better Business Bureau.
- Positions in this field are advertised in the newspaper classified section under headings such as "Radio," "Broadcasting," "Program Director," "Music," "Talk Radio," and "Programming."

- Openings in secondary and major markets are often advertised in radio, music, and other broadcast trade journals. These include *Billboard*, *Broadcasting*, and *Radio and Records*. Opportunities may also be advertised or listed in association trade journals.
- Read the trade magazines to learn about new trends in broadcasting and to keep up with news and current affairs in the industry. Many libraries subscribe to these publications. If your local library doesn't, you might ask the general manager of a local radio station if you can browse through the station's copies.
- Hands-on experience is worth its weight in gold as far as opportunities and advancement. Get involved with your college radio station. Try to find a part-time job with a local station in any capacity.
- Locate an internship program at a radio station. You might either contact radio stations yourself or see if your college has any connections. Often you can receive college credit for these types of programs as well as obtain valuable experience and make important contacts.

MUSIC DIRECTOR—RADIO

Job Description: Select music for shows aired on station; meet with promotion people to discuss new releases.

Earnings: $17,000–$95,000+

Recommended Education and Training: Requirements vary; some stations may prefer college degree or broadcast school training; on-the-job training at radio station helpful.

Skills and Personality Traits: Enjoyment of music; ability to foresee what will be hot and what will not.

Experience and Qualifications: Experience as disc jockey; knowledge of radio stations; understanding of music and music industry.

Job Description and Responsibilities

The main function of the music director of a radio station is to choose the music for programs aired on the station. Responsibilities of the individual vary depending on the station's size and format.

The music director is in charge of selecting the types of music in addition to the specific songs that will be played during a particular show and used for the station's playlist. The playlist is the list of records broadcast regularly on the station.

In order to accomplish this, the individual must listen to a great deal of music. Included are songs already being played as well as new music. New music is brought to the attention of the music director in a number of ways. Record labels send radio stations their new releases in hopes that a music director will listen, like a song, and add it to their playlist. Labels also send promotion people to radio stations throughout the country to meet with music directors. Promotion people try to "push" new records by convincing the music director to listen to their new releases and to add them to the station's playlist. Music videos and television also bring new releases to the attention of radio station music directors.

The music director is expected to conduct research regarding the specific market of the station. This research might include determining the demographics of the listening audience, musical likes and dislikes, the types of music selling in the area, etc.

The music director works closely with the station program director. They discuss research and how new releases will fit into the station's format. They then collectively put together the most effective playlist for the station. At many stations, the music director might also be the program director and might be expected to handle the extra responsibilities as well. Depending on the specific situation, the music director will be responsible either to the program director or the station's general manager.

Additional responsibilities of the individual vary, depending on the station format and size. Music directors may be disc jockeys and have their own radio show or may just be asked to fill in when there is a shortage of on-air personnel. Other responsibilities may include assisting in the training of new DJs and taking part in special appearances and promotions.

For those who enjoy music and the music industry, this type of job is a great opportunity.

Employment Opportunities

Music directors work at radio stations of various sizes, formats, and popularities. Generally, individuals handling the position of music director at a smaller station will also either be the program director or be a disc jockey on a regularly scheduled radio show.

Larger stations in major markets will have more opportunities for full-time music directors. Cities hosting major or primary market radio include:

- New York
- Los Angeles
- Chicago
- Atlanta
- Philadelphia
- Detroit
- Boston

Earnings

Annual earnings for music directors can vary from approximately $17,000 to $95,000 or more. Factors include the size, popularity, and geographic location of the specific station. Other variables include the duties, experience, and reputation of the music director.

Individuals working in smaller markets will be paid salaries on the lower end of the scale. Music directors with a great deal of experience working for popular stations in major markets will have earnings at the higher end of the pay scale.

Advancement Opportunities

Music directors can follow a number of paths to career advancement depending on the direction they want to pursue. Individuals may find similar positions at larger or more prestigious stations. They may also advance to become program director at the same or a larger station.

They may also move up by programming the music for nationally syndicated radio or television shows. Some individuals move out of radio and advance their careers by obtaining jobs with major record labels.

Education and Training

Educational requirements for music directors vary from station to station. Some individuals have a high school diploma and prove themselves as they climb the ranks at radio stations. There are a great many radio stations requiring or prefering everyone involved at the station to have a college background or bachelor's degree. Good choices for majors include music merchandising, music business, communications, journalism, music, and broadcasting. Those who do attend college will also have the opportunity to work on the school's radio station and obtain hands-on training.

Another option for hands-on training is available through vocational and trade schools.

Experience and Qualifications

Music directors must have had experience working at radio stations either professionally or while attending school. Generally, most program directors start out as disc jockeys.

It is imperative that individuals in this type of position like music. In order to perform effectively, they will have to listen to a great many records.

Successful music directors have an uncanny ability to hear a song once or twice and know it will be a hit.

For Additional Information: To learn more about a career in radio contact the National Association of Broadcasters (NAB), the American Federation of Television and Radio Artists (AFTRA), the National Association of Broadcast Employees and Technicians (NABET), and the National Academy of Recording Arts and Sciences (NARAS).

TIPS

- Trade papers and journals often advertise openings for music directors at stations throughout the country. These trades include *Billboard*, *Broadcasting*, and *Radio and Records*.
- Positions are also advertised in the newspaper classified or display sections under the headings of "Music Director," "Programming," "Programming Director," "Radio," "Broadcasting," and "Music."
- Get as much experience working at radio stations and in the music industry as possible. Get involved with your college radio station.
- You might also consider contacting a local station about developing your own show on a specific subject or type of music. In order to persuade them to accept a show, offer to find advertisers.
- Write or call local stations inquiring about internship possibilities. While you won't usually make any money, you will obtain much-needed experience and make important contacts.

DISC JOCKEY

. . . .

Job Description: Introduce records, commercials, news, and public announcements on a radio station.

Earnings: $12,000–$225,000+

Recommended Education and Training: College or vocational training in broadcasting preferred.

Skills and Personality Traits: Pleasant speaking voice; radio personality.

Experience and Qualifications: Experience working on school radio stations helpful.

Job Description and Responsibilities

Disc jockeys work for radio stations. They can have varied responsibilities and duties depending on the structure and size of the station. Stations have an array of formats including various types of music, sports, news, talk, or some combination of these.

Disc jockeys working on stations with music formats are responsible for introducing records. Many DJs offer facts to the listening audience about the recording artists, their tours, and/or their music. Most DJs do quite a bit of ad-libbing in between playing records. At some stations, they may choose the music they play for their shows. At others, the music is chosen by the program or music director of the station. DJs on smaller stations may also be responsible for putting records on turntables or cassettes in tape decks as well as working sound controls. These tasks will be handled by engineers at larger stations.

Other responsibilities of the disc jockey include announcing commercials, giving weather and traffic reports and updates, and reporting the news.

At smaller stations, the disc jockey may also be the program or music director. They may be expected to make public appearances on behalf of the station for charity events, concerts, and the like. Many disc jockeys also do voice-overs for commercials on radio and/or television.

Disc jockeys usually work in three- to five-hour shifts. Most work the same time shift every day so that they can build up a following. Those who project a special or unique style or personality usually become successful and popular. Even in small markets, disc jockeys are often looked upon as celebrities in their area.

Employment Opportunities

Disc jockeys may find employment with stations located in towns and cities throughout the country. Usually, it is fairly easy to find positions in small markets because the turnover is great. Most people seek jobs in these markets to acquire experience. After experience is obtained, they move on to larger markets and more prestigious stations. It is more difficult to obtain employment in major market radio. These stations are located in large metropolitan cities including:

- New York
- Los Angeles
- Chicago
- Atlanta
- Boston

Earnings

Earnings vary greatly for disc jockeys depending on a number of factors. These include the size, prestige, popularity, and location of the station as well as the experience, reputation, and popularity of the DJ. Annual earnings range from approximately $12,000 to $225,000 or more. Those with little experience working in small markets will have earnings on the lower end of the scale. Many disc jockeys augment earnings by doing personal appearances and voice-overs for commercials.

Advancement Opportunities

Disc jockeys advance their careers by obtaining experience, developing a unique personality, and building a following. Those who accomplish this can advance to positions at larger and more prestigious stations. Other methods of career advancement include becoming the music director or program director of a station.

Education and Training

There is no formal education requirement to become a disc jockey. Many stations currently prefer their DJs to have college degrees. Others only require that the individuals have experience and a following.

Those attending college should consider majors or courses in communications and broadcasting. Colleges also afford opportunities including internships and jobs on college radio stations.

There are also vocational technical schools and trade schools located throughout the country offering programs in radio broadcasting.

Experience and Qualifications

Most stations prefer that DJs have some sort of experience in radio. This may be acquired by working at college radio stations, participating in school radio clubs, or interning.

Disc jockeys must have a clear speaking voice. Successful ones have the ability to project an interesting personality over the airwaves to the listening audience.

DJs must usually hold a license from the Federal Communications Commission (FCC). This is obtained by filling out an application and having an employer write a letter stating that the applicant has a job in the broadcasting field.

For Additional Information: There are a number of associations that can provide additional information about a career in this field. These include the National Association of Broadcasting (NAB), the National Association of Broadcast Employees and Technicians (NABET), and the American Federation of Television and Radio Artists (AFTRA).

TIPS

- Experience is helpful in obtaining your first position. Participate in your school radio club or work on your college radio station.
- Try to find an internship program with a radio station. Colleges often have programs in conjunction with local radio stations. If you are not in school, contact the stations directly.
- Positions are advertised in the classified sections of newspapers. Look under

headings such as "Radio," "Disc Jockey," "Broadcasting," "DJ," and "On-Air Personality."

- Openings may also be advertised or listed in trades, including *Billboard*, *Broadcasting*, and *Radio and Records*.
- Many local libraries subscribe to major radio and record trades. You can also locate them in larger magazine or bookstores. Most radio stations also subscribe. Consider asking a local station if you can look through the station's copies.
- If you are considering attending a vocational or trade school, check out its reputation beforehand through your state's attorney general's office and the Department of Consumer Affairs.
- Make a demo tape of your voice announcing records and introducing commercials, news, etc. Send copies with a letter and your resume to radio stations. Depending on the size, you will either send your letter to the personnel director (larger stations) or the general manager (smaller stations). Try to obtain a specific name to send your letter to instead of just "Personnel Director" or "General Manager." Follow up with phone calls a couple of weeks after sending your letter.

RADIO TALK SHOW HOST

Job Description: Discuss subjects of general or specialized interest with guests during radio show; answer call-ins; introduce news, weathercasts, commercials, and public announcements.

Earnings: $12,000–$1 million-plus

Recommended Education and Training: College background or degree preferred.

Skills and Personality Traits: Good speaking voice; radio personality; expertise in one or more areas; gift of gab; ability to think quickly; detail-oriented.

Experience and Qualifications: Experience in broadcasting helpful.

Job Description and Responsibilities

In an effort to attract new audiences, many radio stations throughout the country are adding additional talk shows to their programming or turning to an all talk format. The radio personalities leading the conversation during these shows are called talk show hosts.

Talk shows can center around almost any subject matter. A host may be a broadcasting personality or an expert in a specific field, such as a lawyer, psychologist, veterinarian, stockbroker, or physician.

Individuals can have varied responsibilities and duties depending on the structure, size, and format of the station. Talk show programming is formatted in a number of ways. In some situations, the hosts may be experts in certain fields and have their shows center around those subjects. In others, the shows may invite different guest experts to discuss specific subject matter. Whatever the format, the talk show host must keep the program moving along in an interesting fashion.

The host will usually introduce the subject matter, and the guest or guests, if any, will appear later during the show. Many talk shows also incorporate calls to the station from the listening audience. Callers may comment on the subject or ask questions. Successful talk show hosts have the ability to keep the show interesting by bantering back and forth with guests and callers.

Other responsibilities of the host may entail reading books about the subject under discussion and conducting pre-show interviews. The host also may introduce or read newscasts, weathercasts, commercials, and/or public service announcements.

Talk show hosts may be responsible for hosting a daily show or may host shows only on specific days of the week. Shows can run from one hour to full four-hour shifts. Individuals may perform live or on tape.

At some smaller stations, talk show hosts may also have additional duties such as reporting the news or acting as a disc jockey. They may be expected to make public appearances on behalf of the station.

Employment Opportunities

Radio talk show hosts can work full-time or part-time for radio stations throughout the country. Some individuals have local shows, while other shows are broadcast nationally or syndicated.

Employment opportunities can be increased dramatically if individuals are experts or have credentials in specific areas of interest for a listening audience.

Areas of interest for talk shows are all-encompassing. Some include:

- Business
- Money
- Financial planning
- Cooking
- Food
- Books
- Film
- Television
- Music
- General entertainment
- Current events
- Gardening
- Child care
- Parenting
- Relationships
- Marriage
- Legal issues
- Consumer affairs
- Community events
- The arts
- News
- Politics

Earnings

There can be a tremendous range of earnings for radio talk show hosts. It may run from approximately $12,000 to $1 million or more annually. Compensation depends on the size, prestige, popularity, and location of the station. Other factors include the experience, expertise, reputation, popularity, and draw of the individual as well as the show's following. At some stations, minimum earnings will be negotiated and set by a union.

Usually those having top of the scale earnings are in great demand on national or syndicated shows or stations.

Advancement Opportunities

Radio talk show hosts can advance their careers by locating similar opportunities at larger, more prestigious stations in bigger markets. Individuals may also climb the career ladder by building a following for their show and having it syndicated.

Advancement opportunities are based to a great extent on the type of following individuals build for themselves and their shows. Those who increase their popularity will be in greater demand and will be able to ask for and receive increased earnings.

Education and Training

Most stations require or prefer a minimum of a college background or degree. A formal education and expertise in a specific field is also helpful in lending credibility to the talk show host.

A liberal arts education will be useful in providing individuals with a broad background.

Experience and Qualifications

Experience requirements vary from station to station. They will usually be waived if an individual is an expert in a specific field that is deemed important by station management, and if the applicant meets all other criteria.

Any experience working in radio is useful. This may be acquired by working in other positions at commercial or college radio stations, as a participant in school radio clubs, or as an intern.

A radio talk show host should have a pleasant speaking voice and the gift of gab. The ability to think quickly is mandatory. An expertise in one or more areas is essential to success when hosting a specialty show.

As a rule, radio talk show hosts must usually hold a license from the Federal Communications Commission (FCC). This is obtained by filling out an application and having an employer write a letter stating that the applicant has a job in the broadcasting field.

For Additional Information: Organizations providing additional information about a career in this field include the National Association of Broadcasting (NAB), the National Association of Broadcast Employees and Technicians (NABET), and the American Federation of Television and Radio Artists (AFTRA).

TIPS

- Consider breaking into the field on a small scale. Contact your local radio station and offer to host a show on a subject in which you are an expert. Often, if you offer to find advertisers and are successful, a station will use your show.
- Volunteer to host a show for your school radio club or college station.
- Positions may be advertised in the newspaper classified section under the headings of "Talk Show Host," "Radio," "Radio Talk Show Host," "Specialty Radio Host," "Broadcasting," and "Radio Specialist."
- Opportunities may also be listed or advertised in industry trades such as *Billboard* and *Radio and Records.*
- You can locate major radio and record trades in magazine and/or bookstores. Many local libraries subscribe to them, as do most radio stations. Consider asking a local station if you can look through their trade magazines.
- It is usually fairly easy to find positions in small markets because the turnover is great. Most people seek jobs in these markets to acquire experience.
- Try to find an internship program with a radio station. Colleges often have programs in conjunction with local stations. If you are not in school, contact the stations directly.
- Host a mock show and make a demo tape. Send copies with a letter and your resume to radio stations. Depending on the size, you will either send your letter to the personnel director (larger stations) or the general manager (smaller stations). Try to obtain a specific name to address your letter to rather than just "Personnel Director," "Program Director," or "General Manager." Follow up with phone calls about two weeks after sending your letter.
- Become an expert in one or more fields. Parlay your expertise to send your career in the direction you want. Dr. Joyce Brothers became an expert on boxing (not psychology) to appear on a famous quiz show. Her appearances on that show helped her launch her career as a leading expert and talk show guest in the field of psychology.

NEWS REPORTER—RADIO

Job Description: Develop and report news stories on the air; write copy; check facts.

Earnings: $12,000–$50,000+

Recommended Education and Training: Bachelor's degree.

Skills and Personality Traits: Pleasant speaking voice; articulate; writing skills.

Experience and Qualifications: Experience working in radio or writing news stories for print media.

Job Description and Responsibilities

Radio stations—in varying lengths of air time—report local, regional, state, national, and international news. The major function of radio news reporters is announcing the news on the air. Within the scope of the job, individuals will have varied responsibilities. At smaller stations, there may be only one news reporter who also acts as the news director. Larger stations may have an entire news staff.

Radio news reporters may be responsible for seeking out the news stories, interviewing and securing statements from relevant people, and developing broadcasts. At some stations, news directors and/or editors may select the newsworthy items and assign specific news reporters to cover them. Reporters may also work with editors who review the material and present it in context with other reports.

News stories must be written in a manner that makes them interesting to the listening audience. Reports must be clear and concise. It is imperative that the reporter always check facts for accuracy.

Depending on the structure and size of the station's news department, the news reporter may be expected to go on location and report stories live or to obtain quotes and statements from people involved in specific news stories.

The reporter may tape-record interviews, quotes, and statements either in person or via a telephone hookup. He or she must then edit the interview and decide at that time during a news broadcast to use the recorded pieces. News reporters may do either live or prerecorded news broadcasts.

Other duties of news reporters may include compiling and rewriting stories from wire services. Depending on the station, the individual may just report local news or may be responsible for reporting regional or national news as well. The news reporter might also be responsible for broadcasting sports reports, weathercasts, traffic conditions, etc.

News reporters may work various shifts during the day or night. Their responsibilities might also include attending meetings, events, and functions wherever and whenever news is happening.

Employment Opportunities

Every radio station needs at least one news reporter. Most have more than one. Employment opportunities may be located throughout the country at stations in small towns and large metropolitan cities. Major markets for radio include:

- New York City
- Los Angeles
- Atlanta
- Chicago
- Boston

Earnings

News reporters working in radio can have salaries ranging from approximately $12,000 to $50,000 or more depending on the station's size, location, and prestige as well as the individual's responsibilities, qualifications, and experience. News reporters just beginning their careers at smaller stations will usually earn between $12,000 and $16,000. As they gain more experience and obtain positions at larger, more prestigious stations, their salaries go up considerably.

Advancement Opportunities

Radio news reporters can advance their careers in a number of ways. With experience, individuals can locate similar positions at larger, more prestigious stations, resulting in increased responsibilities and earnings. Individuals may also climb the career ladder by advancing to the position of news director. Some radio news reporters find advancement opportunities handling similar jobs in television or print media.

Education and Training

Most radio stations today require their news reporters to hold a minimum of a bachelor's degree. Good majors for those aspiring to work in this field include broadcasting, broadcast journalism, journalism, communications, and liberal arts. Seminars, workshops, and classes in all aspects of writing will be helpful.

Experience and Qualifications

News reporters working at radio stations usually must have some type of experience working in broadcasting. This is often obtained by working at school radio stations, having summer or part-time jobs at local stations, or going through internships.

Individuals must have excellent writing skills as well as a pleasant speaking voice. The ability to develop stories, check facts, and prioritize news items is required.

For Additional Information: Those interested in a career in radio news can obtain additional information by contacting the American Women in Radio and Television (AWRT), the Association for Education in Journalism and Mass Communications (AEJMC), the National Association of Broadcasters (NAB), the Radio-Television News Directors Association (RTNDA), the National Association of Broadcast Employees and Technicians (NABET), the American Federation of Television and Radio Artists (AFTRA), and the Public Relations Society of America (PRSA).

TIPS

- Obtain experience writing news stories at a part-time or summer job with a local newspaper.
- Positions in this field are advertised in the newspaper classified or display sections under the headings of "News," "Radio News," "Radio," "News Reporter," "Radio News Reporter," "Broadcasting," and "Broadcast Journalist."
- Openings may also be advertised or listed in the radio- and record-oriented trades including *Radio and Records*, *Broadcasting*, and *Billboard*.
- Contact radio stations to locate internships in this field.
- Trade associations and schools may also offer internship programs.
- Send your resume with a short cover letter inquiring about openings to radio stations. Ask that your resume be kept on file.
- If you have little or no experience, try to find a position with a small station. While these stations usually pay their employees very little, the experience and training will be worthwhile in the long run.
- Work at your college radio station to obtain broadcast experience.

PROMOTION DIRECTOR—RADIO

Job Description: Promote interest in station and station talent through the development and implementation of promotions, special events, advertisements, and the like.

Earnings: $12,000–$75,000+

Recommended Education and Training: Bachelor's degree in communications, advertising, business, marketing, public relations, liberal arts, etc.

Skills and Personality Traits: Promotional ability; written and verbal communications skills; creativity; imagination.

Experience and Qualifications: Experience in promotion, publicity, marketing, or sales helpful.

Job Description and Responsibilities

The radio station promotion director is in charge of attracting larger audiences by building an interest in and increasing the visibility of the station. This is accomplished through developing and implementing promotions, special events, and attractions.

The promotion director is expected to come up with interesting, creative, and unique promotions that will attract the interest of the general public, potential advertisers, and other media. These may include contests, sweepstakes, special events, etc., designed to make people want to listen to the station. Sometimes promotions may just involve the station. In other situations, the promotion director may conduct tie-ins, which are promotional ideas involving two or more advertisers or community organizations.

Other projects might include sponsorship of community events such as fundraising telethons, marathons, and entertainment extravaganzas.

The director must bring all promotional ideas and projects to the station management. If the project is approved, the promotion director will determine the appropriate time to run the promotion, rules, prizes, and on-air implementation methods.

Other functions of the promotion director might include developing press releases, announcements, brochures or booklets about the station, programming, specials, and on-air events and promotions. The individual may also be expected to formulate advertisements for print media.

The promotion director is in charge of scheduling public appearances for on-air personalities as well as arranging interviews with magazines, newspapers, and television for feature stories.

Depending on the size and structure of the station, the promotion director may work alone or may supervise one or more assistants. The individual may also function as the public relations or community relations director or sales manager for the station.

Employment Opportunities

Employment opportunities for promotion directors are located throughout the country in both commercial and public radio. Individuals are hired by radio stations with almost every type of format. Every station has someone who handles the responsibilities of the promotion director. However, at smaller stations functions may be handled by the program director, sales manager, public relations director, or station manager.

Employment settings can range from small local radio stations to networks to those in major markets. Cities in which major market stations are located include:

- New York
- Los Angeles
- Chicago
- Atlanta
- Philadelphia
- Detroit
- Boston

Earnings

Earnings for promotion directors at radio stations range from approximately $12,000 to $75,000 or more depending on a number of factors. These include the size, market, and popularity of the station. Other variables include the responsibilities, experience, and expertise of the individual. Experienced promotion directors working for large stations in major markets, who have proven their ability to develop unique promotions that attract a large number of listeners, can demand and receive $75,000 or more. Individuals with limited experience will earn between $12,000 and $25,000.

Advancement Opportunities

Advancement opportunities are based, to a great extent, on the areas of interest of the promotion manager as well as his or her drive and determination.

Many individuals locate similar positions at larger, more prestigious stations. This will result in an increase in responsibilities and earnings. Other individuals advance their careers by becoming sales managers, program directors, public relations or community relations directors, or station general managers. Promotion directors working in radio may also find similar jobs in television.

Education and Training

Most stations require or prefer promotion directors to hold at least an undergraduate college degree. Good choices for majors for this type of career include marketing, public relations, advertising, business, liberal arts, or communications.

Courses, seminars, and workshops in promotion, advertising and publicity techniques, writing, sales, the radio industry, etc., will be useful.

Experience and Qualifications

Experience requirements vary from job to job. Some individuals land positions at smaller stations as promotion directors right after college. Other stations require experience in radio sales, promotion, public relations, marketing, or related fields. Experience working in any facet of radio is a plus.

Promotion directors need excellent communications skills, with the ability to write well and speak articulately. Creativity, imagination, and persuasiveness are necessary. A working knowledge of publicity, marketing, promotion, and public relations is essential.

For Additional Information: Additional information regarding a career in this field can be obtained by contacting the Broadcast Promotion and Marketing Executives, Inc. (BPME), the Broadcaster's Promotion Association (BPA), the Public Relations Society of America (PRSA), the American Advertising Federation (AAF), American Women in Radio and Television, Inc. (AWRT), Women In Communications, Inc. (WICI), the National Association of Broadcasters (NAB), the National Association of Broadcast Employees and Technicians (NABET), and the Radio Advertising Bureau (RAB).

TIPS

- Hands-on experience in radio is valuable when looking for a job. Get involved with your college radio station, handling its promotional aspects.
- While you are still in school, try to find a part-time job with a local station in any capacity.
- Internship programs at radio stations provide training, opportunities, and valuable experience, as well as help you make important contacts. Get in touch with radio stations or inquire whether your college has any connections. Many schools offer college credit for these types of programs.
- It is usually easier to break into the broadcasting field in a small market. While positions in smaller areas usually pay less, the experience will be worthwhile.
- After you get some experience under your belt, start sending your resumes to stations in larger markets.
- Positions in this field are advertised in the newspaper classified display section. Look under headings such as "Promotion Director," "Promotion Manager,"

"Promotion," "Radio," "Broadcasting," "Public Relations," "Special Events," "Advertising," and "Sales."

- Openings may also be advertised or listed in industry trades including *Radio and Records*, *Broadcasting*, and *Billboard*.
- Experience working in publicity, promotion, advertising, sales, etc., is helpful whether it be in radio or another field. Remember to list all relevant experience on your resume.
- Don't forget to send your resume to public radio stations as well as to commercial ones.
- Read the trade magazines to learn about new trends in broadcasting, and to keep up with news and current affairs in the industry. Many libraries subscribe to these publications. If your local library doesn't, you might ask the general manager of a local radio station if you can browse through the station's copies.

COMMUNITY AFFAIRS DIRECTOR—RADIO
· ·

Job Description: Determine community needs; develop programming; write public service announcements; maintain records.

Earnings: $12,000–$40,000+

Recommended Education and Training: Bachelor's degree preferred or required for most positions.

Skills and Personality Traits: Verbal and written communications skills; organization skills; detail-oriented; ability to work well with others.

Experience and Qualifications: Experience working in broadcasting, journalism, public relations, or social service job helpful.

Job Description and Responsibilities

The Federal Communications Commission (FCC) requires every radio station in the country to do a certain amount of public service programming every week. Community affairs directors at radio stations are responsible for determining and developing public service programming for the station. Responsibilities vary depending on the specific station, size, and structure.

In order to be effective, the community affairs director must know the community as well as the audience the station is trying to reach. The individual may be required to do research to gather information on the community and its needs.

The community affairs director will then develop programs and services to meet the specific needs. The individual will work closely with the station manager and/or the programming director in this task. Public service programs may include topics that serve the public interest, such as shows with guests discussing education, community, religious, civic, or government issues. The community affairs director is responsible for developing shows, determining specific show topics, and locating and interviewing appropriate guests. Depending on the station, the individual may also act as the show host.

Another function of the community affairs director is gathering information for public service announcements. These announcements are the blurbs heard on radio which notify the public of community news, upcoming events that benefit the region, and the like. The community affairs director instructs people and organizations to send information regarding public service announcements to the station. He or she will write the public service announcements in the style of the station and have them read by the disc jockey, news staff, or on-air announcer at specific intervals throughout the broadcast day. The individual must keep track of the times each announcement is read and the organizations that benefit from it.

The community affairs director will often represent the station at events and functions sponsored by local not-for-profit organizations, community groups, and public service agencies. The individual may work with the station's promotion department to develop activities that will both promote the station and help a specific cause. This could include raising money for a charitable organization, collecting food, toys, or clothing for the needy, and running telethons.

At small stations, the community affairs director also may be required to handle other tasks such as writing or reporting news stories and developing advertising copy. At larger stations, the individual may supervise a community affairs staff.

Employment Opportunities

Employment opportunities for community affairs directors can be found at radio stations throughout the country. Breaking in is usually easier at smaller stations. More opportunities will be available in large cities hosting a great number of radio stations. Cities hosting major market radio include:

- New York
- Los Angeles
- Boston
- Chicago
- Atlanta

Earnings

Annual earnings for community affairs directors can range from $12,000 to $40,000 or more depending on the size, prestige, and location of the station. Other factors affecting earnings are the responsibilities, experience, and qualifications of the individual.

Individuals with limited experience working at smaller stations will earn between $12,000 and $18,000. As experience and responsibilities increase, so will earnings.

Advancement Opportunities

Community affairs directors at radio stations can advance their careers in a number of ways. Individuals may find similar positions with larger, more prestigious radio stations. Others may climb the career ladder by getting involved in programming, station management, or by becoming an on-air personality. Some advance by locating similar positions in the television industry.

Education and Training

While not all radio stations require a four-year degree, most do prefer it. One will usually find that at least a bachelor's degree is mandatory for advancement. Good choices for majors include broadcasting, communications, journalism, social service, English, public relations, or liberal arts.

Seminars, workshops, and courses in writing, broadcasting, and public relations will be useful.

Experience and Qualifications

Experience requirements for community affairs directors vary from job to job. Experience in broadcasting is helpful, but not always required. Experience can be obtained by working at a college radio station or through internships or part-time jobs with radio stations. Other beneficial experiences include working or volunteering in social service areas, public relations, or journalism.

Community affairs directors need excellent written and verbal communications skills. They should also be very organized and detail-oriented. The ability to understand the type of market their station is trying to reach is another necessary qualification.

For Additional Information: Aspiring community affairs directors can learn more about careers in the field by contacting the National Association of Broadcasters (NAB), the National Association of Broadcast Employees and Technicians (NABET), the American Federation of Television and Radio Artists (AFTRA), and the Public Relations Society of America (PRSA).

TIPS

• Work in your college radio station to obtain broadcast experience.
• Positions in this field are advertised in the newspaper classified section under

the headings of "Broadcasting," "Community Affairs Director," "Community Affairs," "Radio," and "Public Service Director."

- Openings may also be advertised or listed in the radio- and record-oriented trades including *Radio and Records*, *Broadcasting*, and *Billboard*.
- Try to locate an internship with a radio station. Many stations have college credit internship programs. You may also contact radio stations directly.
- Send your resume with a short cover letter to radio stations inquiring about openings. Ask that your resume be kept on file.

TRAFFIC MANAGER—RADIO

Job Description: Supervise and coordinate traffic department; schedule commercials; prepare and/or check daily logs.

Earnings: $14,000–$40,000+

Recommended Education and Training: Educational requirements vary from high school diploma to college background or degree.

Skills and Personality Traits: Word processing skills; computer literacy; organization skills; detail-oriented; supervisory skills.

Experience and Qualifications: Experience requirements vary.

Job Description and Responsibilities

The traffic manager at a radio station has a great deal of responsibility. The individual in this position is in charge of keeping a record of everything that is broadcast on the air each day by logging the information.

Radio stations are required to log everything that occurs during the broadcast day for the Federal Communications Commission. Better known as the FCC, this regulatory agency licenses radio stations broadcasting to the public.

Traffic managers may handle all duties personally or may supervise one or more people depending on the size of the station. In situations where the traffic manager is supervising others, the individual will also be responsible for training assistants or clerks and assigning specific duties to each person.

The traffic manager works with others at the station including the general manager and sales manager to determine the number and sequence of commercials and public service announcements to be aired each hour. If there are too many commercials played during an hour, or they are aired too close together, a station may lose its audience. If there are not enough public service announcements (PSAs) aired, the station may not be adhering to FCC regulations. The traffic manager also works closely with the sales manager and salespeople to try to juggle schedules in order to best fit the advertising sold. The individual must decide the most effective time and way to air each commercial.

Most stations today, even very small ones, are computerized. The traffic manager is required to make sure daily logs are typed and put into the computer correctly. Items that must be listed in the daily log include all commercials, advertisements, public service announcements, programming, and station breaks. These must be provided with the exact time and date they are scheduled to be aired. After the broadcast day, the individual must check the log to be sure that everything that was supposed to have been aired was taken care of by making sure that all announcers, disc jockeys, and other on-air personalities checked off and/or initialed each entry as it was aired.

If a commercial, announcement, or program was not aired or aired at a different time than the log indicates, the traffic manager will authorize changes in the log sheet. There can be no errors. Completed log sheets are sent to the FCC for their review.

Another responsibility of the radio station traffic manager is to review advertisements to make sure that no information contained in the copy might be considered objectionable either by the station or the FCC.

Employment Opportunities

Since every commercial radio station in the country is regulated by the FCC, each station has at least one person handling the duties of the traffic manager. Individuals may work in small, medium, or major market radio. It is often easier to break into this position and obtain experience at a local station in a small market. Once experience is acquired, one may wish to look for a job in a major market. Major market cities include:

- New York
- Los Angeles
- Chicago
- Atlanta
- Philadelphia

Earnings

Earnings for traffic managers working in radio range from approximately $14,000 to $40,000 or more. Factors influencing earnings include the size, location, and popularity of the station as well as the experience and responsibilities of the individual. Those with limited experience working for small, local stations will be compensated on the lower end of the pay scale. Earnings will increase as traffic managers move on to positions with larger, more prestigious stations and their experience and responsibilities increase.

Advancement Opportunities

There are a number of methods by which traffic managers at radio stations can advance their careers. These include locating similar positions at larger radio stations, resulting in increased responsibilities and earnings. Some radio traffic managers may make either lateral moves to work in television or climb the career ladder by finding better positions in the same area in television.

Other possibilities for advancement include changing positions in order to become an advertising salesperson or sales manager at larger stations. This will result in increased earnings for those with sales skills.

Education and Training

Some stations may require only a high school diploma. For those seeking a career in radio broadcasting, a four-year college degree is recommended. While majors can be in any area, courses in radio, broadcasting, advertising, copywriting, marketing, communications, business, English, word processing, and computers will be useful.

Experience and Qualifications

Generally, the larger a station is, the more experience in traffic it will require of an applicant. Small local stations often hire individuals right after college graduation. Any experience working in radio or television will be worthwhile, especially if the work has been in the advertising or traffic department.

Traffic managers should be organized, detail-oriented individuals. Word processing and computer skills are mandatory. Supervisory skills are needed if the individual is working in a large department.

An understanding of the broadcasting industry, advertising, and radio is imperative.

For Additional Information: Individuals interested in pursuing a career in radio traffic management may obtain additional information by contacting their state's broadcasting association, the Radio and Advertising Bureau (RAB), the National Association of Broadcast Employees and Technicians (NABET), the American Advertising Federation (AAF), the National Association of Broadcasters (NAB), American Women In Radio and Television, Inc. (AWRT), and Women In Communications, Inc. (WICI).

TIPS

- Positions in this field are advertised in the newspaper classified section under the headings of "Traffic," "Traffic-Continuity," "Radio," "Broadcast," "Communications," and "Advertising."

- Opportunities may also be advertised in industry trades such as *Billboard* and *Radio and Records.*
- Internships are an excellent method of getting your foot in the door and learning necessary skills. Your college advisor may know of some in this field. You may also locate an internship by contacting radio stations or trade associations.
- Take courses in computers and learn the standard software programs.
- You might want to take classes in copywriting. These will be useful in honing writing skills should you be required to write ad copy, public service copy, etc. The more skills you have, the more marketable you will be.
- Seminars and workshops are often offered by trade associations in radio, advertising, traffic, and continuity. These are valuable for the information and skills you will learn as well as for the contacts you will make.
- If you have limited experience, consider contacting small, local stations. Send your resume and a short cover letter asking about openings.
- As a result of people advancing their careers, there is a great deal of turnover in this position at smaller stations. These stations are good training grounds for the job.

ADVERTISING SALESPERSON—RADIO

Job Description: Sell space to advertisers for radio commercials; service established accounts; bring in new business.

Earnings: $13,000–$150,000+

Recommended Education and Training: Minimum requirement is a high school diploma; most positions require a bachelor's degree.

Skills and Personality Traits: Sales ability; communications skills; numerical aptitude; aggressiveness; personability; being self-motivated.

Experience and Qualifications: Sales experience helpful.

Job Description and Responsibilities

Radio stations make money by selling air time to businesses that want to advertise their products and services. It is the job of advertising salespeople to solicit new advertisers and maintain existing accounts. Advertising salespeople may also be referred to as sales representatives or sales reps.

Advertising salespeople may work in their office one day and be out in the field trying to bring in new accounts or servicing established ones the next. They are responsible for calling or visiting clients on a regular basis to determine their advertising needs. During these calls or visits, the salesperson will offer customers information about rates, discounts, and packages, as well as demographics regarding the station's audience.

Salespeople obtain accounts in a number of different ways. The station sales manager may assign specific territories to the salesperson or the individual might be free to sell advertisements to any advertiser. Instead of geographic territories, salespeople are sometimes assigned categories of advertisers such as restaurants, retail shops, or nightclubs. Depending on the station's size and structure, the salesperson may be assigned to sell to local, regional, or national accounts or may sell to all three.

Whatever the salesperson's territory, his or her main function is to bring in new business. Sometimes the salesperson will be working with businesses who call up and are interested in advertising. In other instances, the individual may have to make "cold calls" to businesses who have expressed little or no interest in advertising. At times, the sales rep may also work with the station's sales, promotion, or marketing manager to develop promotions that can be used to help generate sales.

There is a great deal of paperwork involved in this job. The salesperson will be required to write sales orders as well as pass them on to the appropriate people at the station. The individual will also be required to keep records of when advertisements are aired, insertion rates, discounts, and billing names and addresses.

The radio advertising salesperson is responsible to the station's advertising director. While the salesperson is expected to keep normal business hours, many set appointments at the convenience of clients, even if it means working at night or on weekends.

Employment Opportunities

There are over 10,000 commercial radio stations throughout the country. Without salespeople, these stations would have a much more limited income and have a difficult time remaining in business. Individuals who are aggressive, hard-working, and able to sell are always in demand by radio station advertising departments.

Every commercial radio station has at least one salesperson. At very small stations, the salesperson may also assume the duties of the sales manager, promotion manager, or even an on-air personality. Some larger stations have 25 or more people in this position. Individuals may work in small, medium, or major market radio. Employment options include:

- Local or independent radio stations
- Network radio stations

Earnings

Earnings for radio advertising salespeople are dependent upon a number of different factors, including the individual's experience and selling ability. Other factors affecting take-home pay include the size, location, and prestige of the station. Salaries range from approximately $13,000 to $150,000 or more. Most stations also offer fringe benefit packages to employees.

Radio advertising salespeople may be paid in a number of ways. Options include salary plus a commission on sales, a straight commission, a draw against commissions, and/or a guarantee against sales.

The word *commission* in sales means that the salesperson is paid a percentage of the money earned for the station when selling advertising airtime. When commission is a factor, those who sell more earn more. The percentage of commission varies, but is usually between 10 percent and 20 percent.

Advancement Opportunities

Radio salespeople can advance their careers in a number of ways. One method is to locate a position in a large market or prestigious station. Another is to become a sales, marketing, or promotion manager for a broadcast station.

Education and Training

Educational requirements vary from job to job for radio salespeople. While the minimum requirement for some jobs is a high school diploma, most stations require a bachelor's degree. Individuals in this line of work normally have majors such as advertising, communications, business, marketing, or liberal arts. Useful courses include advertising, sales, business, marketing, speech, math, English, sociology, psychology, writing, and communications.

Successful salespeople also keep up with selling trends and hone their skills by attending workshops and seminars offered by trade associations or other organizations.

Experience and Qualifications

Any type of selling experience is useful for radio salespeople. Sales managers generally believe that highly motivated people who have done well selling any product or service will be successful in this type of position. Individuals just entering the job market might find it easier to break into small or medium market radio. Many jobs at smaller stations do not require any prior experience.

For Additional Information: Associations and organizations that can provide additional information include the American Advertising Federation (AAF), the National Association of Broadcasting (NAB), the Radio and Advertising Bureau (RAB), and the National Association of Broadcast Employees and Technicians (NABET).

TIPS

- Job openings are often listed in the radio broadcast or other entertainment trade papers. If your local library doesn't stock these, contact a local radio station and ask if you can review a few issues. You might also contact the trade journal itself to inquire about obtaining a short-term subscription.
- Positions in this field are advertised in the newspaper classified section under the headings of "Advertising," "Sales," "Salesperson," "Radio," and "Broadcasting."
- Selling is selling. Remember when you prepare your resume to put down every sales job you have ever held.
- Look in the yellow pages of the telephone book to obtain the names and addresses of radio stations in the area. (Check your local library if you are looking for a job in a different geographic location. Many libraries have a supply of phone books from other areas in the country.) Send your resume and a short cover letter to the personnel manager, station manager, or station owner. Try to address your correspondence to a specific name, not just a general title.

ADVERTISING COPYWRITER—RADIO/TELEVISION
. . . .

Job Description: Develop scripts and copy for advertisements to be aired on television or radio.

Earnings: $14,000–$50,000+

Recommended Education and Training: Bachelor's degree in communications, advertising, journalism, English, marketing, public relations, or liberal arts.

Skills and Personality Traits: Ability to write crisp, clear copy; creativity; excellent writing skills; persuasiveness.

Experience and Qualifications: Experience requirements vary; writing experience useful.

Job Description and Responsibilities

Advertising copywriters working in television or radio are responsible for developing the scripts for clients' advertisements. They work in the advertising department of the station. Ads that are aired nationally are usually written and produced by advertising agencies. Local, cable, and/or syndicated ads, however, are generally prepared by the copywriters working at television and radio stations.

Copywriting for television and radio is different from print copywriting. To begin with, there is a time limitation on the ad. Words must be easily spoken, understood, and remembered. In radio, there are no graphics. In television, words must relate to the video.

Copywriters have a number of responsibilities depending on the specific station and the size and structure of the advertising department. Generally, the larger the station, the more specific the responsibilities. An individual might be responsible for conceiving the concept for an ad, writing it, producing it, and getting it on the air, or just for writing the copy.

Sometimes, the copywriter is assigned a client and the responsibility of developing his or her entire broadcast advertising campaign. Other times, one might just develop copy for one ad.

Copywriters are expected to have the ability to write in a variety of styles. These include straight copy as well as dialogue. Dialogue is usually used in scripts in television copywriting. In order for any ad to be effective, it must be written in a crisp, clear language with words that are credible. Television writers may be required to write stage directions as well as instructions for sound effects, voice-overs, etc. Copywriters in these situations often work with a storyboard. The boards make it easier to see which words go with which specific graphics.

Depending on the medium, copywriters will work with directors, producers, senior copywriters, graphic designers, art directors, models, actors, actresses, announcers, and/or camera people. He or she will often work with the advertisers and salespeople to determine the important points to convey and the audience they are attempting to reach.

Copywriters develop one or more drafts of copy for advertisements. After these are done, they are given to the advertiser for approval. The advertiser may accept the copy, reject it, or request changes.

It is important that the copywriter have the ability to condense copy to fit into the required ad time frame. One may be expected to write copy that can be used for both television and radio commercials.

Copywriters usually work under a great deal of pressure, and on several projects at one time. The individuals must have the ability to cope with this while writing effective, creative copy.

Employment Opportunities

Individuals who can write clear, imaginative copy are always in demand at both radio and television stations. Employment opportunities are available throughout the country. Generally, those interested in working in major market television or radio need experience. There is a great deal of turnover at smaller stations as some gain experience and leave for better positions. Employment settings include:

- Radio stations
- Networks
- Network affiliated stations
- Independent television stations
- National cable stations
- Local cable stations

Earnings

Advertising copywriters in television and radio earn between $14,000 and $50,000 or more per year depending on a number of variables. These include the size and location of the specific station as well as the experience, expertise, and responsibilities of the individual.

Copywriters just starting out at small local stations will earn between $14,000 and $19,000 annually. As experience is acquired and they move on to larger stations, or to those located in major markets, earnings go up considerably. Generally, positions in television pay better than those in radio.

Advancement Opportunities

The major route for career advancement in this field is through locating similar positions at larger stations. Another way for advertising copywriters to climb the career ladder is by becoming senior copywriters at the same or at a different station. This results in increased earnings and responsibilities. Some advance their careers by finding positions in advertising agencies.

Education and Training

A college degree is recommended for those aspiring to work in radio or television copywriting. Majors can include advertising, marketing, journalism, communications, English, liberal arts, or public relations.

Seminars, workshops, and classes on copywriting, advertising, and the television and radio industries will prove useful.

Experience and Qualifications

Experience requirements vary from job to job. Those seeking jobs in small market radio and television may find work right out of college. Experience is usually required at stations in larger cities and major markets. Experience can be acquired through working in jobs at smaller stations, positions as assistants, or internships. Others obtain experience writing in other industries.

Successful copywriters must have an exceptional command of the English language. The ability to write clear, concise, and creative copy is imperative. Insight into and working knowledge of the television and/or radio industry, as well as a good imagination, are all necessities.

For Additional Information: Individuals interested in learning more about careers in this field can obtain additional information by contacting the Writers Guild of

America (WGA), the American Marketing Association (AMA), the National Association of Broadcasters (NAB), the Radio Advertising Bureau (RAB), the American Advertising Federation (AAF), the American Women In Radio and Television, (AWRT), Women In Communications, Inc. (WICI), and the National Cable Television Association, Inc. (NCTA).

TIPS

- If you don't have a great deal of experience, you might want to begin your career in a small market station. Send your resume and a short cover letter inquiring about openings to smaller stations. Ask that your resume be kept on file. There is a great deal of turnover at smaller stations.
- As you acquire experience, begin sending your resume to larger stations in major markets. Don't forget cable stations.
- Positions in this field are often advertised in the newspaper classified section under headings such as "Advertising," "Copywriter," "Television," "Radio," and "Broadcasting."
- Opportunities may also be advertised in the industry trades.
- Locate and get involved with internship programs. They can be found at television and radio stations and through college programs.
- Get as much experience as possible writing copy. Consider a summer or part-time job working for a local newspaper in the advertising department.
- Volunteer to handle the advertising needs for local not-for-profit organizations, school activities, and civic groups.
- Try to learn as much as possible about all aspects of broadcasting. Work on your school radio and/or television station. The more you know, the more marketable you will be.
- Take seminars, workshops, and classes in copywriting and advertising from a variety of people. Each teacher can be a source of techniques you might find helpful in the workplace.
- Contact trade associations to see if they offer professional seminars. These are useful for learning new techniques and helping to make contacts.

CHAPTER 4

· · · · · · · · · · · · ·

Careers in Television, Film, and Video

Although nothing can compare to the thrill of seeing live theater, concerts, dance, or other performing arts events, when the show is over, nothing remains for an audience but fond memories. On the other hand, when productions are recorded, a permanent record is established. Not only will the audience be able to re-create its memories, but the record of the production will allow the show to be replayed time after time.

When television first came out, it was a luxury many could not afford. In those days, movies were the family entertainment. Today, the television, film, and video industries are profoundly influential and still growing rapidly. There are few households without at least one television. VCRs are now affordable and commonplace. Camcorders are becoming more affordable, and average people commonly produce their own home videos.

Feature films are released in theaters and are soon after put out on video for people to enjoy at their leisure. The same is true of film classics. Television programming can be recorded to be viewed at the viewer's convenience, not when executives dictate. The advent of cable TV has added new opportunities for more specialized programming.

Although television entered our living rooms almost half a century ago, and the first sound movie was released almost 70 years ago, today's changing audience interests, competition, worldwide events, and other entertainment activities have sparked many new career possibilities in the world of television and film. These include both on-screen and off-screen jobs.

Film and television production take many skilled professionals. Careers in this field are wide-ranging. Many talents, skills, educational backgrounds, and experience levels are required.

Space restrictions limit discussing all possible opportunities. Jobs covered in this section are:

Producer—Television
Director—Television
Production Assistant—Television
Camera Operator—Television
Floor Manager—Television
Location Scout/Location Manager—Film/Television/Commercials
Casting Director—Television/Film
Scenic Designer—Television/Film/Video
Costume Designer—Television/Film
Makeup Artist—Television/Film/Video
Property Master—Television/Films/Commercials

Anchorperson—Television News
Reporter—Television News
Sportscaster—Television News
Weather Reporter—Television News
News Writer—Television
Television Talk Show Host
Video Jockey—Television
Page—Television
Traffic-Continuity Specialist—Television
Public Relations and Promotion Director—Television Station
Director—Film
Production Assistant—Film
Unit Publicist—Television/Film

Individuals interested in careers in television, film, and video should also review entries in other sections of this book. "Careers in the Business End of the Industry" and "Careers in Performing and Writing" both discuss related opportunities.

PRODUCER—TELEVISION

Job Description: Create television productions; develop projects.

Earnings: $20,000–$200,000+

Recommended Education and Training: Bachelor's degree in broadcasting, journalism, communications, theater, or related areas.

Skills and Personality Traits: Detail-oriented; creativity; organization skills; business skills; communications skills.

Experience and Qualifications: Experience in television as director or associate producer.

Job Description and Responsibilities

Every television show has a producer. The producer is the individual that takes the executive producer's ideas and develops them into actual programs. Producers have varied duties depending on their specific station and program responsibilities, and often work jointly with others in the field to produce programming.

Some individuals produce programs that are aired daily such as newscasts, soap operas, and talk shows. Other producers work on a weekly series such as a sitcom, variety show, or drama. They might also be responsible for producing entertainment specials, sports events, or made-for-television movies.

Producers bear ultimate responsibility for the specific program or series of programs from their inception through their creation and airing. Functions include finding scripts and writers, deciding on story lines, choosing talent and guests, selecting locations, determining formats, and supervising promotion.

It costs a great deal of money to produce television shows. The producer must develop budgets and keep projects within these limits. To do so, he or she must calculate the most effective and least expensive ways to handle each detail of a program.

Producers are also expected to keep all business arrangements within a program's budgetary constraints. This includes negotiating fees and making sure all contracts with artists and production and technical people are taken care of correctly and in a timely fashion.

Producers report to executive producers. They may also work with associate producers, who assist with a great deal of the administrative aspects of the job.

Employment Opportunities

Employment opportunities for television producers are more plentiful in large cities with more than one television station. However, it is often easier to break into the field in smaller markets and their independent and local cable stations.

One can produce programming in a variety of areas, including sports, special events, entertainment, news, daytime television, game shows, general programming, sitcoms, talk shows, variety shows, etc.

Television producers work in a number of situations, from major market and networks to small, independent stations or local cable. Employment opportunities may be found with the following:

- Network stations
- Affiliated stations
- Public television
- Local cable stations
- National cable stations
- Independent production companies
- Video production companies

Earnings

Earnings for producers working in television start at approximately $20,000 per year and go to $200,000 or more. Earnings are based on the experience, responsibilities, and qualifications of the individual as well as the station's size, location, prestige, and programming.

Producers just starting out earn between $20,000 and $30,000. As they gain experience and produce more prestigious shows, earnings increase. Those working in public television generally earn less than producers working in commercial TV. Producers of network shows earn salaries at the top of the pay scale.

Advancement Opportunities

Producers advance their careers in a number of ways. Some locate similar positions in larger markets, which results in increased responsibilities and earnings. Others become executive producers. Most aspire to obtain jobs with major networks or with independent production companies that produce programming for networks or major cable stations.

Education and Training

The minimal educational requirement for most television producers is a bachelor's degree. Good choices for majors include broadcasting, communications, journalism, theater, and liberal arts.

Courses, workshops, and seminars in television, producing, and communications will be useful in honing skills and making important contacts.

Experience and Qualifications

Experience working in television is necessary prior to becoming a producer. This can be acquired through internships or through working as an associate producer or director.

To be successful in this type of job, one should be well-organized, detail-oriented, and creative. Verbal and written communications skills are necessary, as are an array of business skills.

For Additional Information: Aspiring television producers can obtain additional information about this field by contacting the National Association of Broadcasters (NAB), the National Association of Television Program Executives (NATPE), the Academy of Television Arts and Sciences (ATAS), the Producers Guild of America (PGA), American Women in Radio and Television (AWRT), the Broadcast Education Association (BEA), the Corporation for Public Broadcasting (CPB), and the International Association of Independent Producers (IAIP).

TIPS

- Join trade associations and attend their meetings. These will provide you with professional support and guidance as well as with opportunities for making important contacts in the field.
- Positions and openings may be advertised or listed in the trades or trade association newsletters.
- Look for internships through your college, trade associations, and television stations. These will offer opportunities to get your foot in the door, learn new skills, and make contacts. Many stations hire their interns after the internship ends.
- Get as much experience as you can working in all facets of television. The more you know, the more marketable you will be.
- Being knowledgeable in a specific field such as entertainment, sports, current affairs, health, consumer affairs, etc., will also increase your marketability.
- Take as many courses, workshops, and seminars as you can find in producing, television, directing, and related subjects.
- Break into the field by taking any job available in television. Learn as you go. Do more than is expected of you and you will advance in your career.
- Begin your career search in small market television or local cable stations. These jobs provide a training ground. There is a large turnover at these stations when people advance to better jobs and higher earnings. The experience factor usually outweighs the low pay for individuals who are just starting out.

DIRECTOR—TELEVISION

. . . .

Job Description: Coordinate and oversee technical and creative aspects of television productions; interpret scripts; prepare production for airing.

Earnings: $20,000–$150,000+

Recommended Education and Training: Bachelor's degree in broadcasting, communications, theater, journalism, or a related field.

Skills and Personality Traits: Detail-oriented; organizational, supervisory, and motivational skills; imaginative; creative.

Experience and Qualifications: Experience working in some aspect of television production.

Job Description and Responsibilities

The director of a television production is in charge of coordinating every facet of the production. The individual will have input with all creative as well as technical aspects of a television production. The director oversees and guides rehearsals as well as the actual shooting of television shows.

Every show has a director, whether it be news, sitcoms, dramas, television movies, specials, or sports. Responsibilities will vary depending on the type of programming involved. The individual works closely with the producer and the writers to create, develop, shoot, and produce television programming of all types. In some instances, the director is also the producer of a show or series of shows.

Choosing the correct cast is important whether the director is working on a newscast, an entertainment special, or a sitcom. The director is expected to choose and hire cast members with or without the help of a casting director. Within the scope of the position, the director will work with costume designers, hair and makeup people, scenic designers, lighting, music, and sound designers, as well as other production people to bring the show to life through the television camera.

Determining who and what should be seen on camera is essential to the success of television directing. The director must plan camera shots, lighting, and sound as well as determine where equipment, props, and people should be on stage in order to get the most effective shots and effects.

Successful individuals have the ability to convey ideas to cast members about the way scripts should be interpreted, lines should be spoken, and physical movements should be accomplished. They also have the ability to choose the appropriate music, sets, lighting, camera shots, and the like.

Directing television shows is a difficult but rewarding job. The director works long hours in an attempt to end up with the best, most polished production possible. Talented, creative directors can turn great shows into hits and even mediocre programs into successes.

Employment Opportunities

While the greatest number of employment opportunities are in large cities hosting more than one television station, it is easier to break into the field in small market television. Individuals may work on staff or freelance. Directors may be assigned a variety of programming or may specialize in particular formats such as sitcoms, news, sports, etc.

Employment opportunities can be found in the following areas:

- Network stations
- Affiliated stations
- Independent production companies
- Video production companies
- Local cable stations
- National cable stations
- Public broadcasting television stations
- School-owned university stations

Earnings

Earnings for directors can range from approximately $20,000 to $150,000 or more depending on a number of variables. These include the type of station or program(s), market, location, and popularity. Other variables include the responsibilities, experience, qualifications, and professional reputation of the individual.

Directors working for networks, many major market stations, and independent production companies may have their minimum earnings negotiated and set by the Directors Guild of America (DGA). Directors may be compensated by the project or on a weekly basis, depending on the specific project and station.

Advancement Opportunities

There are a number of paths for career advancement for television directors, depending on the method individuals take. Some directors become producer/directors. Others become producers. Directors may find similar duties with more prestigious projects or at more prestigious stations. Similarly, individuals may find increased earnings and prestige working for independent production companies.

Directors may also advance their careers by specializing in particular projects that require more complex productions. This will result in increased earnings.

Education and Training

Most employers either prefer or require television directors to hold at least a bachelor's degree. Good majors include broadcasting, communications, journalism, theater, and liberal arts.

Courses and seminars in television, production, communications, theater, film, and related subjects will be helpful in honing skills. A broad knowledge in a variety of subjects will also be useful for directors when working on programming in various areas of interest.

Experience and Qualifications

In order to become a director in television, most usually need some type of experience working in television production. This can be acquired working as an assistant director, unit manager, floor manager, production assistant, or camera operator. Other experience can be obtained through internships or apprenticeships.

Directors must be creative, organized, and detail-oriented individuals. They must have a thorough understanding of television production, camera shots, effects, etc. Interpersonal, motivational, and supervisory skills are necessary for success in this field.

For Additional Information: Individuals aspiring to become television directors can obtain additional career information from the Directors Guild of America (DGA), the National Association of Broadcasters (NAB), the National Association of Television Program Executives (NATPE), the Academy of Television Arts and Sciences (ATAS), American Women in Radio and Television (AWRT), and the Corporation for Public Broadcasting (CPB).

TIPS

- Internships are very useful in getting your foot in the door in this field. Talk to your college advisor or contact television stations, specific television shows, independent production companies, or trade associations to find such programs.
- Apprenticeships are another helpful method of breaking into the field and learning as you go.
- Try to find television and cable stations in small, local markets to use as a training ground. Smaller stations usually offer you the opportunity to learn about all facets of television production instead of just specialized areas. You can also climb the career ladder more quickly as others move on to better positions. After you obtain experience you can send your resume to other stations and production companies.
- You may be marketable if you are highly knowledgeable in a specific field such as entertainment, sports, or news.
- Contacts and networking are helpful in succeeding in this field. Meet important contacts by participating in internships and apprenticeships and by attending seminars, workshops, and trade association meetings.
- Many television directors start out working in theater. Volunteer to direct a school production or work with the director of a community theater production.
- Obtain as much experience as you can working in all facets of television. The more knowledge you acquire, the more marketable you will be.
- Get your foot in the door by taking any job available in television. Learn as you go. Doing more than is expected of you will help you to advance your career.
- Enroll in as many courses, workshops, and seminars as you can find in producing, television, directing, and related subjects.

PRODUCTION ASSISTANT—TELEVISION

· ·

Job Description: Assist in the production of television programming.

Earnings: $12,000–$25,000+

Recommended Education and Training: Bachelor's degree in broadcasting, mass communications, radio-television, theater, or related fields.

Skills and Personality Traits: Detail-oriented; organization and communications skills; word processing skills.

Experience and Qualifications: Experience in theater or television helpful, but not required.

Job Description and Responsibilities

Production assistants working in television are responsible for helping others in the production department produce television programming. They may work in the studio or on location. Specific responsibilities vary with each job. The position is part secretary, receptionist, guy/gal Friday, computer word processor, and helper. At some stations, production assistants move from program to program. At others, individuals are assigned a specific show to work on.

The main function of production assistants, or P.A.s, is to handle duties and thereby free up the time of others on the production staff. Individual responsibilities begin in the preproduction period and go through post-production. Within the scope of the job, P.A.s may work on a variety of things in different areas, which is especially important for those eager to break into the industry. In this job, P.A.s have the opportunity to learn all facets of television production.

Responsibilities can include assisting with research. This is an important function in preparing television programming. Scripts must be developed and facts must be checked for accuracy. Depending on the experience and expertise of the individual, the P.A. might also be allowed to handle some copywriting responsibilities.

Another duty that might be assigned to the production assistant is typing production schedules for filming programs. Once typed, the individual will be responsible for distributing the schedule to the crew.

Production assistants are often in charge of gathering and filing materials used during a production. These can include scripts, photographs, releases, and other documents. Other duties include filling in all necessary production sheets.

Individuals may be asked to help schedule guests, cast roles, or handle similar duties. In many situations, production assistants will do hands-on work setting up monitors and teleprompters, holding cue cards, etc.

Production assistants are expected to pitch in and help wherever and whenever necessary. Through their work, individuals will learn about the various facets of production and find their specific areas of interest.

Employment Opportunities

While individuals can find positions in any area with a television station, the greatest number of opportunities are located in cities hosting more than one station. The job of production assistant is an entry-level position. Therefore, as people move up the career ladder, jobs open up. Every station hires at least one production assistant. Most hire 10 or 12, depending on the size and budget of the station.

Individuals can locate employment opportunities in the following settings:

- Network television
- Independent stations
- Local cable stations
- National cable stations
- Affiliated stations

Earnings

Being that production assistants are usually entry-level employees, salaries, as a rule, are not very high for the industry. Earnings for production assistants range from approximately $12,000 to $25,000 or more. Factors affecting salaries include the size, budget, prestige, and geographic location of the station. Other variables include the responsibilities and experience of the individual.

Advancement Opportunities

Advancement opportunities are endless for production assistants who are eager and enthusiastic. This job gives individuals a basic knowledge of television production. From there, production assistants can move up to become floor managers, camera operators, assistant directors, or associate producers. Most successful people in television production started out as production assistants.

Education and Training

Most stations either prefer or require a bachelor's degree. Good choices for majors include broadcasting, mass communications, radio-television, theater, or related fields.

Courses, seminars, and workshops in all areas of television, production, and film will also be useful.

Experience and Qualifications

Since this is generally an entry-level position, most stations do not usually require experience. However, experience in any aspect of theater or television will be helpful.

Production assistants should be eager to learn and willing to do more than is expected of them. They also need to be extremely organized and detail-oriented. Word processing and computer skills are necessary. The ability to communicate both verbally and in writing is important.

For Additional Information: Individuals can obtain additional information about this career by contacting the National Association of Broadcast Employees and Technicians (NABET), the Directors Guild of America (DGA), the Writers Guild of America (WGA), ABC, NBC, CBS, and the Fox Broadcasting Network.

TIPS

- If you are interested in working at a network, send your resume with a short cover letter to ABC, NBC, CBS, and the Fox Broadcasting Network. Ask about openings for production assistants.
- You might also send your resume and a short cover letter to affiliated, cable, and independent stations.
- If you are attending a college with a major in broadcasting, television, mass communications, etc., find out if the college offers internship programs in conjunction with television stations.
- Read the trades. This will help you keep up with what is happening in the industry.
- Send your resume to television production companies. Ask that your resume be kept on file. Check periodically to see if any positions have opened. Persistence often pays off.
- You might also contact syndicated television shows to see if they have any openings for production assistants. Keep checking. As people get promoted, there may be openings.

CAMERA OPERATOR—TELEVISION

Job Description: Operate the cameras in the studio and on location.

Earnings: $12,000–$45,000+

Recommended Education and Training: High school diploma; hands-on training through apprenticeships, internships, or working as an assistant.

Skills and Personality Traits: Technical skills; aesthetic sense; photography skills; creativity; imagination.

Experience and Qualifications: Experience in television production.

Job Description and Responsibilities

The camera operator's job in television is like the photographer's in still photography. The individual in this position is expected to operate cameras both in the studio and on location. He or she may be responsible for just one camera or be expected to run more than one at the same time.

Camera operators may have varied responsibilities, depending on the specific station structure and size of the department. Some may be required to attend production meetings with others in the production crew, including the director, producers, floor manager, and engineers. They may also be asked to tape program rehearsals as well as actual television productions.

Camera operators may work alone or with one or more assistants. There may also be more than one camera operator working at the same time.

Depending on the situation, cameras can be mounted on a stationary tripod, a dolly, or a portable crane. Camera operators also may use mini-cams or electric news-gathering cameras when shooting a remote on location.

The camera operator is expected to compose, frame, and photograph video images. In order to accomplish this the individual must be sure that the lighting, focus, and angles are correct.

In smaller stations, the camera operator may have extra responsibilities. For example, the individual may double as a driver going on remotes with a news reporter. The camera operator will be expected to pack up and load cameras as well as set them up with lights.

Camera operators may be required to do simple maintenance on their cameras and other related equipment. This is especially important when they are on a remote shoot and something does not work correctly.

Camera operators working in the studio will be expected to listen to instructions from the director and film accordingly. When camera operators are working on remotes or covering news stories, they will often have much more independence.

Employment Opportunities

The greatest number of jobs for camera operators working in television will be located in large, metropolitan cities hosting more than one television station. Smaller stations found in less urban areas offer opportunities for those entering the field. Camera operators may be responsible for shooting any type of programming. However, stations producing a great deal of news will usually have more openings. Employment settings include:

- Networks
- National cable stations
- Local cable stations
- Local affiliated stations
- Independent stations
- Independent television production companies
- Public television stations
- Corporate television studios
- Government television studios

Earnings

Annual earnings for camera operators can range from approximately $12,000 to $45,000 or more. Factors affecting earnings include the size, type, market, and geographic location of the station employing the camera operator. Other variables include the responsibilities, experience, and expertise of the individual.

Camera operators with a great deal of experience working for large stations or networks will have annual salaries at the high end of the pay scale. Individuals working for many stations will have minimum earnings negotiated and set by a union. These unions can include the International Brotherhood of Electrical Workers (IBEW) and the National Association of Broadcast Employees and Technicians (NABET).

Advancement Opportunities

Many camera operators climb the career ladder by locating similar positions at larger, more prestigious stations. This results in increased responsibilities and earnings. Others may become floor managers. Depending on the professional area the camera operator is interested in, the individual may also become a cinematographer or videographer. These positions also result in increased earnings and responsibilities.

Education and Training

While most stations want their employees to have high school diplomas, there are no other specific educational requirements for this job. Some individuals pursue a college education prior to landing a job. Others get hands-on training by participating in internships, apprenticeships, or jobs as production assistants or engineering technicians.

Experience and Qualifications

Experience is essential in this job. This may be acquired through internships or apprenticeships. Other methods of obtaining experience include working as a production assistant or engineering technician at a television station. Any experience working in television production will be useful.

Camera operators need the technical knowledge to operate a video camera as well as the creativity and aesthetic sense to frame and compose shots and angles. Photography skills are helpful.

For Additional Information: Individuals interested in pursuing a career in this field can obtain additional information by contacting the National Association of Broadcast Employees and Technicians (NABET), the International Brotherhood of Electrical Workers (IBEW), and the American Society of Cinematographers (ASC).

TIPS

- You will have an easier time breaking into the field if you apply to small, local stations. While the money will probably be minimal, the experience will be worthwhile.
- Openings may be advertised in the classified section of the newspaper. Look under headings such as "Camera Operator," "Television," "Broadcasting," etc.
- On occasion, jobs may also be listed or advertised in the trades.
- If you are pursuing a college education, try to find a school with a television station. This will offer you the opportunity of hands-on experience while in school.
- Send your resume with a short cover letter to small, local stations, independent stations, and cable stations. Once you acquire some experience, consider affiliates and networks.
- One way to acquire experience is by working for a corporation with a private television department. These are usually only located in very large corporations.
- Join trade associations and attend their meetings. Going to these events is a good way of meeting people in the industry and making important professional contacts.
- Contact the unions and television stations to see if they have internship or apprenticeship programs in this field.
- Learn as much as you can about all aspects of television production. The more you know, the more marketable you will be—especially at the beginning of your career.
- Look for a job as a production assistant. While you might work in a variety

of areas, you will surely be around the camera operator enough to watch, listen, and ask questions.

- A stint as an intern is also a great way to get your foot in the door. Many stations, especially smaller ones, hire interns after the internship has ended.

FLOOR MANAGER—TELEVISION

Job Description: Coordinate director's instructions during rehearsals and show production.

Earnings: $18,000–$60,000+

Recommended Education and Training: Bachelor's degree in mass communications, broadcasting, radio-TV, theater, or related fields.

Skills and Personality Traits: Organization skills; supervisory skills; interpersonal skills; communications skills; calm; detail-oriented;

Experience and Qualifications: Experience working in television production.

Job Description and Responsibilities

While the director supervises the cast and crew of a television production, he or she is usually in a control room. Following the director's instructions, the floor manager directs the cast and crew from the stage floor.

The floor manager is responsible for coordinating a great many of the activities that occur on the studio floor during a production. The job is similar to that of a stage manager in the theater. The floor manager is very visible before, during, and after a television production.

The individual may have varied responsibilities depending on the specific production and size of the crew. Before a production, the floor manager makes sure that the set and cast are prepared and ready for filming. Duties may include preparing and distributing rehearsal call sheets, arranging for rehearsal time and space, and making sure that any required scenery, sets, and equipment are in place. The floor manager may also be expected to lay out and mark with tape areas on the stage floor where actors, actresses, or other performers should stand. The floor manager is responsible for supervising the placement of props, lights, cameras, and monitors as well as all people on the stage floor. The individual is also responsible for checking that the cast, hosts, and guests have makeup on and that any necessary microphones are in place.

The floor manager is very active during production. During this time period the individual will follow the script, cuing performers and other production staff. With the help of the floor manager's signals, performers know how much time is left in a segment, when a segment should begin, etc. The floor manager may also be expected to operate the teleprompter.

After productions have "wrapped," the floor manager will be responsible for overseeing the dismantling of the set, if necessary, as well as for putting away equipment used during the production.

Employment Opportunities

The greatest number of employment opportunities for floor managers are located in cities hosting more than one television station. Floor managers are employed at all stations that produce their own programming. Individuals may work in the following settings:

- Independent television stations
- Local cable stations
- National cable stations
- Networks
- Public television stations

Earnings

Floor managers can earn between $18,000 and $60,000 or more per year. Factors affecting salaries include the type, size, and location of the specific station. Other variables include the experience and responsibilities of the individual. Experienced floor managers at midsized stations average $30,000 to $45,000. Individuals working at larger stations with a great deal of responsibility will earn more.

Advancement Opportunities

There are a number of paths individuals may take to advance their careers. Floor managers may locate similar jobs with larger stations or major markets, which results in increased earnings and responsibilities. Others may find the next step up is to serve a stint as an assistant director or unit manager. Eventually, most floor managers hope they will advance to jobs as directors in television.

Education and Training

Educational requirements vary from job to job. Some stations require only a high school diploma. Others prefer a bachelor's degree. It is especially wise for those interested in career advancement to pursue a college degree. Good majors include mass communications, broadcasting, radio-TV, and theater arts.

Any courses, workshops, or seminars in directing, staging, television production, cinematography, theater arts, and lighting will be useful.

Experience and Qualifications

Experience in television production is mandatory in order to become a floor manager at a television station. Some individuals obtain experience in prior positions as camera operators. Others worked as production assistants.

Floor managers should be organized, detail-oriented people with good communications skills and the ability to supervise others. In order to be successful, individuals need to be able to work under pressure and remain calm in the eye of a storm.

For Additional Information: Individuals interested in working in this area of television can obtain additional career information by contacting the National Association of Broadcast Employees and Technicians (NABET), American Women in Radio and Television, Inc. (AWRT), and the National Cable Television Association, Inc. (NCTA).

TIPS

- The more you know about this industry, the more marketable you will be. Take classes, seminars, and workshops in staging, lighting, camera techniques, television makeup, and television production. These are useful for their educational value as well as for the opportunities to make contacts.
- Positions in this field may be advertised in the newspaper classified section in areas hosting television stations. Look under headings such as "Television," "Floor Manager," "Stage Manager," etc.
- Start your job search in small markets or at local cable television stations. Get some experience and send your resume to larger stations.
- Try to find an internship. If your college does not work with television stations in this capacity, contact television stations directly and inquire about possibilities.
- Contact industry trade associations to find out if they offer seminars or internships.
- When choosing a college, try to find one with a college television station, and then get involved.
- Try to find a job as a production assistant. This is a great way to gain entry into a career in the television industry.

LOCATION SCOUT/LOCATION MANAGER—
FILM/TELEVISION/COMMERCIALS

Job Description: Find, photograph, and secure locations outside the studio for filming; act as liaison between production company, property owners, and neighbors.

Earnings: $75–$500 per day.

Recommended Education and Training: No formal educational requirements.

Skills and Personality Traits: Persuasiveness and negotiation skills; public relations skills; creativity; resourcefulness; photography skills.

Experience and Qualifications: Experience requirements vary; experience as an assistant location scout helpful.

Job Description and Responsibilities

The main functions of location scouts are to find and secure locations to shoot films, television programs, and commercials outside the studio. These outside sites are called "practical locations." They can include anything from the outside of a house to a beach, a highway, an ornate church, or a store interior.

When location scouts are hired, they are told what type of locations are needed for the production as well as other pertinent information about the site. The scout will be told the highest sum that will be paid to rent or use the location. He or she will then be responsible for searching out locations that fit the specifications and visions of the director of the film, television show, or commercial.

The scout may remember a location that is suitable or may call others to see if they know of such a site. Successful location scouts are resourceful in their searches. Individuals in this field often drive around for hours or even days searching for a house, building, piece of property, etc.

Once the scout finds a possible location, he or she must talk to the owners to persuade them to let the production company film on their property. Sometimes this is easy. Other times not. The scout is expected to negotiate a rental price with the owners as well as discuss available dates to shoot. The individual is responsible for taking photographs of the location to show to the director. In most cases, the scout attempts to find a number of options so that the director has a choice of locations.

The location scout may be asked to accompany the director and others from the production company to the sites to choose the most appropriate one. After a location has been chosen, the scout will finalize negotiations, have releases signed by property owners, and secure any necessary permits from the local, state, or federal government.

Once that is done, the job of the location scout may be completed. In some situations, the individual is kept on as the location manager. In this capacity, the individual acts as a liaison between the property owner, the community, and the production company. While filming is exciting to most people, those living in an area surrounding the location site may have their routines upset. The location scout/manager is expected to make sure that the production company gets the required shots with the least amount of inconvenience to the property owners and their neighbors.

It is imperative that everyone be kept satisfied during the filming. Handling this task often requires quite a bit of public relations with the property owner and neighbors.

Employment Opportunities

The greatest number of opportunities for location scouts are found in areas where there is a great deal of film, television, and commercial production. The main locations for these projects are in New York City and Los Angeles. However, many films and television shows are shot in other localities.

Location scouts may find employment searching out practical locations for the following:

- Motion pictures
- Music videos
- Educational films
- Industrial films
- Advertising agencies (for commercials)
- Cable productions
- Television shows (dramas, television movies, sitcoms, game shows, etc.)
- Miniseries
- Television production companies

Earnings

Earnings for location scouts can vary from approximately $75 to $500 per day or more. Earnings are based on experience, expertise, reputation, and levels of responsibility as well as the type of production and its budget. Individuals working as assistants may earn between $25 and $75 per day helping full-fledged location scouts in their work.

Location scouts that also handle the duties of a location manager can earn up to $500 or more per day.

Advancement Opportunities

Location scouts can advance to the position of location manager. Other advancement opportunities include finding more prestigious productions with which to work.

Education and Training

While there is no formal educational requirement to become a location scout, many individuals in this field have a college education. Degrees and majors vary with each individual. Some, pursuing a career in film or television, have gone to school and majored in theater, film, or television. Others have degrees in fields that are totally unrelated to the entertainment industry.

Courses in film and television are useful in learning about the industry and making contacts. Classes in photography may also be helpful in honing skills in that area.

Experience and Qualifications

Experience requirements vary from job to job. Those aspiring to work on major films or television shows should have some experience in the field. This can be acquired by working as an assistant location scout, production assistant, or intern. Other experience can be obtained by working in this area with student films and low-budget productions.

The ability to negotiate, persuasiveness, and public relations skills are mandatory for this career. Successful location scouts should also be resourceful people with a creative eye.

Individuals must be adept at photography. In order to find locations, a car and driver's license are necessary.

For Additional Information: Individuals interested in working in this field can obtain additional information by contacting the Directors Guild of America (DGA) and the National Alliance of Broadcast Engineers and Technicians (NABET). Other information can be obtained by contacting the state film commission.

TIPS

- Make sure you read the trades to keep up with what is happening in the industry, learn about new productions, film industry trade shows, etc. Industry trades include *Daily Variety* and *The Hollywood Reporter*.
- Contact production companies and inquire about openings as an assistant location scout. Names of production companies are listed in production directories. The money will be minimal, but the experience will be worthwhile.
- Call or write your local film liaison office to inquire about location scouts or location managers working in your area. Get their addresses and send your resume. Offer your services as an assistant. Follow up with a phone call— persistence helps.
- Until you get some experience, stress your willingness to work for low wages.
- There are many low-budget films under production. Many people working on these would be glad to have someone help them, but they don't have the finances to do so. All experience in this area will help you learn how to do

this job and to make contacts. You might consider a short stint as an intern if you can't find a paying position.

- Low-budget or student films may hire you as a full-fledged scout. The money may be minimal. However, you will learn about the industry, how to do your job, and will make important contacts.
- Get yourself listed in film production resource directories. (This is usually free.) You might also consider placing a small advertisement for your services in one or more of these directories.
- Another way to advertise your services as a location scout is to print business cards with your name, address, phone number, and area of expertise. Send them to production companies with a short letter and your resume.
- Attend film industry trade shows with your business cards in hand. These shows are often advertised or listed in the trades.
- Contact the government film office in your area and inquire about the possibilities of being added to their lists of local location scouts. Many companies coming into your area will prefer a local scout with less experience to one from out of the area, even if he or she has more experience.

CASTING DIRECTOR—TELEVISION/FILM

Job Description: Audition talent; recommend actors and actresses to director; negotiate contracts and salary.

Earnings: $1,000–$100,000+ per production.

Recommended Education and Training: No formal educational requirement; training may be obtained in college or through internships, apprenticeships, or on-the-job training.

Skills and Personality Traits: Communications skills; organization skills; detail-oriented; good memory; ability to match the right person with the right part; insight; intuition.

Experience and Qualifications: Experience working as an assistant casting director.

Job Description and Responsibilities

Casting directors working in film and television are responsible for finding talent for movies, television programming, commercials, music videos, etc. To accomplish this they must determine exactly what types of actors and actresses are needed for specific productions. This is done by reading the script and talking to the director. This information will help match the look, voice, and personality of an actor with the right role.

Individuals may cast the major roles, supporting roles, and/or extras for the production. In some cases, the director or producer has already decided who he or she would like to fill the major roles. In this situation, the casting director might call the agent of the actor or actress and have him or her come in to read a scene. Major superstars, however, often do not even audition. If they agree to the part after reading the script, negotiations begin.

Supporting roles and other cast members, as a rule, come in and read for the casting director. The casting director may read the other parts while the actor or actress auditioning reads his or her part from a section of the script. First auditions may or may not be videotaped. Usually if the casting director asks someone to come back for a second audition, there is a screen test done to see how the individual looks on film.

Casting directors often develop advertisements announcing casting calls and requirements. These are placed in industry trades, newspapers, and other publications. They may also hold open auditions.

As people audition, casting directors and their assistants keep notes that are filed for later use. This information is kept for the current as well as future projects the individual may be casting.

Casting directors select one or more actors or actresses who fit the bill for each role. These people are then called back to audition in front of the director and/or producer. While casting directors recommend talent, they do not have the final say. That is usually up to the director and/or producer of the production.

In addition to auditioning and recommending performers, a major responsibility of casting directors is negotiating with the performer's agent regarding the contract and salary.

The most successful casting directors have a unique talent for choosing the actor or actress that is most suitable for each role in the production.

Employment Opportunities

The greatest number of opportunities for casting directors in television and film are located in Los Angeles, Hollywood, and New York City. Casting directors may work on staff or freelance. Individuals may find employment opportunities working in a variety of settings. These include:

- Private casting companies
- Independent television production companies
- Independent film production companies
- Networks
- Motion picture studios

Earnings

Earnings for casting directors working in television and film vary depending on a number of factors. These include the budget and prestige of projects as well as the responsibilities, experience, and reputation of the casting director. Earnings are dependent on whether the individual is on staff or working on a per-project basis. Casting directors can earn between $1,000 and $100,000 or more per project depending on whether they are casting a major motion picture, television show, music video, or commercial.

Advancement Opportunities

Casting directors can advance their careers by locating staff positions that result in more consistent work. Other advancement opportunities include finding either a larger number of projects to work on or more prestigious projects to cast.

Education and Training

While some individuals hold college degrees in broadcasting, television, theater, or film, there are no formal educational requirements necessary for becoming a casting director in television or film. Training can be acquired by stints as interns, apprentices, or assistants to casting directors.

Experience and Qualifications

Experience is usually required to become a casting director in television and films. Some acquire this through internships, apprenticeships, and jobs as assistants. Many casting directors held other jobs in television, film, and/or theater prior to their current positions. Familiarity with the industry is essential.

Casting directors must have the insight to know exactly what producers and directors are looking for and then find actors and actresses to fit the parts.

Some casting directors are members of the Casting Society of America (CSA). There are a number of requirements necessary to join this organization. These include sponsorship by members of the group, having credits for casting for a specified number of years, and being voted on by the membership.

For Additional Information: Individuals interested in learning more about careers in casting can contact the Casting Society of America (CSA).

TIPS

- Apprenticeships are one of the best ways of entering the business and learning about the field.
- Internships are another good method of learning the business.
- Most casting directors require at least one assistant. There is a great deal of turnover in the industry because unless they are on staff, casting directors usually only need assistants when they are working on a project.

- Find out about the membership requirements necessary to join the CSA. This association offers useful seminars, conferences, and information. They also provide professional guidance and support to members.
- Try to locate a mentor working in casting who will help guide your career.
- Look for a part-time or summer job working for an entertainment industry personal manager, theatrical agent, booking agent, etc. This will help you get experience in the industry as well as to make contacts.
- Contact casting offices and casting directors to find internships, apprenticeships, and training programs.
- Offer to cast school or community theater productions to gain experience.
- Try to find a job as an assistant to a casting director working in television or film. Watch, listen, and learn. Ask questions. Do more than is expected of you.
- Audition at one or more casting calls for film or television shows. When you do, it will help you understand the demands of casting directors as well as allow you to view the casting process from a different angle.
- Watch television shows, films, and plays. Look at the actors and actresses playing the parts. Try to understand why they were chosen.

SCENIC DESIGNER—TELEVISION/FILM/VIDEO

Job Description: Design, develop, and create scenery and sets for television, film, and/or video productions.

Earnings: $15,000–$85,000+

Recommended Education and Training: Bachelor's degree in theater arts, art and design, television production, or related fields.

Skills and Personality Traits: Artistic flair; creativity; interpersonal skills; ability to conceptualize and translate ideas.

Experience and Qualifications: Experience working in theater, television, film, or video production; internships and apprenticeships helpful.

Job Description and Responsibilities

All television and film productions require the expertise of scenic designers. The major functions of these individuals are to develop and design sets and scenery for television and film productions. A well-designed set can make the difference between a mediocre, unremembered production and a production that no one can forget.

Scenic designers may also be called scenic directors, set designers, art directors, or production designers. The individual's responsibilities begin in the preproduction period. During that time, the designer meets with the director and often with the producer to discuss their ideas. The individual will also read the script to determine the physical setting(s) that must be developed.

In order to translate ideas into reality, scenic designers often draft sketches and illustrations as well as create models of sets. In many productions, more than one set is used. The individual must develop floor plans specifying where each set will be located. As cameras, lights, and other major equipment must also be situated, it is important to determine where everything will be located and placed.

Scenic designers work closely with a great many people. These include set dressers, property masters, lighting designers and directors, costume designers, the director, and often the producer as well. They must also work with carpenters to oversee set construction.

Other responsibilities of scenic designers include keeping track of sets, scenery, backdrops, and the large props in inventory. In some situations, scenic designers must do research to make sure that the details of a set relate to those of a particular time period. This might occur when designers are working on sets for productions of old-time westerns, Victorian age pieces, or the 1940s or 1950s time periods. For example, scenic designers would not use VCRs on the set of a television show or movie set in the 1960s. Individuals may be expected to create sets for time periods that have not yet occurred or for science fiction or surrealistic productions. This is often a great challenge.

Talented scenic designers can watch movies or television programs and know that their efforts played an integral part in the artistic success of the production.

Employment Opportunities

The greatest number of opportunities for employment for scenic designers are in Hollywood, Los Angeles, and New York City. However, television stations as well as independent television and film production companies throughout the country may offer opportunities.

Individuals may work on staff or, more frequently, freelance. Scenic designers are employed by independent film, television, commercial, and video production companies. They may also be employed by independent, local, and cable stations as well as networks and other production companies handling television programming.

Types of television shows using the services of scenic designers include:

- Soap operas
- Dramas
- Made-for-television movies
- Game shows
- Sitcoms
- Entertainment specials
- Variety shows
- Talk shows

Earnings

Scenic designers working on a fairly consistent basis earn between $15,000 and $85,000 or more annually. Factors affecting earnings include the type and prestige of the production as well as the experience, reputation, and responsibilities of the individual. Annual compensation is also greatly affected by the amount of work the scenic designer does. Those who work on staff will have more secure incomes than individuals who freelance.

In most situations, minimum earnings are negotiated and set by either the United Scenic Artists (USA) union or the International Alliance of Theatrical Stage Employees (IATSE).

Advancement Opportunities

Advancement opportunities for scenic designers include locating more consistent full-time staff positions with television or film production companies. Other individuals advance their careers by obtaining a larger number of jobs per year. Scenic designers can also climb the career ladder by becoming involved with more prestigious projects in television or film.

Education and Training

While a college degree is not essential for all jobs in this field, it is recommended. There is a great deal of competition in this area. College often offers opportunities to make contacts, hone skills, and obtain experiences that the individual might not otherwise have.

Good choices for majors include theater arts, art and design, television or film production, or related fields. Courses, seminars, and workshops in television and film production, drafting, graphic arts, stagecraft, and architecture will be useful.

Hands-on experience and on-the-job training provide a helpful training ground for individuals interested in pursuing a career in this field.

Experience and Qualifications

Experience is usually required for this position. The degree of experience necessary varies from job to job. As a rule, the more prestigious the job and production, the more experience is required. Hands-on experience is always valuable.

Experience can be obtained in a number of ways. Some individuals work as assistant scenic designers in television, film, or theater. One may also acquire experience through apprenticeships and internships.

Those working in unionized situations must become members of the USA union. To join, individuals must take and pass an examination and go through an interview process.

Scenic designers should be creative people with an artistic flair. They should also have the ability to conceptualize and translate ideas. A knowledge and understanding of television and film production techniques is also required.

For Additional Information: To learn more, individuals can contact the USA union and Set Designers and Model Makers (SDMM).

TIPS

- Consider breaking into the field on a small scale. Offer to design sets for local or cable television stations.
- Get experience handling the set design for school or community theater productions.
- Read the industry trades. Look for low-budget productions to find opportunities to obtain experience. These productions often do not have enough financial backing to hire experienced professionals and may offer you the chance to work at a lower fee.
- Never turn down an opportunity to get experience, even if the salary is low or nonexistent. All productions that you work on can be listed on your resume.
- Another good method of acquiring experience and making industry contacts is to become a production assistant.
- Send your resume and a short cover letter to networks and film, video, commercial, and television production companies.
- Get listed in film production resource directories.
- Join the USA union. In addition to negotiating and setting minimum fees for scenic artists, the union provides professional guidance and support to its members.

COSTUME DESIGNER—TELEVISION/FILM

Job Description: Design costumes for television and film productions; outfit actors and actresses.

Earnings: $20,000–$75,000+

Recommended Education and Training: Bachelor's degree in fashion or costume design helpful.

Skills and Personality Traits: Sense of style; drawing and sketching skills; graphic arts skills; sewing skills; creativity; imagination.

Experience and Qualifications: Experience in costuming, wardrobe, and related areas in television, film, and/or theater.

Job Description and Responsibilities

Costume designers are responsible for dressing the cast of a television or film production. Individuals may rent or purchase costumes or may design original ones. In the scope of the job, they are expected to work within the budget allowed for costumes. Costume designers may work alone or may supervise one or more assistants.

Costume designers have many responsibilities. They usually begin their job by reading the script and talking to the director. In this way, designers can learn about the characters and the time period and determine the costuming requirements. They may do research by reading books, visiting museums, going through magazines, etc., so that costumes accurately reflect the time period in which the production is taking place. They then work on ideas for costumes.

Generally, the individual is responsible for costuming the entire cast from the extras to the lead characters. Depending on how elaborate the production is, the designer may also be costuming characters who change scenes frequently. This is especially true in feature films where time periods are often extended.

Sometimes the characters of the production will be wearing normal, everyday street clothes. In these situations the designer may not have costumes made. Instead, costumes such as suits, dresses, etc., can be chosen from a clothing store. This often occurs when costuming a contemporary television show or film. The designer may shop with the actors or actresses or may supervise assistants who shop for these items.

In other situations, the individual may determine that some of the actors and actresses should be wearing their own clothing. This might occur when there are a lot of extras involved in a production. The designer will then be expected to check and approve the clothing of those characters.

In addition to purchasing or borrowing costumes and clothing from stores, designers might also find appropriate costumes at theatrical costume supply houses or in the studio's stock. Occasionally, costumes that are in stock are altered and/or redesigned.

One of the most challenging and interesting parts of a costume designer's job is actually designing the costumes. When required, the designer will make sketches and do drawings. The designer may also photograph samples and have models made. Fabrics and colors are chosen for each costume and these are shown to the director. The director may approve the sketches or may have more concrete ideas of costumes that might bring out the character's personality. The costume designer may also collaborate with the production designer.

Once the designer gets approval on the costumes they must be constructed. This may be done by an outside company or handled by one of the designer's assistants. After costumes are sewn, they must be fitted to each actor and actress.

Costume designers must consider many factors when planning costumes. These include the lighting and set design as well as the movements of the actors and actresses in the production. For example, if the character will be running through a busy street during a scene, the designer must not make the costume so tight that the individual cannot move comfortably.

Other things that must be taken into account include the size and body shape of the actors and actresses who will be wearing the costumes, as well as the costume's coloring.

A great part of the costume designer's time is spent after costumes are completed. During production, the costume designer will supervise assistants doing final fittings and fixing costumes that need alterations, changes, or repairs. Often what looks good to the eye may not photograph well. Things may need to be changed. The designer must be able to work quickly within time constraints.

Talented costume designers are very creative people. A good one makes characters more believable in their roles. Through their ideas and designs they are able to bring out the personalities of characters as well as help to bring characters to life.

Employment Opportunities

The greatest number of employment opportunities for costume designers interested in working in the film and television industries are found in Los Angeles, Hollywood, and New York City. Costume designers can either freelance or work as salaried employees in a number of settings. These include:

- Networks
- Independent television production companies
- Independent film production companies
- Motion picture studios
- Independent costume design companies

Earnings

Costume designers working on a fairly consistent basis in television and film can earn between $20,000 and $75,000 or more annually. Earnings are dependent on the amount of work the individual does as well as the prestige of the project. Other factors determining earnings include the reputation, responsibilities, and experience of the costume designer.

Individuals usually have minimum earnings negotiated and set by one of the unions representing costume designers in these industries. These include the United Scenic Artists (USA) union, the Costume Designers Guild (CDG), and the International Alliance of Theatrical and Stage Employees (IATSE).

Individuals working on a television series, for example, will earn a minimum of approximately $1,300 to $1,400 per week. Similar minimums are earned by those working in film. However, creative costume designers who have established a good reputation in the industry can negotiate earnings well over minimum scale. Many successful costume designers earn upwards of $75,000 per year.

Advancement Opportunities

Costume designers can advance their careers by locating more prestigious projects. Individuals can also advance by finding a job with an ongoing television series or by costume designing for a major motion picture.

Education and Training

While there is no formal educational requirement for this career, a bachelor's degree in costume design or fashion is helpful. Courses might include fashion design, costuming, drawing, sketching, color theory, theater arts, design, art history, history, sewing, staging, lighting, and television and film production.

Experience and Qualifications

Experience is mandatory for costume designers working in television and film. This can be acquired through internships and apprenticeships in the costuming department of television and film productions. Similar experience can be obtained by working in this area in theater. Many costume designers began their careers as dressers or wardrobe assistants. With the passage of time they may have worked as sketch artists, tailors, and the like.

Costume designers working in this industry should be creative people with a sense of style. The ability to work under pressure is essential. Unlike theater where things can be changed more easily, designers cannot change something the day after shooting even if they come up with a better idea. These individuals must know how to research, sew, sketch, and draw.

For Additional Information: Individuals interested in pursuing a career in costume design can obtain additional information by contacting the USA union, the CDG, the IATSE, and the Motion Picture Costumers (MPC).

TIPS

- It is easier to acquire experience in costume design in theater than in television and film. Even though there are a number of differences in the jobs of costume designers in the various media, experience in theater will be helpful.
- Offer to handle the costume design for school and community theater productions.
- Look for apprenticeships with costume designers, wardrobe assistants, dressers, etc., in theater, film, and television.
- The more you know about the entire process of filmmaking, television production, and theater, the better. Try to take classes, workshops, and seminars in acting, directing, set design, and lighting as well as in costuming, costume design, etc.

- While you might not have to sew at this stage of your career, you should have sewing skills. Take sewing classes to learn new techniques.
- Go to the library and look through books and magazines to get ideas on costumes, dress, clothing, accessories, and so forth.
- You should also visit museums to view period costumes. While you're there, check out period paintings.
- Watch television shows and view films, keeping an eye out for the costuming of characters.
- Put together a portfolio of your best sketches. You will need them when applying for a job. Try to have a varied collection of sketches illustrating your skill at designing for different situations.
- Send a short letter with your background sheet or resume to the networks, independent film and television production companies, studios, etc. You might also contact independent costume designers or costume design companies to see if they are looking for assistants.
- Keep in mind that you will probably have to start at the bottom and work your way up the career ladder.
- A good way to get your foot in the door and learn as you go is to find a job as a production assistant in the area of costume design.
- Read the trades. You will often read about low-budget films that are getting ready to go into production. Contact the production company to see if there are any openings for work in costume design. If you offer to work for low wages, you might find a position. While the money will be minimal, it will help you get experience and credits.

MAKEUP ARTIST—TELEVISION/FILM/VIDEO

Job Description: Improve or alter the appearance of actors and actresses in film, television, or video through the design and application of makeup.

Earnings: $20,000–$100,000+

Recommended Education and Training: Training through college, professional makeup school, or courses in television, film, and stage makeup.

Skills and Personality Traits: Creativity; proficiency in television and film makeup design and application.

Experience and Qualifications: Experience with television, film, and theatrical makeup through apprenticeships, internships, etc.

Job Description and Responsibilities

Makeup artists working in television and film use makeup to improve, enhance, or alter the appearance of actors and actresses. There is a great deal of lighting used in television and film production, which often washes out features of the cast and exaggerates their flaws. Proper application of makeup can make the cast look more appealing to viewers.

In some instances, such as news, talk shows, and commercials, makeup artists make sure that the physical appearance of the anchors, reporters, hosts, and models appears more natural under the harsh studio lighting. In other instances makeup artists must create a multitude of illusions and special effects in order to portray characters more vividly. These can include scars, deformities, blood, wounds, black eyes, artificial features, etc. Makeup artists may be required to make characters appear older, younger, heavier, or thinner.

Individuals may be asked to help create the appearance of an entire character in a television show, film, or video. In order to do this the makeup artist may do research, read the script, analyze the character, talk to the director and actors, etc. In many cases, the characters will resemble "real" people; in others, makeup artists may have to employ a great deal of creativity and skill to design elaborate makeup for specialized productions, such as science fiction shows or films.

Makeup artists are responsible for applying makeup to the face as well as the arms, legs, and any other exposed portions of the body. For example, actors portraying characters who have been in a major car accident might need to be made up so that the body looks mangled.

Individuals apply makeup before the scenes are shot. This often means the makeup artist must be at work very early in the morning. Many of the morning news shows have production people coming in at 11 P.M. or midnight to get ready. Makeup artists must be on hand to apply makeup for hosts, anchors, and guests. Soap operas or films may also have early calls for performers, resulting in even earlier calls for makeup artists.

Makeup artists work closely with the production hairstylist, director, production designer, costume designer, and costumer. In some cases, the makeup artist may also assume the duties of hairstylist. This usually occurs in low-budget films, production companies, and local television.

An important function of makeup artists in television and films is re-creating makeup for actors and actresses so that the appearance of the character being portrayed remains consistent throughout lengthy or out-of-sequence filming. In order to re-create makeup, artists often take Polaroid photos and use notes.

Experienced makeup artists working in television and film usually have their own makeup kits filled with a variety of makeup and appliances used to create illusions as well as to enhance appearances.

Employment Opportunities

Individuals pursuing a career as makeup artist in television or film will find the greatest number of opportunities in Los Angeles and New York City. Productions may use one or more makeup artists, depending on the size, type, and budget. Makeup artists working in this medium may work on staff or freelance for:

- Networks, local, independent, or cable newscasts
- Entertainment and variety shows
- Sitcoms
- Dramas
- Soap operas
- Television movies
- Independent television production companies
- Motion pictures and films
- Industrial shows
- Videos
- Advertising agencies
- Producers of commercials
- Local affiliated television stations
- Independent television stations
- Cable stations

Earnings

Annual earnings for individuals working on a fairly consistent basis in television and films range from $20,000 to $100,000 or more. Factors affecting earnings include the size, type, and budget of a production as well as the expertise, qualifications, experience, and responsibilities of the makeup artist. Annual earnings are also based on how often individuals work.

Makeup artists working in television and film earn between $500 and $2,500-plus per week. There are some working on major films who earn $2,500 or more per day.

Individuals working in television and film may have minimum earnings negotiated by the International Alliance of Theatrical Stage Employees (IATSE) union or the National Association of Broadcast Employees and Technicians (NABET).

Advancement Opportunities

Makeup artists working in television and film can advance their careers in a number of ways. Some find consistent work on a television series, resulting in a steady income. Others advance by locating positions on more prestigious projects requiring greater expertise. One can also climb the career ladder by landing a position as the department head or key makeup artist of a production.

Education and Training

Educational and training requirements vary from job to job. Many old-time makeup artists working in television and film were self-taught or learned from apprenticing with others. Today, there are a variety of ways to learn the skills needed for this profession. A college degree with a major in television, film, or theater arts is helpful in learning skills and providing experiences that individuals might not otherwise have the opportunity to participate in.

There are also makeup schools specializing in television, film, and theatrical makeup. Courses, workshops, and seminars in television, film, and stage makeup offered at colleges, universities, and many television or film studios are useful in honing skills and making contacts.

Experience and Qualifications

Experience is usually required to become a makeup artist in film and television. This can be acquired through internships or apprenticeships. Experience can also be obtained by working in community, regional, stock, or dinner theater productions, local or cable television, or with student films. Many makeup artists start their careers as assistants to full-fledged makeup artists and learn the ropes as they go.

Individuals must be proficient in the design and application of television and film makeup. Many areas of the country require makeup artists to hold state licenses. These are usually obtained by attending a licensed school of cosmetology and hairstyling, as well as by taking and passing a written and practical state exam.

Makeup artists working in unionized situations may also be required to be members of the IATSE. To become a member, individuals will have to take and pass a practical exam illustrating their skills in various theatrical makeup techniques.

For Additional Information: Individuals aspiring to have careers as makeup artists in television and film can obtain additional information by contacting the IATSE, Makeup and Hairstylist Local 798, Makeup and Hairstylist Local 706, the Cosmetologists Association, and the National Hairdressers and Cosmetologists Association (NHCA).

TIPS

- Get experience by offering to do the makeup for fashion shows, community or school theater productions, and the like.
- Contact television stations, film production companies, studios, etc., to find internship or apprenticeship programs.
- Take as many seminars in film and television makeup as you can. These are often offered by production companies, studios, etc. They are an excellent means of learning new skills, honing old ones, and making important industry contacts.
- Read the trades. You will often find valuable information in these papers and magazines that can be useful to your career.

- There are also a great many books on the subject of television and film makeup that can teach you new techniques.
- Look for new films, videos, or television shows that are under production. This information can be found in industry trade papers.
- If you haven't acquired a great deal of experience, contact low-budget productions to see if they will use you. While the compensation will probably not be great, the experience will be worthwhile.
- Try to get copies of all finished films, videos, commercials, shows, etc., in which you have worked on the makeup. Use these when applying for other jobs. Often, low-budget productions, student films, or college television stations will give you the film instead of all or part of your compensation.
- Prepare a portfolio of photographs of actors, actresses, models, etc., whose makeup you have done. Offer to do the makeup of these individuals free of charge in exchange for the opportunity to photograph them for your portfolio.
- Work on student films and shows. Many students go on to become major film and television producers, directors, and the like. The world of television and film is a small one.
- Write to makeup artists, production companies, studios, television stations, etc., to see if they would be willing to hire you as an assistant. Look in television and film industry directories to get names, addresses, and phone numbers.

PROPERTY MASTER—
TELEVISION/FILMS/COMMERCIALS

Job Description: Locate and maintain props which help scenes come alive and become more realistic in television, film, video, and commercial productions.

Earnings: $100–$500+ per day.

Recommended Education and Training: No formal educational requirements; college degree or courses in broadcasting, television, film, or theater arts helpful.

Skills and Personality Traits: Resourcefulness; mechanical ability; artistic ability; detail-oriented.

Experience and Qualifications: Experience as an assistant prop person, production assistant, runner, stagehand, set dresser, etc.

Job Description and Responsibilities

Property masters are responsible for locating and maintaining props used on film, television, video, and/or commercial sets. Individuals may have varied duties depending on the specific job.

Property masters, or prop masters as they are often called, are expected to get all the items used to decorate and enhance sets. These items include everything that is ornamental as well as functional in a scene and that might help bring it to life. The individual handling props for an interior living room scene might be responsible for finding draperies, lamps, furniture, magazines, framed pictures, vases, flowers, plants, etc. Depending on the story, plot, and scene, other items might include food, cigarettes, ashtrays, matches, glassware, silverware, toys, etc.

In some situations, the props are easy to find. The property master may just be responsible for finding out what the director or set designer needs and locating the items from a storage area. In other situations, the individual must rent or buy items or have them constructed. The prop master may be expected to search through secondhand stores, thrift shops, and junkyards to find props from other time periods.

Another function of the property master is to make sure that all props are clean and maintained to stay in working order. When food is needed, the property master will often need to know how to make it look fresh and appetizing. Experienced property masters learn the tricks of the trade needed to keep food looking fresh after hours under hot lights. The individual may be expected to fix soft drinks so that they have more bubbles than normal, concoct water or juice so that it looks like an alcoholic beverage, or fix a steak so that it has more sizzle.

Property masters may be responsible for placing props in the correct locations for each scene as well as for removing or striking them from the set after the scene has been shot.

After scenes have been completed and props are no longer needed, the property master is also expected to return them to storage or to the location from where they were borrowed or rented.

Property masters may work at a studio or on location. Those working on location often have a more difficult job finding the required props. Whether individuals are responsible for handling prop requirements for a television talk show, sitcom, or drama, or for a film, video, or commercial, the finished tape will reflect their work.

Employment Opportunities

The greatest number of employment opportunities for property masters can be found in Hollywood, Los Angeles, and New York City. However, opportunities may be available in other large, culturally active cities hosting television stations, production companies, etc. Individuals may work in a number of settings. These include:

- Television stations (networks, local, independent, cable, etc.)
- Television production companies
- Video production companies
- Film production companies

Earnings

The range of earnings for property masters is dependent on a number of variables. These include the type and budget of the production. Other factors include the experience, reputation, and responsibilities of the individual. Property masters can freelance or be employed by a production company on a full-time basis. Those employed on a full-time basis will have a more secure, consistent earning pattern.

Earnings for property masters can range from approximately $100 to $500 per day or more. In most situations their minimum earnings are negotiated and set by a union. The International Alliance of Theatrical Stage Employees (IATSE) and the National Association of Broadcast Employees and Technicians (NABET) are two of the most prevalent unions negotiating for property masters.

Successful property masters who work on a steady basis often earn up to $60,000 or more per year.

Advancement Opportunities

Property masters can advance their careers by locating work on a more consistent basis, finding more prestigious productions to work on, or by becoming staff property masters. Other advancement opportunities include becoming a scenic designer for productions. Many of the possibilities for advancement depend on the individual's training, experience, and talents.

Education and Training

While there is no formal educational requirement to become a property master, many feel a college degree or background helps to provide experiences and opportunities that will be useful in breaking in and excelling in this career. Courses, workshops, seminars, etc., in film, theater arts, theatrical production, scenic design, construction, and the like will be of great value.

Other useful forms of training for aspiring property masters are apprenticeships, internships, and on-the-job training.

Experience and Qualifications

Experience is usually required to become a property master. Individuals can acquire this experience in a number of ways. Some start out their careers as set dressers, stagehands, or grips. Others begin as assistant property masters, runners, or production assistants.

Since property masters are often required to find hard-to-locate items, they must be extremely resourceful. Woodworking and carpentry skills are helpful, as is an artistic flair.

For Additional Information: Aspiring property masters can obtain additional information by contacting the local affiliate of the IATSE or the NABET.

TIPS

- Consider breaking into the field on a small scale. Contact a local television or cable station to see if there are any opportunities as an assistant property master.
- It is important to get your foot in the door and learn by watching, helping, and doing. Try to do as much as you can, not just what is expected of you.
- Visit thrift shops, secondhand stores, antique shops, etc., to see what is available. Take notes and keep them for future reference.
- Take courses in woodworking, carpentry, and other related subjects. In a small production company, the ability to create, build, and repair props is helpful.
- Contact the local affiliate of IATSE to see if there are any opportunities for apprenticeships.
- You might also consider contacting television, film, and video production companies regarding internships, apprenticeships, or jobs as assistants.
- Make sure you read the industry trades. Keep up on happenings in the industry. Look for student and low-budget film productions that are starting up and contact them about job possibilities.
- There are a number of production directories that have listings for each specialty. Contact them to find out the requirements for listing yourself.
- You might place a small ad advertising your specialty in the trades or in a production directory. People in the industry read and look through these publications.
- Send your resume and a short cover letter to production companies, television stations, property masters, etc., inquiring about jobs as assistants.
- Print business cards with your name, phone number, and the words ''Property Master.'' Hand them out to everyone in the industry who might help you.
- Find opportunities to meet industry people by joining and attending meetings of unions and trade associations. You might also make contacts at seminars, workshops, and classes in the field.

ANCHORPERSON—TELEVISION NEWS

Job Description: Report news and introduce reports on weather, traffic, special interest stories, etc., during newscast.

Earnings: $20,000–$1.5 million-plus

Recommended Education and Training: Bachelor's degree in broadcasting, journalism, mass communications, liberal arts, or political science.

Skills and Personality Traits: Pleasant appearance and speaking voice; communications skills; understanding of news developments; ability to analyze and/or interpret major news events.

Experience and Qualifications: Experience working in television news.

Job Description and Responsibilities

Anchorpersons on television news programs are the hosts of the newscasts. They have a number of responsibilities depending on the specific station. Some newscasts have one anchorperson while others have two. The anchors are the center of the newscast.

Anchorpersons are responsible for reading news reports. They often offer voice-over comments with taped reports of news events that occurred in the course of the day.

In addition to reading news reports, anchorpersons introduce reporters and their stories and other segments of the newscast. These can include the weather, sports, business news, and so forth.

In some situations individuals may be expected to research stories, write reports, and compile information from wire service copy. In other situations, news writers, researchers, and reporters handle these tasks. Anchorpersons may rewrite stories to make them more clear. At certain times they go into the field to report on special stories and events. They may also conduct interviews in the studio prior to newscasts for use during the show, or do it live during newscasts.

Other duties of anchorpersons include handling special news reports and bulletins as well as acting as hosts for documentaries or special news shows. At smaller stations, the anchorperson may also be the news director. Individuals may be required to determine the importance and sequence of stories used in the newscast.

Anchorpersons may be expected to discuss current news situations and developments as well as analyze and explain them to the viewers. They inspire interest in stories by the way they tell the news. Anchors who appeal to viewers and have the ability to report the news in a believable and satisfying way will build a following.

Employment Opportunities

An anchorperson may find employment at television stations throughout the country. Those with little experience will find it easier to break into the field in a small market or at local cable television. Employment opportunities include:

- Network television
- Independent stations
- Local cable stations
- National cable stations
- Affiliated stations

Earnings

Anchors can earn between $20,000 and $1.5 million or more annually. Factors affecting earnings include the station market, size, location, prestige, and popularity. Other variables include the individual's experience, popularity, and responsibilities.

There are a number of network anchorpersons who have developed a large following over the years and they earn the highest salaries. Individuals working in major markets for network affiliates can earn $200,000 or more. Those working in very small markets start out at approximately $20,000. Salaries go up with experience, popularity, and market size.

Advancement Opportunities

Advancement opportunities for anchorpersons are, to a great extent, based on the popularity and following they can build. They advance their careers by locating similar positions at larger, more prestigious stations or networks. This results in increased popularity and earnings.

Education and Training

The minimum educational requirement to become an anchorperson is a bachelor's degree. Good choices for majors include broadcasting, journalism, mass communications, political science, and liberal arts. Workshops and seminars in television broadcasting, news writing, speech, and related subjects will be useful.

Experience and Qualifications

Most anchorpersons were television reporters prior to their current position. Experience working in the newsroom gathering, writing, and reporting news is necessary. Some also have experience working in radio or print news.

Experience can be garnered through internships or working in small market or local television.

Anchors must not only look good on camera, but have a pleasant, clear speaking voice as well. Those successful in this field have the ability to let their personality shine through the camera to viewers.

For Additional Information: Aspiring anchorpersons can obtain additional information about careers in this field by contacting the Radio-Television News Directors Association (RTNDA), the Writers Guild of America (WGA), the American Federation of Television and Radio Artists (AFTRA), and the Society of Professional Journalists (SPJ).

TIPS

- Internships are a great way to get your foot in the door in this field. Stations often hire interns after their program ends. If your college does not have a program, contact television stations yourself and inquire about possibilities.
- Get as much experience as possible in a newsroom. If you can't find a job working in television news, begin in radio or print journalism.
- Depending on your geographic location, positions may be advertised in the newspaper classified section. Look under headings such as "Anchorperson," "TV Newscaster," "Television," "Reporter," "Anchorman/woman," etc.
- Openings may also be listed or advertised in the trades.
- It is easier to break into the field in small markets. Get some experience and start sending out tapes and resumes.
- Look for seminars and workshops in news writing, broadcasting, and similar subjects.
- Make sure you keep up on current events and news. Many interviews include questions and opinions regarding these topics.
- After you obtain some experience, you might consider finding an agent to help you locate better jobs and to negotiate earnings.

REPORTER—TELEVISION NEWS

· ·

Job Description: Report news and feature stories live on the air or via tape; research facts and gather information; develop stories.

Earnings: $18,000–$200,000+

Recommended Education and Training: Bachelor's degree in journalism, mass communications, broadcasting, political science, or liberal arts.

Skills and Personality Traits: Pleasant appearance and speaking voice; good verbal and written communications skills; inquisitive; curious.

Experience and Qualifications: Experience writing news for radio, television, or print media.

Job Description and Responsibilities

Television reporters are responsible for reporting news stories and features for news broadcasts. They may report news live in the studio or on location in the field. They may also tape segments and do voice-over reports.

A news story can relate to society in a number of ways. The reporter is the individual responsible for determining the slant of each story. Sometimes reporters may emphasize the human angle. Other slants may be business- or consumer-oriented. In some situations, the reporter may take a national story and find a local angle. The trick is to make the story as interesting as possible for the greatest number of viewers.

In order for reporters to do their job they must gather information about news stories. This can be done through interviews, investigations, searching out leads, checking facts for accuracy, and organizing the report. Finished news reports must be easy to understand, credible, and accurate. Good reporters can make even a boring, run-of-the-mill story seem interesting.

Reporters may be expected to handle either general or specialized areas of news. These include health, entertainment, politics, business, consumer information, sports, etc. Depending on the size and structure of the station, reporters may be required to cover local functions and events or stories of national importance. They will be expected to attend and cover press conferences, events, and functions that affect the station's area. Many reporters are also expected to travel in order to handle breaking stories throughout the country or the world.

Some reporters are assigned stories by the news director or assignment editor. Others have more flexibility and are able to develop stories and features. Most reporters work shifts. They may work overtime to investigate reports and gather information for important stories. TV reporters may also be called in to work additional hours when there are emergencies requiring special news reports.

Employment Opportunities

Television reporters may find employment opportunities throughout the country in any area that hosts television or cable stations. Depending on the size of the station, there may be one or more reporters. Individuals with knowledge about special subjects such as health, business, entertainment, sports, consumer affairs, etc., will often be more marketable.

Reporters may work in a variety of settings in major, midsize, and small markets. Employment opportunities include:

- Network television
- Independent stations
- Local cable stations
- National cable stations
- Affiliated stations
- Public television stations

Earnings

Earnings for television reporters can range from approximately $18,000 to $200,000 or more annually. Factors affecting earnings include the popularity, size, market, type, and location of the station. Other variables include the experience, responsibilities, qualifications, and popularity of the reporter. Generally, reporters with little experience working in smaller market television will earn between $18,000 and $28,000 a year. As one gains experience and begins working in larger markets and at more prestigious stations, income increases. Reporters for major cable stations, networks, and major market television affiliates will earn the highest salaries.

Advancement Opportunities

Reporters can advance their careers in a number of ways. Some individuals obtain experience, build a following, and locate similar positions in larger markets or at more prestigious stations. Others go on to positions as assistant news directors or news directors. Most reporters aspire to advance their careers by becoming an anchorperson.

Education and Training

Most television stations require their reporters to have a minimum of a bachelor's degree. Good choices for majors include broadcasting, mass communications, journalism, political science, and liberal arts.

Seminars, workshops, and classes in news writing, broadcasting, and television news will be useful in honing skills and making contacts.

Experience and Qualifications

Experience requirements vary from job to job. Individuals working in small-market television may find jobs straight out of college. More experience is required for jobs at larger, more prestigious stations. This may be obtained through internships or through working in the news department of a television station as a desk assistant or news writer.

Reporters should have a pleasant appearance and speak in a clear, articulate manner. Successful ones are inquisitive and curious. Excellent written and verbal communications skills are imperative.

For Additional Information: Individuals aspiring to work in this field can obtain additional information by contacting the Writers Guild of America (WGA), the

American Federation of Television and Radio Artists (AFTRA), the National Association of Broadcasters (NAB), and the Radio-Television News Directors Association (RTNDA).

TIPS

- Get experience working in the news field. Even if you can't find a job in television, look for one in print or radio journalism.
- Positions in this field are advertised in the newspaper classified sections under such headings as ''Reporter,'' ''Television,'' ''News,'' ''Correspondent,'' ''Cable Television,'' ''Special Reporter,'' etc.
- Openings may also be listed or advertised in the trades.
- Try to find an internship. If your college does not work with television stations in this capacity, contact television stations directly and inquire about possibilities.
- If your school has a college television station, get involved. If there is no campus television station, seek work on the school's radio station and/or newspaper.
- Start your job search at a small-market or local cable television station. Get some experience, make a tape, and send out your resume to larger stations.
- Look for seminars and workshops in news writing, broadcasting, and the like.
- Make sure you stay informed about current events and news. Many interviews include questions and opinions regarding these topics.
- After you have obtained some experience, consider hiring an agent to help you locate a better job and to negotiate earnings.

SPORTSCASTER—TELEVISION NEWS

Job Description: Report sports news and events to television audience; write sports reports; select information for sportscasts.

Earnings: $15,000–$1.5 million-plus

Recommended Education and Training: Bachelor's degree in broadcasting or journalism.

Skills and Personality Traits: Communications skills; broad knowledge of sports; writing skills.

Experience and Qualifications: Experience in radio, television, or print journalism; clear speaking voice.

Job Description and Responsibilities

Television sportscasters report sports news to television audiences, whether live or on tape. Individuals may anchor the sports segment of one or more news shows during the broadcast day. They may also be responsible for reporting sports briefs or scores as they occur.

In some cases, TV sportscasters may be assigned to cover events, games, or matches in the field. In other instances, they may report or provide commentary on video other people have brought or sent into the station. Some sportscasters are lucky enough to have their own television show geared specifically to sports.

Duties of TV sportscasters, also called sports reporters or sports announcers, will depend greatly on the size and prestige of the station where he or she is working. Large stations with larger staffs may have a sports director, writers, color commentators, and a number of sportscasters. Smaller stations may just have a sports director and one sportscaster. At very small stations, the sportscaster will be responsible for handling all sports-related functions.

These individuals must be adept at writing their own copy. The copy should be written in a style that is easy to read and understand. Other duties of sportscasters include attending press conferences; developing sports-related features; interviewing athletes, coaches, managers, promoters, and fans; and announcing play-by-play sports activities.

Sportscasters working for small local or cable stations will be required to report on school, college, and amateur sports activities as well as on major developments in the professional sports world.

This is an ideal job for individuals who are passionate sports fans interested in a career in broadcast journalism. Work hours will vary depending on assignments. There may be a great deal of overtime involved, since the sportscaster might be required to attend luncheons, dinners, press conferences, and sporting events. However, for those who enjoy sports and the people involved in this profession, overtime work hours can be fun.

Employment Opportunities

Television sportscasters may anchor the sports segment of the news on a regular basis during the week, or part-time on weekends and/or holidays. They may also cover sporting events like games, press conferences, matches, etc. Job opportunities are found at:

- Local television stations
- Independent television stations
- National cable sports stations
- Local cable television stations
- Networks

Earnings

Annual earnings for television sportscasters can range from approximately $15,000 to $1,500,000 or more. Salaries are, to a great extent, determined by the type of market the individual works in as well as by the specific station and geographic location. Earnings are also determined by the responsibilities, experience level, and prestige of the given individual.

While local and cable stations often pay salaries on the lower end of the scale, many people take such jobs to obtain experience. As they gain experience and acquire positions in larger markets, earnings rise considerably and can range between $25,000 and $50,000. Television sportscasters with a large audience in major markets can earn up to $200,000 annually. Those working for network television may have earnings of $1.5 million or more.

Advancement Opportunities

The most common method of advancement for television sportscasters is to obtain a position with a larger or more prestigious station. Depending on their career level, sportscasters may also be assigned to better news shows, receive a promotion to station sports director, or earn their own sports-oriented show. Some sportscasters become color commentators for major sports events and become media personalities in their own right.

Education and Training

To most people interested in sports, a job revolving around sports events and news would be heavenly. Therefore, competition in the world of broadcast journalism is fierce. While a four-year degree is not required for all jobs, it is most often preferred. A bachelor's degree with a major in broadcasting, journalism, or communications is ideal. A degree in liberal arts would be acceptable. Some colleges also offer degrees or courses in sports administration. Courses, seminars, and workshops in writing, broadcasting, sports, etc., will be extremely useful. Colleges and universities with their own television stations will offer the opportunity to obtain hands-on experience.

Experience and Qualifications

Television sportscasters need a broad knowledge of the world of sports. Experience working in television and/or radio is beneficial. The ability to speak clearly and articulately, as well as feel comfortable in front of a camera, is mandatory.

For Additional Information: There are a number of associations, organizations, and unions that can provide additional information about careers as a television sportscaster. These include the American Federation of Television and Radio Artists (AFTRA), the National Sportscasters and Sportswriters Association (NSSA), the Radio-Television News Directors Association (RTNDA), the Writers Guild of America (WGA), and the American Sportscasters Association (ASA).

TIPS

- An internship or training program is your best opportunity for locating a job. These may be found at television stations or through trade associations. These programs offer you on-the-job training as well as assistance in making contacts.
- Make it known in the newsroom that you are always available. Some sportscasters get their break by working weekend or holiday shifts.
- If you are in college, become involved in some capacity with your school television station. If the school does not have a TV station, make sure you are at least involved in the school's radio station.
- Another way to obtain hands-on experience if you are in school is to inquire about the possibility of covering school sports for your local television station.
- Positions for local, independent, or small cable stations may be advertised in the newspaper classified section under the headings of "Broadcasting," "News," "Newscaster," "Sportscaster," "Broadcast Journalism," "Journalism," "Television," "Sports," "Announcer," or "Sports Reporter."
- Jobs for other stations may be advertised in the trades or association periodicals.
- Local and cable television stations have a high turnover rate. A job at either type of station in any department will give you valuable experience. Additionally, you will be among the first to know when the station's sportscaster is planning to leave.

WEATHER REPORTER—TELEVISION NEWS

Job Description: Report weather conditions and forecasts during newscasts or special reports; gather information.

Earnings: $18,000–$200,000+

Recommended Education and Training: Bachelor's degree preferred by many stations; others may only require high school diploma.

Skills and Personality Traits: Pleasant appearance and speaking voice; articulate.

Experience and Qualifications: Public speaking experience helpful.

Job Description and Responsibilities

Television weather reporters are responsible for reporting the day's weather and providing forecasts during news programs and special reports. Responsibilities will vary depending on the qualifications of the individual and the specific television station's structure.

Individuals as a rule will report weather conditions such as wind velocity, barometric pressure, temperatures, and meteorological changes. Within their reports they may also offer pollen counts, smog alerts, temperature extremes, or other conditions that may affect the health of viewers.

Weather reporters perform in a number of ways. Some are required to read the weather while sitting at a desk. Others may announce the weather with a voice-over tape of the day's weather highlights. Many use visual devices to help illustrate weather conditions. Most commonly, weather people stand in front of an image of a map or plastic overlay and point out various weather conditions and temperatures.

Weather reporters compile weather information in a variety of ways. Some have people in the field gathering information, while others use information provided by satellite weather services and wire services. Information may also be compiled from local, regional, state, or national government agencies. Larger stations often have their own equipment set up to monitor and gage weather conditions.

Individuals try to make their portion of the news as interesting as possible. To do this, they may work with other departments at the station to develop interesting, funny, or unique art to illustrate weather conditions and forecasts. Weather reporters generally do not read a script. Instead they report the weather and ad-lib as they go. A great deal of the success of weather reporters rests on their ability to ad-lib with wit.

Individuals working at smaller stations are usually only responsible for gathering and reading the weather information. At larger stations, weather reporters may be meteorologists who have a great deal of knowledge in this field. These individuals often also explain weather patterns, conditions, and their effects.

Weather reporters usually work specific shifts. Individuals appear during newscasts, special reports, and weather briefs scheduled throughout the day.

Employment Opportunities

Weather reporters may work full- or part-time for television and cable stations throughout the country. The largest number of opportunities are available in cities with more than one television station. However, small-market television is much easier to break into. Individuals may find employment opportunities in the following:

- Network television
- Independent stations
- Local cable stations
- National cable stations
- Affiliated stations

Earnings

There is a wide range of earnings for television weather reporters, depending on a number of factors. These include the specific station and its size, market, and popularity, as well as the qualifications, experience, responsibilities, and popularity of the weather reporter. Approximate annual earnings for full-time weather reporters range from $18,000 to over $200,000. Those with little experience working in small-market and local cable television can expect to earn between $18,000 and $25,000 annually. Earnings increase with experience as individuals build a following and locate positions in larger, more prestigious markets. Weather reporters for networks and major national cable stations have earnings at the high end of the scale.

Advancement Opportunities

The most common path for career advancement as a weather reporter is to locate a similar job with a larger, more prestigious station. This will result in increased visibility and earnings. Some weather reporters also go on to become general news reporters.

Education and Training

Educational requirements for weather reporters vary from job to job. While many smaller stations only require a high school diploma, individuals seeking a career in the broadcast field should have a college degree. Those who aspire to become a weather reporter should look towards either a four-year or graduate degree in meteorology. Those who think they might start out as weather reporters and then go into general reporting might also consider a major in broadcasting, journalism, mass communications, liberal arts, or political science.

Courses, seminars, and workshops in communications, writing, meteorology, and public speaking will be useful.

Experience and Qualifications

Some positions, especially those in small-market or local cable television, may not require any experience of a weather reporter. An indication that the individual can speak in front of the camera is all that might be needed. As individuals seek positions in larger markets, more experience will be necessary. This can be acquired through internships or through working in television studios in other capacities such as announcer, news writer, desk assistant, or reporter.

A great deal of the job of a weather reporter is to make the report interesting. Successful weather people have a rapport with the viewing audience. They may build this by explaining weather patterns in easy to understand language or by having unique methods of announcing the weather. Some individuals, for example, use cartoon figures or drawings to illustrate weather patterns. Others may have special vocal styles or physical mannerisms that help people enjoy watching their forecasts.

Weather reporters must be articulate and have a pleasant voice and appearance.

For Additional Information: Aspiring weather reporters can obtain additional information about careers in the field by contacting the American Meteorological Society (AMS), the American Federation of Television and Radio Artists (AFTRA), the Radio-Television News Directors Association (RTNDA), and the National Association of Broadcasters (NAB).

TIPS

- Contact the AMS and inquire about membership requirements. Join if you can. This association offers professional guidance and support to its members and may be helpful in finding leads for jobs.
- Positions may be advertised in the newspaper classified section under headings such as "Weather Reporter," "Television," "Broadcasting," "Meteorologist," and "Weathercaster."
- Job openings are also advertised and listed in the trades.
- After you obtain experience, you might consider an agent to help you locate better jobs and to negotiate earnings.
- Take courses, workshops, and seminars in public speaking, broadcasting, and meteorology. These will help you learn new skills and hone old ones.
- Do as much public speaking as you can. This will help you learn how to ad-lib and speak with style.
- Look for internships. Inquire about programs at your college, at television stations, and through trade associations.
- If your school has a college television station, get involved. If no college television is available, work on the school's radio station handling weather reports.
- Start your job search at a small-market or local cable television station. Get some experience, make a tape, and send it out with your resume to larger stations.

NEWS WRITER—TELEVISION

Job Description: Write and develop news stories for newscasts.

Earnings: $12,000–$40,000+

Recommended Education and Training: Bachelor's degree in journalism, communications, or related field.

Skills and Personality Traits: Writing skills; research skills; ability to prioritize facts; interview skills; creativity; curiosity.

Experience and Qualifications: Experience writing news for any type of media.

Job Description and Responsibilities

Television news writers are responsible for writing the news stories or scripts read by reporters and/or news anchors. Individuals may have varied duties depending on the size and structure of the station and the newsroom. Scripts or stories written by news writers are usually read by anchors or in-studio reporters. At smaller stations, news writers may also be reporters and/or anchors themselves.

Individuals may obtain information for news stories in a number of ways. These include gathering information from reporters, wire services, press releases, or research. News writers must check information and details for accuracy. This may be accomplished through research, telephone calls, interviews, etc.

In addition to writing news stories, individuals may also be expected to develop introductions for stories, commentaries, and transitional phrases that lead anchors from one story to the next or to various parts of the newscast.

Writing news for any medium entails some similarities. However, writing for television must be done in a manner that is clear and concise and in a language that is easily read by reporters and anchors. It must also be done in a fashion that integrates the news story with the visual picture. Because each topic is given a specific amount of time, the individual must be able to write the story in a manner that can be understood by the audience with a minimal amount of words.

Writing for television news is a demanding task. Stories often break with little warning. Individuals in this profession must have the ability to write a story or lead for the news quickly without becoming panicked and flustered.

In addition to writing for scheduled newscasts, a news writer may be expected to write news briefs, special reports, and the short "teases" that are aired to peak interest before the news is shown. They may also be required to develop scripts for news documentaries, specials, and public affairs programs.

Employment Opportunities

While television news writers may find employment in any area throughout the country that hosts a television station, the greatest number of opportunities are located in areas with more than one station. It is generally easier to break into the field at smaller independent or cable stations. Individuals may work in the following settings:

- Independent television stations
- Local cable stations
- Networks
- National cable stations
- Affiliated stations
- Wire services

Earnings

Individuals may earn between $12,000 and $40,000 or more as television news writers. Factors affecting salary include the size, budget, location, and type of television station the individual is working with. Other variables include the responsibilities, experience, and professional reputation of the writer.

Those just beginning their careers with little or no experience and working at small stations will earn between $12,000 and $18,000 annually. As they obtain experience and move into jobs at larger or more prestigious stations, their earnings go up considerably.

Advancement Opportunities

There are a number of paths for career advancement in this field. Some individuals locate similar positions at larger stations, resulting in increased responsibilities and earnings. News writers may be assigned additional projects such as documentaries or news specials.

Other methods of advancement include becoming news directors or producers. Some news writers also advance their careers by locating positions as news reporters.

Education and Training

A bachelor's degree is usually required by most stations for positions as television news writers. Good choices for majors include journalism, communications, English, and political science.

Experience and Qualifications

Experience requirements for television news writers vary. Many stations prefer people to work as desk assistants prior to the job of news writer. Some obtain experience as interns which can land them a job right after college. Experience may also be acquired by working as a news writer for either print media or radio.

Television news writers must have excellent writing skills and command of the English language. The ability to write simple, clear, concise, crisp copy that reporters can easily read is essential. Creativity is helpful.

Individuals must know how to research and check facts. The ability to work within tight deadlines is another necessity in this field.

For Additional Information: Individuals interested in pursuing a career in this field can obtain additional career information by contacting the National Association of Broadcast Employees and Technicians (NABET), the Writers Guild of America (WGA), and the Radio-Television News Directors Association (RTNDA).

TIPS

- A summer or part-time job at a local station in the newsroom will provide useful experience.
- Openings may be advertised or listed in the trades.
- Try to attend a college with a school television station.
- If your college does not have a television station, get involved with the school's radio station to obtain broadcast experience.
- Positions in this field may be advertised in the newspaper classified sections under the headings of "News Writer," "Television News," "Television," and "Broadcasting."
- Other openings may be advertised or listed in industry trade magazines and papers.
- Contact television stations to locate internships in the field.
- Another way of obtaining useful experience is to get a summer or part-time job with a local newspaper in order to write news stories.
- Trade associations and schools may also offer internship programs.
- Send your resume with a short cover letter inquiring about openings to television stations. Ask that your resume be kept on file.
- It may be easier to break into this field in the newsroom of a small local station.
- Keep abreast of current affairs, news items, etc. Interviewers may ask questions before they hire you.
- You should put together a portfolio of scripts and other news stories you have written. Bring these to any job interviews.

TELEVISION TALK SHOW HOST

Job Description: Introduce and interview guests and performers; discuss relevant topics; lead show segments and guests in discussion.

Earnings: $20,000–$5 million-plus

Recommended Education and Training: Educational requirements vary; college degree preferred.

Skills and Personality Traits: Good conversationalist; articulate; research skills; inquiring mind; comfortable in front of television camera; pleasant appearance; personable; witty.

Experience and Qualifications: Experience working in television.

Job Description and Responsibilities

One of the current trends in television programing is the proliferation of talk shows. Flipping through the channels, almost anytime during the day or evening, it is evident that people like to watch and hear about other people's lives and experiences. What began years ago with just a couple of shows has now ballooned into talk show mania. The shows cover a variety of subjects ranging from general interest to more specialized areas. Some shows are strictly informational. Others include entertainment. The shows may be live or taped, with or without audiences.

Shows such as *Oprah Winfrey, Donahue,* and *Sally Jesse Raphael* usually focus on one main topic daily. Early morning shows such as *Good Morning America, This Morning, The Today Show,* and many local A.M. shows are divided into segments, with each centered around a specific topic. Nighttime talk shows such as *The Late Show* and *The Tonight Show* are formatted to include monologues, interviews, and entertainment. There are many variations of these formats.

Talk show hosts may work alone or with co-hosts. Responsibilities vary depending on the specific show and its format. The major duties of talk show hosts include introducing and interviewing guests, discussing subjects relevant to the specific show, and keeping the show moving in an interesting manner.

Within the scope of these responsibilities, talk show hosts may be expected to banter back and forth with guests and audience members about the topic of the day. They will make comments and ask interesting and pertinent questions. In order to perform their jobs effectively, show hosts often do research so that they fully understand and can talk about the subjects being discussed. Research can include gathering information from books and articles, interviewing people, and visiting relevant places. Hosts may be responsible for doing research on their own or may have assistants who handle this task and then report the facts to them.

Depending on the type of show, hosts may perform monologues, appear in skits, sing, etc. They may be responsible for leading segments on most any subject, including cooking, health, relationships, current events, and news.

Talk show hosts are usually required to attend production meetings, rehearsals, run-throughs, blocking, and the like. They work with the producer or guest coordinator to book guests and develop subject matter for shows.

Employment Opportunities

The greatest number of employment opportunities for television talk show hosts are located in areas with more than one television station. Although it is very difficult to get a break hosting a network talk show, opportunities are often open on a local level. Many small independent and cable stations produce some of their own programming. This might include either an early morning or noon talk show. Employment settings include:

- Networks
- Network affiliated stations
- Local cable stations
- Local independent stations
- Syndicated talk shows produced through independent television production companies

Earnings

Earnings for talk show hosts are based to a great extent on the specific market and show as well as the experience, popularity, and draw of the individual.

Compensation can start at approximately $20,000 for a host appearing on a show produced by a local independent station. Those hosting popular network shows earn millions of dollars annually. Hosts at many stations have minimum earnings negotiated and set by a union.

Advancement Opportunities

Television talk show hosts can advance their careers in a number of ways. Those with a track record drawing large viewing audiences may climb the career ladder by being lured to more popular shows. Others locate similar positions at larger, more prestigious stations or shows. Hosts may also have their show syndicated, resulting in increased exposure and earnings. An example of this is *Oprah Winfrey*.

Education and Training

While there is no formal educational requirement to become a television show host, a college degree is recommended. Television is an extremely competitive field. The better prepared the individual is, the more opportunities will open. A strong liberal arts background with courses in broadcasting, journalism, English, television, and communications will be useful. Workshops in performing and comedy might also be helpful.

Experience and Qualifications

Experience in front of a television camera is usually required. Many television-show hosts have worked in broadcasting, journalism, and/or news prior to their current positions.

Others started in entertainment. For example, Jay Leno and Joan Rivers came from comedic performance backgrounds.

Talk show hosts must be witty and able to think quickly. A broad knowledge in many fields is helpful. Individuals should be comfortable in front of a camera and know their way around a television studio.

A pleasant appearance and clear speaking voice are necessary. Talk show hosts should be articulate with good communications skills. The ability to relate well to others and encourage conversation is imperative.

For Additional Information: Individuals interested in pursuing a career in this field can obtain additional information by contacting the American Federation of Television and Radio Actors (AFTRA), the National Association of Broadcasters (NAB), and Women In Communications, Inc. (WICI).

TIPS

- If you live in an area where there are television stations, look for openings advertised in the classified section of newspapers. Look under headings such as "Television," "Broadcasting," and "Show Host."
- Job openings are often advertised and listed in the trades.
- After you have obtained experience, consider an agent to help you locate better jobs and to negotiate earnings.
- Take courses, workshops, and seminars in public speaking, broadcasting, and comedy. These will help you learn new skills and hone old ones.
- Do as much public speaking as you can. This will help you learn how to speak with style and ad-lib.
- Look for internships. Inquire about programs at your college and television stations, as well as through trade associations.
- If your school has a college television station, get involved. If it doesn't, work on the school's radio station.
- Start your job search at a small market or local cable television station. Obtain some experience, make a tape, and send it along with your resume to larger stations.
- If you have a special skill, you may find opportunities as an expert segment guest on local shows. This will help give you experience working on the air

as well as provide exposure. For example, many talk shows have segments geared towards cooking, childcare, relationships, gardening, consumer affairs, crafts, etc.

VIDEO JOCKEY—TELEVISION

Job Description: Discuss and introduce music videos on television.

Earnings: $12,000–$250,000+

Recommended Education and Training: No formal educational requirement; college degree or background may be preferred.

Skills and Personality Traits: Articulate; comfortable working in front of cameras; knowledge of music and music industry.

Experience and Qualifications: Experience working in or around music industry, television, or radio.

Job Description and Responsibilities

Video jockeys work on television introducing music videos and discuss artists, performers, music, and news of the industry. Their jobs are comparable to radio disc jockeys.

Individuals may have regular shows broadcast live or prerecorded. Shows cannot usually be taped too far in advance because of the continual changes occurring in music. To become successful, most VJs develop and project a unique style and personality. Like DJs, they must build a following of people.

Responsibilities vary depending on the specific station and show. The sole responsibility of some VJs is to introduce the music videos. Others are expected to interview acts or review new videos as well. The video jockey may have the option of choosing the videos that will be aired or may be required to follow the format prescribed by the program or music director.

Individuals working at smaller stations may often be expected to handle duties not related to the VJ job. These might include anything from writing copy for commercials to promoting products themselves. Some prefer to find ways to stay in front of the camera. They become the station's entertainment reporter, news reporter, etc.

One of the best things about working as a video jockey, even at a small local or cable station, is that the VJs usually become local celebrities. This often results in being asked to do public appearances, host concerts, act as an emcee for major acts performing in the area, and perform an array of other activities that can lead to bigger and better opportunities.

Employment Opportunities

Opportunities for video jockeys are increasing as more stations begin to air music video shows. Employment may be located in any area hosting one or more television stations. Opportunities may be available in smaller markets throughout the country, or in major music markets such as New York City, Los Angeles, Washington, D.C., and Nashville. While the largest employer of VJs are cable stations, including MTV, VH1, and CMT, individuals may find employment in additional settings including:

- Other cable stations
- Syndicated shows
- Network television
- Local television stations
- Independent stations

Earnings

Earnings for video jockeys range from approximately $12,000 to $250,000 or more a year. Variables include the size, type, location, and prestige of the specific station as well as the particular show. Other factors affecting earnings are the responsibilities, experience, professional reputation, and popularity of the VJ.

Generally, the larger the market and more popular the station or show, the higher the individual's earnings will be. Video jockeys working for many stations will have their minimum earnings negotiated and set by unions. Many VJs augment their incomes with public appearances.

Advancement Opportunities

Video jockeys can advance their careers in a number of ways. Some individuals find similar positions at larger, more prestigious stations. As they obtain exposure and popularity, they often find jobs in other areas of television such as broadcast news. VJs may also be lured to high-paying jobs in radio.

Education and Training

There is no formal educational requirement necessary to become a video jockey. However, some stations may prefer their employees to hold college degrees or at least have some college background. Those who opt for college might consider a major in television, broadcasting, or the music business.

Courses, seminars, and workshops will be useful in learning new skills and making important contacts.

Experience and Qualifications

Individuals aspiring to work as video jockeys should have experience working in the music industry, radio, or television. This experience may be obtained through prior jobs, internships, college, etc. To be successful, video jockeys need to keep abreast of trends, music, and acts in the industry.

Individuals should be articulate with a pleasant speaking voice and the ability to project their personality over the air. They should also be comfortable working in front of a camera and around microphones and studio lights.

For Additional Information: Additional information about careers in this field can be obtained by contacting the National Academy of Recording Arts and Sciences (NARAS), the American Federation of Television and Radio Artists (AFTRA), and the National Association of Broadcast Employees and Technicians, AFL-CIO (NABET). Individuals might also contact the three major music video networks: MTV, CMT, and VH1.

TIPS

- It may be easier to break into this career at a small local station.
- Consider suggesting a music video show as a possible program format to the program director of a small local or cable station. Remember to indicate that you are interested in hosting the show.
- If you live in an area where there are television stations, you might find openings advertised in the classified section of the newspapers. Look under headings such as "Video Jockey," "VJ," "Television," "Television Personality," "Music Television," and "Broadcasting."
- Positions may also be advertised or listed in the trades.
- If you are planning on attending college, look for one with a school television station. Once there, get involved in as many aspects of station operation as you can. The more you know, the more marketable you will be.
- If the school you are going to does not have a television station, make sure you get involved with their radio station.
- Being on the air in any capacity will be helpful. Consider a job as a radio disc jockey to obtain experience.
- Every station offers internships. These provide one of the best types of experience you can get. Contact stations and inquire about possibilities.
- Make a video demo to showcase your talent. Make copies and send them along with your resume and a cover letter inquiring about openings and other possibilities.

PAGE—TELEVISION

Job Description: Work in various departments of television station assisting and filling in for people; learn about various departments at a station or network.

Earnings: $15,000–$22,000+

Recommended Education and Training: Bachelor's degree in broadcasting, communications, journalism, public relations, liberal arts, or related fields.

Skills and Personality Traits: Communications skills; enthusiasm; eager to learn.

Experience and Qualifications: Experience working for college or local television station helpful, but not required.

Job Description and Responsibilities

Pages work at major networks, network-owned affiliates in major markets, major independent stations, and national cable stations producing their own programming. The main aspiration of almost all pages is building a career in the television industry in some capacity.

Individuals are hired for a period of time ranging from six months to two years. During this time, pages are exposed to the various departments at the station or network and learn the functions, duties, and responsibilities. Depending on the structure of the station and the page program, individuals may move from department to department in a scheduled fashion or may be assigned tasks assisting departments as they are needed, filling in for vacationing or ill employees.

Responsibilities can include filling in for or acting as a receptionist or secretary in any department, delivering teleprompter scripts and copy, giving studio tours, helping talk show guests feel comfortable, showing guests to the "green room", monitoring reception lines of audiences for television shows, showing audience members to their seats, etc. Pages can be assigned almost any task.

Through their work, pages can see which department interests them, make contacts, and hopefully land a job. For individuals interested in a career in television, this is probably the best way to make contacts and get their foot in the door.

Employment Opportunities

Employment opportunities for pages are most plentiful in New York City, Los Angeles, and Chicago. Opportunities exist for this position in the following employment settings:

- Major networks (ABC, CBS, and NBC)
- Network-owned and -operated television stations in major markets
- Large, major market stations such as Fox
- National cable stations

Earnings

Earnings for pages range from approximately $15,000 to $22,000 or more. Variables affecting earnings include the experience, responsibilities, and qualifications of the individual as well as the specific station and geographic location.

Advancement Opportunities

This job is an entry-level position. Advancement opportunities are endless, depending on which area in the television industry individuals are interested in pursuing. Many people in television started their careers as pages and moved up to become successful in many different parts of the field. Some include meteorologist and television personality Willard Scott of *The Today Show,* news anchor Ted Koppel of *Nightline,* and many other major television executives, producers, directors, writers, actors, actresses, and comedians.

Advancement is based on experience, expertise, qualifications, luck, and being in the right place at the right time. Most television stations and networks like to promote from within.

Education and Training

In most instances, a college degree is necessary in order to become a page. Good choices for majors include television/radio broadcasting, communications, journalism, liberal arts, public relations, or related fields.

Experience and Qualifications

As this is an entry-level position, there generally is no formal experience requirement. However, any experience in television or broadcasting acquired in school or at local stations will be useful. Most stations require pages to be college graduates. Individuals should be eager and enthusiastic with good communications skills.

For Additional Information: Additional information regarding jobs as pages can be obtained by contacting ABC, CBS, NBC, their local affiliates in major markets, or the Fox Broadcasting Network, American Women In Radio and Television (AWRT), and the National Association of Broadcasters (NAB).

TIPS

- Send your resume and a short cover letter to the director or manager of pages or personnel director of the major networks. Query network-owned stations in major markets, major cable stations, and major market independent stations as well.
- If you have any contacts, use them to help you obtain an interview.
- Positions may be advertised in the newspaper classified section under the headings of "Television," "Broadcasting," "Entertainment," or "Pages."
- Positions may also be advertised or listed in the trades.
- Your college advisor, professor in communications, broadcasting, journalism, etc., or placement office may know about possibilities after graduation.
- Get as much experience as you can while you are still in school. Work on your college station or a local television or cable station. While experience is not always a requirement, working around television will help you make contacts, which will in turn make it easier to obtain a position as a page.
- Look for an internship program to gain experience and make contacts.

TRAFFIC-CONTINUITY SPECIALIST—TELEVISION

Job Description: Schedule programs, commercials, station breaks, and public service announcements; prepare daily station log.

Earnings: $14,000–$45,000+

Recommended Education and Training: Educational requirements vary from high school diploma to college background/degree.

Skills and Personality Traits: Detail-oriented; organized; written communication skills; computer skills.

Experience and Qualifications: Computer experience helpful.

Job Description and Responsibilities

Television stations are monitored by the Federal Communications Commission. They must therefore adhere to FCC rules and regulations. Traffic-continuity specialists or representatives at television stations are responsible for scheduling programs, commercials, public service announcements, and station breaks. They are also responsible for developing and preparing the FCC log, which details on paper the entire broadcast day at the station. Other duties may include developing copy to use during station breaks or between programming.

The position of traffic-continuity specialist may also be referred to as traffic-continuity representative or continuity copywriter. Specific duties of individuals may vary depending on the size of the station. At very large stations, functions may be broken up. For example, individuals may be hired only to handle the traffic functions or to handle copywriting duties.

The traffic-continuity specialist may also be expected to schedule on-air personalities or announcers to record station breaks, station identifications, and public service announcements. In certain situations, the individual may be required to work with the production department to develop video material that will coincide with voice-over announcements.

Traffic-continuity specialists work with the program director or manager as well as with the station sales manager. With their help, the individual determines what time slots are available for advertisements and which ones have been sold. The individual also makes sure that similar products are not being advertised right before or after each other. It is the responsibility of the individual to gather all information and type it into the computer so that the daily log can be prepared. In this manner, the station will have a report of what was aired every minute of the broadcast day.

Employment Opportunities

Since every television station employs traffic-continuity specialists, employment opportunities are plentiful. In many situations this is an entry-level job. The greatest number of opportunities will be found in areas hosting more than one television station. Employment settings can include:

- Network television
- Independent stations
- Local cable stations
- National cable stations
- Affiliated stations

Earnings

Annual earnings for traffic-continuity specialists range from approximately $14,000 to $45,000 or more. Factors affecting earnings include the size, type, and location of the station as well as the experience and responsibilities of the individual. Generally, those just starting out at small, local stations will be compensated at the lower end of the scale. Individuals with experience working at large stations in metropolitan areas will have earnings between $35,000 and $45,000.

Advancement Opportunities

There are a great many opportunities for advancement in this field. One may find a similar position at a larger, more prestigious station with a resulting increase in both responsibilities and earnings. Traffic-continuity specialists may also advance their careers by moving into positions such as advertising salesperson, sales coordinator, sales manager, or even operations manager.

Education and Training

Educational requirements vary from job to job. Some stations may only require a high school diploma. Others may require or prefer a college background or degree. Good choices for majors include broadcasting, marketing, advertising, and mass communications. Courses in advertising, copywriting, broadcasting, and computer usage are also helpful.

Experience and Qualifications

At many stations, especially smaller ones, this position is an entry-level job that requires no experience. At larger stations, previous experience may be necessary. One of the major qualifications essential to this job is computer literacy. The applicant should have a working knowledge of a variety of programs.

The ability to write copy is helpful, as are other written communication skills. This job also requires an extremely organized and detail-oriented individual.

For Additional Information: Those interested in pursuing a career in this field can obtain additional information by contacting the National Association of Broadcasters (NAB).

TIPS

- Offer to handle the traffic-continuity responsibilities at your school station.
- Positions in this field are advertised in the newspaper classified section under headings such as ''Television,'' ''Broadcasting,'' ''Traffic,'' ''Continuity Specialist,'' etc.
- Contact smaller local, independent, and cable television stations. Inquire about openings. Send your resume and a short cover letter asking about openings. There is a great deal of turnover in this position at smaller stations as a result of people moving up the ladder.
- Look for internships in this department with television stations.
- Take classes in copywriting. They will be useful in honing writing skills.
- Become familiar with widely used computer programs. This will give you an edge over others.

PUBLIC RELATIONS AND PROMOTION DIRECTOR—TELEVISION STATION

Job Description: Handle public relations, publicity, and promotions for a television station.

Earnings: $15,000–$75,000+

Recommended Education and Training: Bachelor's degree in public relations, communications, journalism, advertising, English, liberal arts, etc.

Skills and Personality Traits: Written and verbal communications skills; creativity; detail-oriented; organized; imaginative.

Experience and Qualifications: Public relations, publicity, promotion, or journalistic experience necessary.

Job Description and Responsibilities

The public relations and promotion director of a television station has a number of responsibilities. He or she is integral to the development and implementation of public relations campaigns as well as the handling of publicity and promotion for the station, its personalities, and programs. Specific duties vary depending on the station.

The public relations and promotion director is expected to keep the station in the public eye. This can help to attract viewers as well as advertisers. To accomplish this, the director develops special promotions to attract media and public attention. These may include contests or events co-sponsored by affiliates or other businesses in the community. The director may arrange for station personalities to appear at public functions or other events to help promote the station. Sometimes the individual will also schedule interviews with station personalities.

As part of the job, the public relations and promotion director is expected to write press releases, feature articles, fact sheets, etc., for media distribution. The p.r. director will also be required to develop press kits, flyers, and other written material. This may be done personally or by assistants supervised by the director. The individual may also be expected to develop written materials about the station, its programs, and personalities for public consumption.

The successful p.r. director must determine the audience the station is trying to reach and find the best ways to attract its attention. The individual will often be asked to supervise research on demographics as well as on audience and community needs.

Other functions of a television station public relations and promotion director include acting as the station's spokesperson and attending community or industry events on behalf of the station.

The p.r. director works with a number of other departments. These include traffic and continuity, advertising, community relations, and programming. Working with other departments, the public relations and promotion director can help attract new viewers and advertisers. He or she can help make a station more visible in the community while improving its public image.

Employment Opportunities

Individuals interested in pursuing this type of career can find employment opportunities throughout the country in any city hosting a television station. The largest number of opportunities will be located in larger, metropolitan areas hosting more than one station. Employment will be found in the following settings:

- Networks
- Affiliated stations
- Local independent stations
- National cable stations
- Local cable stations
- Public television stations

Earnings

Public relations and promotion directors of television stations earn between $15,000 and $75,000 or more annually. Factors affecting earnings include the specific station and its prestige, size, and location. Other factors include the experience, expertise, and responsibilities of the individual.

Public relations and promotion directors with increased experience and responsibilities working at larger stations earn between $35,000 and $50,000. Those working at networks or national cable stations may earn between $45,000 and $75,000-plus.

Advancement Opportunities

Public relations and promotion directors at television stations can advance their careers in a number of ways. Many individuals climb the career ladder by finding similar positions at larger, more prestigious stations. This results in increased responsibilities and earnings.

Others find public relations and promotional positions in radio, film, or in totally unrelated fields. Some may strike out on their own and begin a public relations or publicity agency.

Education and Training

Most stations require their public relations and promotion directors to have a minimum of a bachelor's degree. Good choices for majors include public relations, communications, journalism, advertising, English, and liberal arts.

Courses, seminars, and workshops in all facets of public relations, writing, promotion, photography, journalism, etc., will be useful.

Experience and Qualifications

Experience requirements vary from job to job. Generally the larger the station, the more experience required for the position. Experience in all facets of public relations, promotion, and advertising is usually needed. This can be acquired through internships or by working as public relations, publicity, or promotion assistants at television or radio stations or in an unrelated field.

Public relations and promotion directors at television stations should have a reasonable working knowledge of public relations, publicity, promotion, and advertising techniques. Written and verbal communications skills are necessary. Creativity is imperative. Individuals should have the ability to develop promotional ideas from inception through fruition. An understanding of the television industry will benefit the successful promoter.

For Additional Information: Individuals interested in a career in public relations and promotion for television stations can obtain additional information by contacting the Broadcast Promotion and Marketing Executives (BPME) and the Public Relations Society of America (PRSA).

TIPS

- Contact the PRSA to find out about membership requirements. A student membership is available. This trade association provides professional guidance and support. They also offer many seminars and workshops that are useful in honing skills, learning new techniques, and making important contacts.
- Internships are an excellent way of getting your foot in the door and making professional contacts. Write or call television stations to inquire about internship possibilities.
- The PRSA and the BPME may also know of available internships.
- Job openings may be found in the classified section of newspapers. Look under headings such as "Public Relations," "Promotion," "Publicity," "Television," and "Broadcasting."
- Jobs may also be advertised or listed in industry trade magazines and newspapers.
- Get experience by contacting local television stations to see if they have any openings for assistants in your area.
- Experience can often be acquired through a summer or part-time job working as an assistant to the public relations or promotions director of a local radio station.

DIRECTOR—FILM

Job Description: Interpret script; prepare production for filming; coordinate and oversee technical and creative aspects of film; guide actors and actresses in performance.

Earnings: $5,000–$1 million-plus per production.

Recommended Education and Training: Film school or a degree in film, theater arts, drama, or related field useful.

Skills and Personality Traits: Artistic skills; detail-oriented; leadership skills; organizational skills; supervisory skills; motivational skills; imagination; creativity.

Experience and Qualifications: Experience working in some aspect of film or television production.

Job Description and Responsibilities

Every film has a director. The director is responsible for pulling together every detail of the film, from the creative to the technical. As the project's artistic director, the individual works closely with the producer and writers, as well as with the entire cast and crew, to develop and shoot the film. Collaborators include the actors and actresses, costume designers, scenic designers, hair and makeup people, lighting, sound, and music designers, etc. In some instances, the director may also be the producer of the film.

The director is expected to bring the production to life through the eye of the camera. The end result of the film expresses the director's vision. The director supervises both rehearsals and the actual shooting of television shows and/or films. As part of the job, he or she must determine who and what should be seen on camera at each moment. The individual is required to plan camera shots, lighting, and sound, as well as determine where equipment, props, and the actors and actresses should be on stage. The goal is to end up with the most effective shots possible.

Once a producer has retained a director, the work begins. Normally, this is before the cast is chosen, rehearsals start, or filming begins. In some situations, however, the director will be brought in after this process is well underway.

A great deal of the director's work is accomplished soon after being retained. The director will become familiar with the script, assist in casting, and work with scenic, costume, and lighting designers.

There are many people involved in the making of a film, most with a large number of responsibilities. The director relies to a great extent on the first and second assistant directors and the production manager to help with the vast myriad of details. These include arranging the shooting schedule; making sure the cast, crew, and equipment are correctly positioned; handling paperwork; and administering the financial aspects of the production.

The director is expected to oversee and instruct during rehearsals and the actual shooting of each film. The individual must communicate with and motivate actors and actresses to play their roles appropriately. Sometimes the director may read a part and have specific actors or actresses perform their parts so that the director's ideas can be translated more easily.

Directors who make a name for themselves have a number of unique abilities that set them apart from the rest. These individuals know how to convey their unique interpretation of scripts to the cast members. This might include indicating how lines should be spoken or what physical movements would be likely to improve the production. They also have a special proficiency when choosing the music, sets, costumes, lighting, and camera angles. Talented and creative directors perform miracles by turning the script into a monster box office hit as well as a creative achievement.

Employment Opportunities

The majority of opportunities for film directors are found in Hollywood. While the chance of directing a major feature film without any experience is unlikely, one can break in by directing student films or low-budget productions. Employment possibilities include:

- Independent film production companies
- Independent producers
- Video production companies
- Studios

Earnings

Earnings for film directors vary greatly. Variables include the experience, expertise, and reputation of the director, as well as the budget of the film. Individuals may earn approximately $5,000 to $1 million or more directing one film.

In certain situations directors will have their minimum earnings negotiated and set by the Directors Guild of America (DGA). Minimum earnings for the DGA are based on, among other factors, the budget of the film and the minimum number of weeks the cast and crew will be employed. For example, directors working at least 11 weeks on films with budgets of $500,000 or less can earn a minimum of approximately $5,100 per week. Those working at least 13 weeks on feature films with budgets over $1.5 million can earn a minimum of slightly over $8,000 weekly. These are minimums. Many directors earn considerably more. Some also negotiate percentages on box office revenues.

Advancement Opportunities

Film directors can advance their careers by working on more prestigious projects with larger budgets. Most in this field aspire to direct a critically acclaimed, award-winning feature film that becomes a box office hit.

Education and Training

While a college degree will not insure a career as a film director, it is helpful for a number of reasons. A college education is useful for the credibility it lends and the education, experience, and opportunities it affords. Many colleges have film schools. In addition to film, other helpful majors include theater arts, drama, and related fields.

Those who do not pursue college often obtain training by working with and watching other directors on the job and by participating in internships.

Courses and seminars in all aspects of film production, lighting, directing, stagecraft, set design, screenwriting, theater arts, acting, and related subjects will be helpful in honing skills

Experience and Qualifications

Experience is required in order to become a film director. This may be acquired through working in various facets of film production. Individuals may also obtain useful experience by working as an assistant director, directing student films, or participating in internships. Some directors worked in television prior to moving over to film. Others began their careers as actors, actresses, screenwriters, and the like.

Directors need to be particularly artistic, creative, and imaginative people. They must also be well-organized and detail-oriented. A thorough knowledge of film, production, camera angles, lighting, effects, etc., is imperative.

For Additional Information: Individuals aspiring to become film directors can obtain additional career information from the Directors Guild of America (DGA).

TIPS

- Read the trades. Look for information on new, low-budget films that are going into production. Work for minimum wage if you have to. The experience will be well worth it.
- View movies and films of all types to see how other productions have been directed.
- Attend performances at the theater to learn the different techniques of directors of theatrical productions.
- One of the best ways to start your career is by getting involved in student films.

- Internships are helpful in getting your foot in the door, making contacts, and gaining experience. Contact independent film production companies and studios to see if they offer programs.
- Apprenticeships are another way of breaking into the industry and learning as you go.
- Take courses, workshops, and seminars in film, lighting, set design, producing, directing, and related subjects.
- Many film directors start out working in theater or television. Volunteer to direct a school production or work with the director of a community theater production.
- Get as much experience as you can working in all facets of film. The more experience you have, the better a director you will be.
- Break into the field by taking any job available in film. A job as a production assistant is a good way to start. Watch, ask questions, and learn as you go.
- The DGA offers professional support and guidance. Contact them to learn about any programs or opportunities which might be useful in your career.

PRODUCTION ASSISTANT—FILM

Job Description: Assist other members of crew in the production of films, video, and commercials.

Earnings: $25–$250 per day.

Recommended Education and Training: No formal educational requirements; college degree or background may be helpful in career advancement.

Skills and Personality Traits: Ability to take direction; detail-oriented; organized; interpersonal skills; communication skills; typing and/or word processing skills; enthusiastic; energetic.

Experience and Qualifications: No experience required; car and driver's license necessary.

Job Description and Responsibilities

Production assistants help crew members before, during, and after a film production. This is an entry-level job, similar to that of a guy or girl Friday. Responsibilities vary depending on the specific production, budget, time frame, and size of the crew.

Productions may hire 1 to 10 production assistants, or P.A.s, as they are also called. They may be assigned a multitude of tasks. One of the main functions of the production assistant is running errands to free up others on the production crew who may be performing more specialized tasks. Errands can include getting coffee and donuts, delivering scripts, making phone calls, taking messages, photo-copying, typing, parking cars, or locating hard-to-find props. Other duties may include moving equipment, props, or sets; escorting cast members from dressing rooms to the set; or cleaning up the set after a day of shooting.

Production assistants may be assigned to help in one department throughout an entire production or may float in between various departments, helping where and when needed. P.A.s who are assigned tasks that involve a great deal of running errands are called "runners." Those handling other tasks and assisting in various departments are full-fledged production assistants.

The reason many people who want a career in film try to obtain P.A. jobs is that these positions provide superior learning experiences and a valuable train-ing ground. Production assistants have the opportunity to learn about the film business as well as make important contacts. Once an individual gets a foot in the door as a production assistant, the opportunities and possibilities for advance-ment are endless.

Employment Opportunities

P.A.s may work on a freelance basis or may be employed on staff full-time by production companies. Production assistants working in film may work for a number of different types of employers. These include production companies for:

- Commercial films
- Music videos
- Educational films
- Industrial films
- Advertising agencies
- Cable productions

Earnings

Production assistants may earn between $25 and $250 per day. However, unless P.A.s are working full-time for a production company, they usually do not work on a year-round basis. They must continually find new projects.

Advancement Opportunities

Since the job of production assistant is looked upon as a stepping stone to other careers in film, advancement prospects are endless. One can advance by becoming a production manager or coordinator. Some who began their careers as production assistants have gone on to become directors and producers, having held a vast array of positions along the way.

As a rule, production assistants are exposed to a variety of departments and jobs. Eventually, they find one or two specific areas that they are interested in pursuing further.

Education and Training

There is no specific educational requirement necessary to becoming a production assistant in film. Many, however, are college graduates. Courses, seminars, and workshops in all the aspects of film production will be useful in learning the necessary skills and techniques, as well as for making important contacts.

The job of a production assistant is a learning experience in itself. It teaches the practical basics of film making as untrained individuals watch and assist professionals in a variety of situations.

Experience and Qualifications

While this is an entry-level job, any experience in film production will be helpful. The best qualifications are an eagerness to do whatever is asked when assisting others in production and the ability to take direction without question.

A car and a clean driving record are essential to this position. Production assistants should be both personable and tolerant. Strong interpersonal, verbal, and written communications skills are also necessary. Individuals in this line of work should be detail-oriented and able to handle many projects at once. The ability to work under pressure is a must.

Successful production assistants should always be ready to do more than is expected of them without grumbling.

For Additional Information: Individuals interested in working in this field can obtain additional information by contacting the Directors Guild of America (DGA) and the National Alliance of Broadcast Engineers and Technicians (NABET). Other information can be obtained by contacting the state film commission.

TIPS

- Network as much as possible. If you know anyone in film, make sure he or she knows you are looking for a job as a production assistant.
- Read the trades. Look for companies that are beginning or are currently in production.
- Call production companies to inquire about openings for production assistants. Ask to speak to the production coordinator.
- Send your resume to production companies. Ask that your resume be kept on file. Check with them periodically to see if any positions have opened—persistence often pays off.
- Names, addresses, and phone numbers of production companies are located in production directories. These are available through state film commissions or motion picture liaison offices.
- You can get your name and phone number listed as a production assistant in production directories. Contact your state's film commission or a local motion picture liaison office to find out when the next directory is coming out.

• Consider going to a location where a production is being shot and meeting the production manager. This usually only works if the production is being shot in a public location. Do not make a nuisance of yourself. Simply ask to see the production manager. When introduced, ask if you can send a resume.

UNIT PUBLICIST—TELEVISION/FILM

Job Description: Promote and publicize television shows, films, movies, etc.

Earnings: $15,000–$75,000+

Recommended Education and Training: Bachelor's degree in public relations, communications, journalism, English, or liberal arts.

Skills and Personality Traits: Written and verbal communications skills; telephone skills; ability to work under pressure; persuasive; aggressive; creative; personable.

Experience and Qualifications: Experience in public relations, publicity, journalism, and/or entertainment.

Job Description and Responsibilities

Unit publicists are responsible for the publicity for television shows, movies, and feature films. The major function of the person in this position is to create interest and excitement in the TV show or film to attract a large audience and media attention.

Unit publicists are often hired before a new film or television show is released. It is their responsibility to develop ways to create interest in the project. One of the major methods used by unit publicists is arranging media interviews with the stars of the production. These may include interviews with editors, reporters, and columnists from the television, radio, and print media. Depending on the specific project, these interviews may be set up with local, national, network, cable, or syndicated media.

The unit publicist may travel with the stars of the television show or movie promoting the project, or may assign an escort or assistant to handle these responsibilities. The individual makes sure that the stars arrive at the interview on time, and provides press releases, photographs, video clips, and press kits to the reporter, editor, or producer. The publicist may talk to the interviewer ahead of time in order to point the interview in a positive direction.

As part of the job, the unit publicist will be responsible for writing press releases and developing press kits, fact sheets, and biographies of film and/or show stars. The individual will also be responsible for arranging for still shots that can be used in print media and video clips for television. All this information must be distributed to the appropriate media.

The publicist works very closely with the studio, production company, producer, and/or networks producing the show or film. Often, in order to obtain media attention, the unit publicist will schedule major press conferences and parties. The individual will also arrange for screenings of the show or film for critics and reviewers. Excerpts from positive reviews are quickly duplicated and sent to other media to obtain additional publicity.

Generally, unit publicists are assigned or retained for specific projects. Once a film has been out for a period of time, it no longer needs exposure. The unit publicist must therefore find or be assigned to another project. Television shows often retain unit publicists for longer periods of time.

To be successful in this profession, unit publicists must constantly generate tremendous amounts of publicity and gain a great amount of exposure for the movie or television show. Even then, as a result of a number of variables, the project may not be successful. Often, the unit publicist is blamed.

However, individuals with a thick skin and a positive attitude can have careers that team the glamor of the movie and television industries with the skills of publicity, promotion, and public relations.

Employment Opportunities

The greatest number of employment opportunities for positions in this field are located in Los Angeles, Hollywood, and New York City. Individuals may work in the following capacities:

- Freelance
- Public relations, press agent, or publicity agencies
- Independent publicists or press agents
- Networks
- Independent film production companies
- Independent television production companies
- Television and/or motion picture studios

Earnings

Earnings for unit publicists can range from approximately $15,000 to $75,000 or more annually. Variables affecting earnings include the experience, reputation, and responsibilities of the individual. Other factors include the specific project and work situation. Individuals who are freelancing or working independently, for example, may not have as steady an income as those on staff with a public relations or publicity firm, studio, or production company.

Experienced unit publicists handling the publicity for major motion pictures or successful television shows can earn $1,500 or more weekly. Those with little experience in the industry may start out earning $250 to $300 per week.

Some publicists belong to the Publicists Guild (PG). This group negotiates and sets minimum earnings for members working for studios, television stations, agencies, production companies, etc., that have agreements with the Guild. The minimum earnings for individuals handling publicity run between $1,100 and $1,300 per week depending on the specific type of employment.

Advancement Opportunities

Advancement opportunities for unit publicists are to a great extent based on being in the right place at the right time, talent, drive, and determination. One way to climb the career ladder is to locate more prestigious films, movies, and television shows to publicize. Another is to find a position with a larger public relations company, press agent, or publicity agency, studio, production company, etc. Many individuals employed by a company advance by striking out on their own and becoming independent or freelance unit publicists.

Education and Training

A college degree is recommended for this type of position. Good choices for majors include public relations, communications, English, journalism, and liberal arts. Courses, seminars, and workshops in publicity, the entertainment industry, film, television, writing, promotion, entertainment marketing, public relations, etc., will be very useful.

Experience and Qualifications

In order to become a unit publicist, one is usually required to have experience in publicity, public relations, journalism, and/or some facet of the entertainment industry. This may be acquired by working as an entertainment journalist, publicist, assistant unit publicist, intern, or publicity or press agent assistant or trainee.

To be successful in this field, unit publicists must be creative, imaginative, and persuasive, and know how to come up with and implement unique ideas that will attract media attention. Excellent communications skills, both verbal and written, are imperative. Since the phone is a lifeline for the publicist, strong phone skills are a must. The ability to work under pressure is mandatory in this line of work.

For Additional Information: Individuals interested in obtaining more career information can contact the National Entertainment Journalist Association (NEJA), the Public Relations Society of America (PRSA), and the Publicists Guild (PG).

TIPS

- This is a difficult career to try to work in without contacts in the entertainment industry—especially if you are freelancing. If you know anyone in the business, discuss your aspirations.
- Obtain experience handling publicity for school, community, and local entertainment events including concerts, plays, and other performances.
- Contact a local television or cable station to see if there is a position open to handle station publicity. If there is not, try to create one.
- Join trade associations and attend their meetings. Network as much as possible.
- Keep up on what is happening in the industry by reading the trades. In addition, look for job opportunities in industry trade papers.
- A good way to break into the industry and obtain experience is by handling the publicity for a low-budget film. The trades often have articles and notices about new low-budget films going into production. Contact the production company to inquire about these opportunities.
- Have business cards printed and distribute them to as many people in the industry as possible, including entertainment journalists and critics.
- Volunteer to handle publicity for community organizations putting on entertainment extravaganzas. This will be good experience, good exposure, and an excellent opportunity to make contacts in the industry.
- Become an entertainment critic, reviewer, or reporter for your local or school paper. This will provide you with many opportunities and ways to make contacts. Whenever entertainers or entertainment events come into town, you can get your foot in the door by calling managers, agents, or the stars.
- Similarly, you might consider working for a school or local radio or television station.
- Internships are another excellent method of breaking into the field and making contacts. Larger entertainment public relations agencies often offer summer work programs. The same is true for television and film production companies and television stations. Write a letter to the personnel department inquiring about possibilities. Include your resume. If you don't hear back from them within a couple weeks, call. Even if a position doesn't exist, you might be able to talk someone into creating one.

CHAPTER 5

. . . .

Careers in Recording and
the Record Business

In the early days of recording, gramophones were wound up to play 78s in parlors and sitting rooms while young men courted young women. Over the years, records evolved from 78s to 33s to 45s, and then to eight tracks. Compact discs and cassettes have now all but replaced single records and albums.

The recording industry is still an evolving and growing field of the entertainment business. In addition to major recording companies, there are more and more independent labels springing up throughout the country. MTV, CMT, and other music video television and cable programs have made it possible for hit recordings to be created almost instantly. Affordable electronic audio equipment makes it easy to create demos at a relatively low cost.

Careers in this field are all-encompassing. A wide variety of people with a multitude of talents, skills, expertise, educational backgrounds, and experience levels are required.

Space restrictions limit discussing all possible opportunities. Jobs covered in this section are:

Record Producer
Arranger
Recording Engineer
A & R Representative
Promotion Representative—
  Recording Company
Staff Publicist—Recording
  Company

Artist Relations and Development
  Representative—Recording
  Label
Marketing Representative—
  Recording Label

Individuals interested in careers in the recording industry should also review entries in other sections of this book. "Careers in the Business End of the Industry" and "Careers in Performing and Writing" describe related opportunities.

RECORD PRODUCER

Job Description: Produce recordings for groups and solo performers; supervise recording sessions.

Earnings: $16,000–$250,000+

Recommended Education and Training: No educational requirements; apprenticeships helpful; sound recording school may be useful.

Skills and Personality Traits: Ability to select hit songs before they are recorded; ability to communicate musical ideas; creativity.

Experience and Qualifications: Experience working in various facets of the music industry; knowledge of music business.

Job Description and Responsibilities

Record producers are responsible for overseeing all facets of making a recording. Their main function is to produce a record that will appeal to a wide audience. Within that function, individuals have numerous responsibilities on both the creative and the business ends. Responsibilities will vary depending on whether the producer is on staff at a label or freelancing as an independent.

The job of a record producer starts before the recording begins. In this prerecording stage, the producer must determine the direction that the label and the artist want a recording to take. This is done through meetings with both parties.

The next step—an extremely important consideration for the producer—is to help the act choose the material to be recorded. Successful producers often have an ability to hear a "raw" tune and know what it will sound like after it is recorded with the act's special flavor and sound. The producer must develop a realistic budget for the project and then keep within it during the recording.

The individual will be expected to hire a contractor who will then hire the background musicians and vocalists needed for the recording. An arranger and an engineer must also be selected. Studio time is expensive. The producer will make sure that the act has rehearsed the song and is ready to record. When the act is ready, the producer chooses a studio and books time.

During the recording session the producer has a great deal of responsibility. The producer supervises the entire recording session, working with the engineer and determining what special effects to use in order to end up with just the right sound.

After the recording is completed, the producer may mix and edit the tracks, or engineers or mixers may be hired for the job. Good mixing is essential to the success of a recording. The individual may also choose the song that will be released as a single and help select the order of songs on a compact disc or cassette.

Other business duties of the producer include clearing mechanical licenses; checking on copyrights; and making sure that consent forms and releases are signed and in order and that bills are paid to the studio, musicians, vocalists, engineers, etc.

Whether it is the sound effects unique to a producer, a special blend of instruments, or a specific way vocalists harmonize, record producers each have a way of adding their own personal trademark to every song they are involved with.

Employment Opportunities

Record producers can be on staff at major record companies or independent labels. Individuals may also freelance as independent producers. The greatest number of opportunities will be available in cities where there are a large number of recording companies and recording studios. Recording capitals of the country include:

- New York City
- Los Angeles
- Nashville

Earnings

Earnings for record producers are dependent on a number of factors, including the level of success and professional reputation of the individual. Earnings also vary depending on whether or not the individual is on staff or freelancing.

Record producers can earn annual salaries ranging from approximately $16,000 to $250,000 or more. Individuals on staff at recording companies may be paid a straight salary or a salary plus royalties on sales of recordings that have been produced. Depending on the label, staff producers can average between $16,000 and $55,000 or more per year.

Independent producers who freelance are paid a fee plus royalties on recordings they produce. The fee is paid by either the artist(s) or the artists' recording label. Royalty rates can be negotiated and vary from producer to producer. The more successful a producer is, the higher the royalty rate that can be negotiated. Producers with a number of hits under their belts can earn over $250,000 a year.

Advancement Opportunities

Producers advance their careers by working on recordings that become hits or, at the very least, attain some degree of popularity. Individuals can then find positions at larger labels, work with more prestigious acts, or freelance depending on the options they are interested in. As producers climb the career ladder in this field, they can demand and receive higher earnings.

Education and Training

There are no formal educational requirements necessary to become a record producer. Skills are learned through watching others. Apprenticeship programs are useful in learning the techniques as well as in making much-needed contacts.

Music training is helpful. There are also trade and vocational schools offering programs in sound recording. Many colleges and universities also have programs that focus on the recording and technical aspects of the music industry.

Experience and Qualifications

Most people who become producers have worked in various capacities in the music industry prior to their current vocation. In order to be good at producing, individuals must have an almost innate sense of what song and arrangement will be a hit before it is recorded. A good musical ear is necessary to determine what will sound good.

For Additional Information: Associations and organizations that can provide additional information about a career as a record producer include the National Academy of Recording Arts and Sciences (NARAS), the Country Music Association (CMA), the Gospel Music Association (GMA), and the Recording Industry Association of America (RIAA).

TIPS

- Look for apprenticeships and internships. These can be obtained through trade associations and organizations and through recording studios and labels. Many colleges and universities offering music industry programs with specialties in recording may also provide industry contacts and opportunities for internships and apprenticeships.
- Consider an entry-level job in a recording studio. This will give you the opportunity to watch producers at work.
- People who are successful are often happy to help a newcomer. Try to find a mentor who can take you under his or her wing and help guide your career in a positive direction.
- You might also try to find a job with a small independent record label in any

capacity. Duties in smaller companies are not as specific as those in larger ones. Once you get your foot in the door, you can learn as you go.

- Another way to break into the field is to locate an act that has a song you believe can be a hit. Help finance the recording session in exchange for producing the song. Then try to find a label that believes in both of you.
- Things have changed dramatically in the recording industry. Today, independent labels as well as major ones are turning out top hit tunes. If you believe in yourself and have experience in various aspects of the music industry, you might try to find some backers to help finance a new label.

ARRANGER

Job Description: Arrange new musical compositions or create new arrangements for established songs.

Earnings: $12,000–$150,000+

Recommended Education and Training: Music training through private study, conservatories, colleges, universities, workshops, seminars, etc.

Skills and Personality Traits: Ability to read music; proficiency playing one or more instruments; ear for music.

Experience and Qualifications: Experience as musician; ability to compose music helpful.

Job Description and Responsibilities

The main job of an arranger is to arrange the various parts of a musical composition. Individuals may work with new music or create different versions of songs that have already been recorded or performed.

Desired effects are achieved by determining what voice, harmonic balance, instrument, rhythm, tone, and tempo should be used in the composition. Specific duties will depend on the type of work the arranger is doing.

Arrangers may develop arrangements for songs that are to be recorded. They may also work on arrangements of musical compositions that are to be performed live.

In some situations, individuals may be asked to take songs that have been previously recorded with lyrics and do an instrumental arrangement. Music arrangers on staff at music publishers are often expected to find different ways to write or play music.

Another duty of arrangers is to transcribe musical compositions for entertainers, orchestras, bands, etc. This is generally done when an act wants to perform a song in a style different from what was originally written. For example, a symphony might want to perform a composition originally performed by a pop artist. The song would probably have to be arranged in a completely different way to make it work.

Many recording stars use the services of arrangers to develop new arrangements of previous hits. These remakes, also called "covers," often become hits again and again. Arrangers may take a song with a country flavor and do an arrangement for a pop star. In the same vein, the arranger may take a hit originally done by an R & B artist and create an arrangement that makes the song a country hit.

Arrangers need to be aware of current music trends in order to develop arrangements for today. Things have changed dramatically in music over the years. Pieces that worked musically in the 1950s will not always be accepted in the 1990s. The arranger must also have enough creativity and confidence to explore new ideas and musical concepts. Sometimes the mere addition of certain instruments such as strings or horns can make all the difference and turn a song into a hit.

Employment Opportunities

Arrangers can either freelance or work as salaried employees in a number of settings and for different types of employers. These include:

- Music publishers
- Print music licensees
- Music services
- Recording artists
- Recording studios
- Singers or musicians
- Musical shows
- Television
- Motion pictures

Earnings

Annual earnings for arrangers vary greatly depending on the degree of success the individual has attained. Salary is also dependent on the type and amount of work the arranger receives. Staff arrangers will have steadier earnings than freelance workers. With freelancers, the more they work, the more money they earn.

It is often difficult at the beginning of a career to earn enough money to live on. Once an arranger gets a foot in the door he or she may earn between $12,000 and $19,000 annually. Those who begin to achieve mild success can earn up to $40,000. Top arrangers earn $150,000-plus annually.

Minimum fees for arrangers working on recordings, films, or television are set by the American Federation of Musicians (AFM). Top arrangers with a proven track record may demand fees well over scale. In addition to fees, individuals may also be paid a royalty on each record, cassette, CD, and piece of sheet music sold.

Advancement Opportunities

Arrangers can advance their careers in a number of ways. The first (and probably most common) is by working with more prestigious acts. Advancement opportunities occur when a record or other piece of music the arranger has worked on is recognized for its artistic merits or hits the top of the charts.

Some individuals find that they can experience more success by composing and arranging their own material for records, television show themes, film scores, or Broadway shows.

Education and Training

Arrangers must have training in music theory, orchestration, harmony, composition, arranging, and electronic music. They must also be proficient in playing one or more instruments. While arrangers are highly skilled at their profession, there is no formal educational requirement. Training can be accrued through private study, attendance at music conservatories, universities, or colleges, and through workshops or seminars.

Experience and Qualifications

Most arrangers have experience writing and composing music on either a professional or an amateur level. Many individuals start their career in arranging as musicians, playing one or more instruments.

Arrangers need a good musical ear as well as the creativity to develop musical ideas into arrangements.

For Additional Information: Associations, organizations, and unions that can provide additional information regarding a career as an arranger include the American Society of Music Arrangers (ASMA), the National Academy of Recording Arts and Sciences (NARAS), and the AFM.

TIPS

- Consider breaking into the field on a small scale. Offer to arrange music for entertainers who have not yet achieved success.
- Openings for staff positions may be advertised in the newspaper classified section under headings such as "Arranging," "Arranger," "Music Publisher," "Music Service," "Recording," and "Music." These positions will usually only be advertised in large, culturally active cities that host large numbers of music publishers, music services, recording studios, etc.
- Join the local affiliate of the AFM. Their trade journal, *The International Musician*, often lists or advertises opportunities. People in the union office might also know of possibilities.

- Contacts are important in this field. Attend seminars, workshops, union meetings, etc., in order to develop a network.
- Consider a part-time job in a recording studio. This will be helpful in learning a great deal about the industry and about arranging. You will also make important contacts.
- Get as much experience as possible. Offer to arrange and/or compose music for your school musical or a local community production.
- Compose music for new acts or for yourself if you are also an entertainer.
- Find and take seminars, workshops, and classes in arranging. Even if you think you know everything there is to know about arranging, you will probably learn a new technique, get a new idea, or make a new contact.
- If you have your own group, you might arrange their music.
- Take advantage of internships and apprenticeships offered through trade associations, colleges, universities, etc. These are a great way to get your foot in the door.

RECORDING ENGINEER

Job Description: Operate sound board during recordings; mix recorded tracks; set up studio.

Earnings: $12,000–$125,000+

Recommended Education and Training: College or technical school training in sound engineering or recording technology; apprenticeships.

Skills and Personality Traits: Musical ear; mechanically and electronically inclined.

Experience and Qualifications: Experience working in recording studio.

Job Description and Responsibilities

Recording engineers have varied responsibilities depending on their experience, the structure of the studio, and the number of engineers working on a session. They are responsible for assisting in the creation of the total "sound" of a recording.

Very large studios have a chief recording engineer, as well as a recording assistant and a mixing engineer. Responsibilities of engineers include preparing the studio before the recording artists arrive by setting up instruments and microphones, turning them on, and checking to make sure everything is working correctly. Recording engineers may also be required to repair the equipment in the studio.

One of the main responsibilities of the engineer is to operate the sound board, electronic devices, and other equipment during recording sessions. While doing this, the engineer must determine what "sound" the act and producer are looking for. The individual will then use the various audio controls on the board to create the correct sound, tempo, etc.

Another important duty of a recording engineer is to mix the recording tracks to create a master tape. This ability is an art that must be learned. The individual, working closely with the producer and the artist, must decide the volume of each track and then balance them. Instruments may need to be added to attain the desired sound. The result of this work is the master tape, which is used to make the act's CDs, cassettes, and records that are sold in stores.

Employment Opportunities

The most employment opportunities will be located in the recording capitals of the country including New York City, Los Angeles, and Nashville. Recording engineers can work in a variety of situations. These include:

- Staff position at a record company
- Staff position at a recording studio
- Freelance

Earnings

Approximate annual earnings for recording engineers range from $12,000 to $125,000 or more depending on the specific situation. Individuals on staff with little experience at recording studios or record labels usually earn between $12,000 and $18,000. As recording engineers obtain more experience their salaries go up.

Well-known engineers with a great deal of experience can earn up to $75,000 a year. The most successful engineers working with top recording artists earn over $125,000 annually.

Advancement Opportunities

Recording engineers advance their careers in a number of ways. Some move up by becoming head or chief engineer at a studio. This results in increased responsibilities and earnings. Others go from working on staff to becoming successful freelance engineers. Many engineers advance their careers by becoming engineer-producers for top acts.

Education and Training

Recording engineers can get training in several ways. Some individuals take college courses in sound engineering and recording technology. Others attend technical or vocational schools in the subject area. Many recording engineers apprentice in a recording studio and learn the trade by watching and working with experts in the field.

Experience and Qualifications

Experience working in a studio is necessary in order to become a recording engineer. This may be obtained by going through internship programs or apprenticeships. Some individuals acquire experience by locating a job as a recording assistant, helping the engineers set up the studio before artists arrive.

It is imperative to the success of recording engineers to have a good musical ear. Individuals must also have the ability to translate the musical concepts of artists and producers onto tape.

For Additional Information: Individuals aspiring to work as recording engineers can obtain additional information by contacting the Society of Professional Audio Recording Studios (SPARS), the National Academy of Recording Arts and Sciences (NARAS), the Country Music Association (CMA), and the Gospel Music Association (GMA).

TIPS

- Look for an internship program in this area. Contact record companies and colleges to see if they offer programs.
- You may find job opportunities as recording studio set-up workers in the classified section of newspapers in cities hosting a large number of recording studios, such as New York, Los Angeles, and Nashville. Look under headings such as "Recording Studio," "Recording Set-up Worker," and "Engineer Assistant."
- Many record companies offer minority training programs. If you qualify, take advantage of the opportunity.
- Look for seminars and workshops for recording engineers. These may be offered by trade associations, colleges, or vocational and technical schools.
- Visit recording studios to see if you can find someone willing to hire you as an apprentice.

A & R REPRESENTATIVE

Job Description: Locate new talent to add to record company roster; find songs for artists signed to label; act as liaison between artist and label.

Earnings: $18,000–$85,000+

Recommended Education and Training: College degree may be preferred.

Skills and Personality Traits: Ability to see potential in raw talent; communications skills; interpersonal skills.

Experience and Qualifications: Experience working in music or recording industry or radio.

Job Description and Responsibilities

A & R stands for "artist and repertoire." A & R representatives work for record labels. Their main functions include locating talent that will be an asset to the specific label, getting the artist(s) to sign a contract with the company, and finding songs that will be appropriate for the artist(s). Within this capacity, A & R reps have many responsibilities.

New talent may be located in a number of ways. The A & R rep is expected to go to clubs and attend concerts and talent showcases in order to hear and see groups or solo artists. The individual also reviews solicited and unsolicited tapes, demo records, and music videos that are sent to the company by acts hoping to land a recording contract.

A & R representatives might also try to coax established artists who are with other labels to switch to a new label. In some cases, the label will wait for the artist's current contract to expire. In others, the label may negotiate to buy out the existing contract.

Successful A & R reps are those who can attract successful artists to sign with the label. In order to get performers to sign with their company instead of a competitor, the A & R rep will try to make their contract more attractive. Money is not always the only factor involved. Contract negotiations can also involve the amount of development, promotion, publicity, advertising, and tour support a record will receive.

After the A & R representative has successfully signed new talent to the label's roster, he or she will need to work closely with them. The individual is expected to help find the ideal material for the artist to record. Sometimes, the artist is a composer or already has songs in mind. If not, the A & R rep might review tapes of new songs that are sent to the company by aspiring songwriters to see if there are any possibilities for the artist. The individual might also find one or more former hits that need only to be arranged in a different fashion. In some instances, a staff writer is brought in to compose a potential hit song for a specific artist.

The A & R representative does everything possible to make sure that the artist achieves success while at the label. The individual will work with various departments, including publicity, artist development, and promotion, to attain that goal.

While artists are under contract with a label, the A & R representative is their liaison with the record company. If they are unhappy with anything that has to do with the label, the individual will try to rectify the situation, or at least make the artists feel that the problem is being taken care of.

Employment Opportunities

A & R representatives work on a full-time basis for record companies. The majority of opportunities will be located in the recording capitals. These include:

- New York City
- Los Angeles
- Nashville

Earnings

A & R representatives have annual salaries ranging from approximately $18,000 to $85,000 or more. Factors affecting earnings include the size and prestige of the record label as well as the experience, responsibilities, and professional reputation of the individual. A & R reps may also receive bonuses for signing superstars and other artists who have made big hits.

Advancement Opportunities

A & R representatives advance their careers by signing performers who produce hit records. Individuals may locate similar positions at more prestigious companies or may advance to become an A & R director at a label.

Education and Training

There are no formal educational requirements. However, competition is keen in the recording industry. A candidate with a college degree will usually be preferred over one with just a high school diploma. Good choices for majors include music merchandising, music business, public relations, communications, marketing, liberal arts, and English. Classes, seminars, and workshops in any of these areas will also be useful.

Experience and Qualifications

A & R representatives usually must have some sort of experience working in the music or recording industry or in radio.

The most important qualification for an individual in this field is the ability to see the potential in raw talent. A & R reps should also like music—they will be listening to a lot of it and spending a great deal of time around it. Good communications and interpersonal skills are needed to succeed in this industry.

For Additional Information: Individuals interested in a career as an A & R representative or director can obtain additional information by contacting the National Academy of Recording Arts and Sciences (NARAS), the Country Music Association (CMA), and the Gospel Music Association (GMA).

TIPS

• Try to locate an internship in a record company. Contact record labels as well as trade associations to inquire about programs. Many colleges and universities with music business or music merchandising programs have contacts within the industry.

• On occasion, openings may be advertised in newspaper classified sections under the headings of "A & R Rep," "A & R Coordinator," "Artist and Repertoire Coordinator," "A & R Staffer," "Talent Acquisition Rep," "Record Company," and "Music." The majority of ads in this field will probably be found only in New York, Los Angeles, and Nashville newspapers.

• Read the trades. Not only will they advertise openings, but they will keep you up on new trends and activities in the industry.

• When looking through the trades, you will often read about people who have been promoted or have left one company for another. This is a good way to find possible openings.

• Send your resume and a short cover letter to the personnel director of record companies. Try to get a specific name to whom you will send your letter. Ask that your resume be kept on file if there are no current openings. Contact them again every couple of months.

• Keep your options open when applying to record companies. Take any job you can get. Most labels promote from within. Get your foot in the door and try to move into the position you are seeking.

• Obtain experience by locating local up-and-coming talent. Work with them as their manager or agent.

PROMOTION REPRESENTATIVE—RECORDING COMPANY

Job Description: Attempt to obtain airplay for label's recordings; visit and call station music and program directors.

Earnings: $16,000–$50,000+

Recommended Education and Training: Minimum of high school diploma; bachelor's degree preferred.

Skills and Personality Traits: Sales ability; persuasiveness; aggressiveness.

Experience and Qualifications: Experience in sales, radio, or music industry helpful.

Job Description and Responsibilities

In order for record companies to make money, they must sell records, cassettes, and CDs. To get people to want to buy these products, they must first hear them. The individuals who try to get airplay for the label's recordings are called promotion representatives.

Prior to the success of music television stations such as MTV, VH1, and CMT, the usual way to "break" a record was to try to get airplay in important markets or geographic areas of the country. Once a release was being listened to and gaining popularity in one of these markets, the audience would spread throughout the country until a national hit was created. The process often could and usually did take time.

Today, videos aired on national television mean that a new release can become a national (if not international) hit almost instantly. When fans like songs, they call their local stations and request them.

Promotion reps have a number of responsibilities. Their main function is to call or visit radio station music directors, program directors, and disc jockeys to persuade them to listen to and play the label's material.

There may be a great deal of travel involved in this type of position. Individuals are usually assigned specific categories of music as well as geographic territories in which to work. Promotion reps will be responsible for making appointments to visit all the radio stations in that geographic location that play the type of music that fits in with their category. While major markets are located in New York City, Los Angeles, and Nashville, depending on the label and the release, promotion reps may be assigned territories in areas throughout the country.

During the visit, the promotion representative will give the station's program or music director copies of new releases, promotional material on the artists who made the recordings, and any documentation on airplay reaction. If reps are lucky, the music or program director will listen to the release while they are in the studio and will like it enough to add it to the station's playlist. In smaller areas, promotion reps might call radio station personnel and send promotional copies of releases and press material.

Since television videos are such an important force in the development of hits, instead of dealing with radio stations some promotion reps may be assigned to contact the music or program directors of music video television stations and stations with similar programming. Duties will be similar to those involving radio stations.

Promotion reps visit or call record and music stores in their assigned area and throughout the country to check the sales of the records they are promoting. If sales are good, they will report this information to music directors with hopes that it will convince them to add the release to their playlist or put it into a more frequent rotation.

Promotion representatives do a great deal of socializing and entertaining. Individuals are expected to wine and dine music directors, program directors, and disc jockeys from radio and television. This can include anything from lunches and dinners to attending concerts with key personnel to hear the actual audience response to music.

Employment Opportunities

Promotion representatives can find employment opportunities in a variety of settings. These include:

- Staff positions at major labels
- Staff positions at independent labels
- Independent positions for small labels
- Independent positions for major labels in areas outside of major geographic markets

Earnings

Promotion representatives earn between $16,000 and $50,000 or more annually. Factors affecting salaries include the size and prestige of the label for which the individual is working, as well as the responsibilities, reputation, and experience of the individual.

Advancement Opportunities

Promotion representatives can climb the career ladder by locating similar positions at larger, more prestigious labels or by being assigned to larger, more important markets. To do this, individuals must establish a track record by having releases added to station playlists and increasing the frequency of their airplay.

Promotion reps may also move into other record company departments. Those with supervisory skills can advance their careers by moving up to a regional promotion manager position or by becoming a label's director of promotion.

Education and Training

Some labels will hire promotion representatives with a minimum of a high school diploma. Usually, major labels prefer or require at least a college background or bachelor's degree. Good choices for majors include music merchandising, music business, business, communications, advertising, and liberal arts.

Experience and Qualifications

Most promotion representatives are excellent salespeople. They have the ability to persuade key personnel at radio stations not only to listen to their recordings, but also to add them to their playlist. Prior to the position with a recording label, a promotion rep may have had experience in a variety of sales jobs or involvement in some area of the radio or the music industry.

Promotion reps must be knowledgeable about trends in music, the recording industry, and the music business in general.

For Additional Information: Contact the National Academy of Recording Arts and Sciences (NARAS), the Country Music Association (CMA), and the Gospel Music Association (GMA) for additional information about promotion representatives and other careers in the recording industry.

TIPS

- Colleges and universities hosting music merchandising and music business majors and programs usually have work-study programs in the industry.
- Positions in this field may be advertised in the newspaper classified section under the headings of ''Promotion Rep,'' ''Records,'' ''Recording Industry,'' ''Music,'' ''Independent Promotion Rep,'' and ''Promotion.''
- Openings are also often advertised in the trade magazines.
- Contact record companies to locate internship programs. If labels write and tell you that there are no internships available, contact them again and try to create one for yourself. These are valuable for the education and experience as well as for the opportunity to make important contacts.
- Send your resume with a short cover letter inquiring about openings to the personnel directors of recording companies. Ask that your resume be kept on file.

- Contacts are vital. If you have any in the recording industry or music business, use them to help you obtain an interview.
- A part-time or summer job at a radio station might help you make contacts with recording company promotion reps. Talk to them about their jobs. Many people may be happy to take you under their wings and help you with your career.
- Many major recording labels have minority training programs available. If you fulfill the requirements, take advantage of the opportunity.

STAFF PUBLICIST—RECORDING COMPANY

Job Description: Obtain publicity for artists signed to recording label; write press releases; develop publicity campaigns.

Earnings: $15,000–$85,000

Recommended Education and Training: Bachelor's degree.

Skills and Personality Traits: Verbal and written communications skills; knowledge of publicity and promotion; creativity.

Experience and Qualifications: Experience working in publicity or public relations.

Job Description and Responsibilities

Staff publicists at recording companies are responsible for handling publicity for the label's artists. As staff publicist the individual must consistently work towards getting the artists and/or their recordings into the public eye and then to concentrate on ways to keep them there.

Staff publicists often work with an act, their personal publicist, and the management company to formulate publicity campaigns for selling recordings. The difference between staff and personal publicists or press agents is that staff publicists try to develop publicity to sell more records. Personal publicists or press agents develop campaigns to create an image for the act. In addition, it is not uncommon for staff publicists to be assigned to work with up to 10 different artists. Personal publicists usually can give more specialized attention to their clients.

The publicity department handles all the publicity and press requirements for all of the artists on the label's roster. Responsibilities will vary depending on the size and structure of the publicity department as well as the experience level of the individual. In large publicity departments, staff publicists will have more specific duties. In smaller departments, individuals will usually be expected to handle a multitude of general responsibilities.

Staff publicists with little experience often handle the clerical work. They gather information for and compile press kits, collect and check information for news releases, make calls for supervisors, etc. More experienced publicists are expected to develop ideas and write press releases for the act or individual.

Writing a press release is one thing; getting it to the media and persuading them to use it is another. After staff publicists send out press releases, they must follow up with calls. A great deal of the publicist's day is often spent on the phone talking to the media about acts and recordings that have been assigned to him or her. Individuals will be expected to set up interviews with newspapers, magazines, radio, and television. Publicists will also try to arrange personal appearances for artists on television talk and variety shows in conjunction with new releases.

Publicists may schedule and organize press parties and conferences to announce important events regarding the label, the artists, or major releases. Staff publicists may send out promotional copies of upcoming releases to media to try to spark their interest.

When acts go on tour, the staff publicist will be expected to set up media appearances. The individual will work closely with the artist's management and tour personnel to coordinate tour publicity and promotion.

Perks may include occasional traveling with an act, attending parties and other functions to mingle with the press, and attending concerts to hear acts the label represents.

Staff publicists work closely with the director of the department as well as other departments within the company including A & R, promotion, marketing, and artist development. The objective is to work together to give every artist and recording the best possible chance of success. The more recordings that sell, the more money both the artist and the label earn.

Employment Opportunities

If an individual is creative, understands publicity, and can write well, the publicity department is one of the easiest to enter at a recording label. There is a great deal of turnover in this department because people are either promoted to other positions or move on to other labels. Small recording companies can be located in cities throughout the country. Larger companies located in the recording capitals of the country will offer the most opportunities. These are found in:

- Los Angeles
- New York City
- Nashville

Earnings

Staff publicists working at recording labels will earn between $15,000 and $85,000 annually. Factors affecting earnings include the experience level and responsibilities of the individual as well as the size, structure, and prestige of the label. Entry-level jobs in this field range from $15,000 to $19,000. Individuals with more experience will earn between $25,000 and $45,000 annually. Staff publicists with a great deal of experience and responsibility working at large labels can earn up to $85,000 a year.

Advancement Opportunities

One of the great things about working in the publicity department of a recording company is that as individuals gain experience and prove themselves, they can easily advance to better positions. Staff publicists might, for example, advance by being assigned more prestigious clients or supervising others in the department. Individuals might also locate similar positions at larger, more prestigious labels, which results in increased earnings and greater responsibilities. Some climb the career ladder by becoming the director of the publicity department at a recording label.

Other paths of advancement include becoming an independent publicist or press agent or seeking a position at a large, prestigious, music-oriented public relations firm.

Education and Training

A bachelor's degree is recommended for this position. While not all labels will require a degree, in order to advance it is usually necessary.

Good choices for majors include public relations, marketing, music business, music merchandising, advertising, communications, and journalism. Seminars, workshops, and classes in all aspects of writing, journalism, communications, publicity, and the music industry will be especially useful.

Experience and Qualifications

In some instances, individuals can land an entry-level job in the publicity department of a recording label if they have a college degree in a related field. It is usually helpful to have experience handling publicity on some level, whether it be for people in entertainment or in an unrelated field.

Media contacts in music as well as in other areas are important. If publicists don't have the contacts, they need the ability to "schmooze" in order to establish good contacts.

Verbal and written communications skills are imperative. A creative mind is essential in developing new strategies, angles, and hooks to get and keep the act's name, face, and music in the public eye.

For Additional Information: Additional information about careers in publicity and recording companies can be obtained by contacting the Public Relations Society of America (PRSA) and the National Academy of Recording Arts and Sciences (NARAS).

TIPS

- If all that is available is an entry-level job in the publicity department of a recording company, consider taking it. This way, you will get your foot in the door. Recording companies try to promote from within the ranks. Those who show initiative and are good at what they do will quickly move up into a better position.
- Send your resume and writing samples to the personnel directors of recording companies. Ask that they keep your resume on file if there are no current openings. Contact them again every couple of months.
- Contact recording companies and trade associations to inquire about internship programs. These will offer you great experience, help you make important contacts, and give you a really good chance at being hired after the program ends.
- If you can't find an internship in a recording company, consider one in a music-oriented public relations firm. At this point, experience and contacts are what you are after.
- Newspapers in New York City, Los Angeles, and Nashville may advertise job openings in their classified sections. Look under headings such as "Publicity," "Publicist," "Press Agent," "Public Relations," "Music," "Record Company," and "Staff Publicist."
- Trade papers and magazines also advertise openings.
- There are a small number of employment agencies specializing in jobs in the music industry. They are usually located in New York City and Los Angeles, but may also be in other culturally active cities. Look in the yellow pages of the phone book and Sunday newspaper classifieds to see if there are any agencies advertising music as their specialty.
- Get experience writing publicity. Offer to do publicity for your college student activities department, local talent, community productions, etc.
- Take seminars, workshops, and the like in areas related to publicity, music, and the record industry. These are good learning opportunities as well as aides in making more important contacts.

ARTIST RELATIONS AND DEVELOPMENT REPRESENTATIVE—RECORDING LABEL

Job Description: Act as liaison between recording company and signed artists.

Earnings: $18,000–$40,000+

Recommended Education and Training: Bachelor's degree preferred.

Skills and Personality Traits: Interpersonal skills; knowledge and understanding of music business and recording industry; written and verbal communications skills.

Experience and Qualifications: Experience in music industry promotion, publicity, public relations, or artist management.

Job Description and Responsibilities

Artist relations and development representatives act as the liaison between the recording company and its artists. Once artists sign with recording labels, they need to feel and know that the company is doing everything possible to help their music and careers. They also need to feel special throughout the life of a recording contract. Without it, those who become successful may be enticed to sign with another label.

The recording business is unique. The business life and social life of artists are often meshed into one. One of the main functions of the artist relations and development rep is to build a good relationship between the artist and the recording company on both a business and social level. This may be accomplished in a number of ways, depending on the specific label and artist. For example, the rep may make sure that flowers are sent to female artists on their birthdays or that champagne is delivered to a group before an important concert. The individual may also be expected to get tickets to a big sporting event for members of a label's act.

Another important function of the artist relations and development representative is to make sure that the act is kept satisfied at all times. The individual will talk and meet with the act and its management on a consistent basis, making sure that there are no potential problems involving the label. If there are problems, it is up to the representative to solve them personally or bring them to the attention of someone who will.

Part of the job of the artist relations and development rep is helping the recording artist or group build their careers to the fullest potential. The individual works with every department at the label to coordinate tours and publicity with new releases. The rep will often attend concerts and offer suggestions on improvements in performance and stage presentation. The individual does everything possible to help the artist become successful and sell the greatest number of recordings.

One of the reasons many people like to work in this field is that they tend to build long-lasting friendships with the act and their management team. These friendships often last even after artists have changed labels.

Employment Opportunities

Positions in artist relations and development can be located at larger recording companies as well as at many smaller independent labels. Some companies delegate the responsibilities of this position to people in other departments including, A & R and publicity. Most major recording companies are located in the recording capitals of:

- New York City
- Los Angeles
- Nashville

Earnings

Earnings for artist relations and development representatives range from $18,000 to $40,000 or more. Factors affecting earnings include the size and prestige of the company as well as the responsibilities, experience, and qualifications of the individual.

Advancement Opportunities

Advancement opportunities for artist relations and development representatives include becoming the director of the department or moving into an advanced position elsewhere in the company. Some individuals advance into publicity or promotion while others move into the A & R department.

Education and Training

While there are no formal educational requirements for this position, most recording companies now prefer or require employees to have a bachelor's degree or at least a college background. Good majors to consider include music business, music merchandise, communications, journalism, public relations, business, and liberal arts. College programs often also offer experience and other opportunities such as internships with recording companies that might not otherwise be open.

Seminars and workshops in all aspects of promotion, publicity, and the music industry are also beneficial and help to cultivate contacts.

Experience and Qualifications

Experience in publicity, public relations, promotion, or artist management is usually required for this position. Experience may be acquired through internships or work as an administrative assistant in one of the departments in the recording company. Other experience may be obtained by working with personal managers or publicists in the music or entertainment industry.

Individuals need a thorough understanding and knowledge of the music and recording industries. Interpersonal skills and the ability to deal with a variety of people are also required.

For Additional Information: Individuals interested in pursuing a career in this field can contact a number of associations for more information. These include the National Academy of Recording Arts and Sciences (NARAS), the Country Music Association (CMA), and the Gospel Music Association (GMA).

TIPS

- Promotions in recording companies are often filled from within the company. Take any position that is open to get your foot in the door. Work hard and do more than is expected of you.
- If you get an entry-level job, volunteer to handle tasks that others don't want or don't have time to finish.
- Try to find an internship in the artist relations department of a recording company. Many labels have summer programs. Others have programs in conjunction with colleges. You will learn new skills, find out about the industry, and make valuable contacts.
- Look for seminars, workshops, and courses related to the music industry. These are additional ways to learn skills and make contacts.
- Send your resume and a short cover letter to the personnel directors of recording companies. Inquire about openings. Ask that your resume be kept on file and follow up frequently.
- Positions may be located in the classified sections of newspapers in the major music capitals. Look under headings such as "Music," "Record Company," "Record Label," "Artist Development," and "Artist Relations and Development."
- Some recording companies have minority training programs. Take advantage of them if you qualify.
- There are a small number of employment agencies in the country specializing in jobs in the music and recording industry. These agencies are usually located in New York City, Los Angeles, and Nashville.

MARKETING REPRESENTATIVE—RECORDING LABEL

. . . .

Job Description: Develop ways to market and sell a label's recordings.

Earnings: $18,000–$40,000+

Recommended Education and Training: College degree or background may be preferred or required.

Skills and Personality Traits: Verbal and written communications skills; marketing skills; interpersonal skills; creativity.

Experience and Qualifications: Experience in music or recording industry helpful, but not always required.

Job Description and Responsibilities

Marketing representatives for recording companies are responsible for developing and implementing ways to market and sell the label's music. Individuals may work on a local or regional level. There are many responsibilities within the scope of the job.

Marketing reps are assigned to work in specific geographic areas. Individuals visit and call on music stores and departments in their assigned area. There is a great deal of travel involved. Reps must determine what recordings are selling well in their area and make sure that there are sufficient quantities at each location to meet demand. This is especially critical when the label's acts appear on television shows, on radio shows, or in concerts; win awards; or make the news in any way.

Marketing representatives are expected to report sales of recordings by the label's artists to radio stations in the area. Sales are reported in major radio and music trades and tip sheets. This information is used by radio stations to determine what recordings to add to their playlist. This information is also important because it is used by many music stores, radio stations, and trades to develop the music charts.

Marketing representatives assist in the execution of all marketing concepts and programs utilized by the recording label. This could include setting up promotional appearances of one or more of the label's acts in large music stores or with major radio stations in the area; providing giveaway prizes such as recordings, concert tickets, T-shirts, etc., of label artists; or delivering point of purchase or window displays promoting the label's artists to music stores in their assigned area.

The marketing representative will ultimately be responsible for overseeing the marketing of the label's artists and recordings in their assigned areas. While the individual works under the supervision of the director of marketing, most labels welcome suggestions that will help recordings sell. Those with creative, unique ideas to sell music in a specific area can be very successful in this field.

Employment Opportunities

Most major recording labels hire large numbers of marketing representatives. Smaller labels hire fewer people, but it is usually easier to obtain a job with them. While recording companies may send representatives to various cities in the country, the greatest number of opportunities can be located in the major recording capitals. These include:

- New York City
- Los Angeles
- Nashville

Earnings

Marketing representatives earn approximately $18,000 to $40,000 or more annually. Factors affecting earnings include the size and prestige of the specific label as well as the responsibilities, qualifications, and experience of the individual.

Advancement Opportunities

Marketing representatives can advance their careers by locating similar positions in larger, more prestigious companies. Individuals may also become regional reps or regional directors of marketing.

Education and Training

Educational requirements vary for marketing reps depending on the label. While some smaller labels may only require a high school diploma, many companies prefer or require a bachelor's degree or at least some type of college background. A college education is often helpful in preparing for a job in this industry and offers opportunities that individuals might not otherwise be afforded.

Good choices for majors include music business, music merchandising, marketing, business, communications, and advertising. Courses and seminars in any of these areas will also prove useful.

Experience and Qualifications

Experience requirements will vary with the job. Any experience working at a recording company, whether as a receptionist or in a clerical position, will be useful. Experience as an intern is also extremely helpful in obtaining a job.

Marketing representatives should be creative with their marketing skills. A thorough understanding of the recording industry is necessary in order to be successful. Verbal and written communications skills are essential.

For Additional Information: Associations that can provide additional information on this career include the National Academy of Recording Arts and Sciences (NARAS), the Country Music Association (CMA), and the Gospel Music Association (GMA).

TIPS

- A good way to break into this field is to get a job in a large music store in a major music market. Marketing reps from various labels will visit and call the store. Try to hook up with a couple of people in the field and discuss your aspirations. They may be willing to set up an appointment for you or give you a name to call or write to.
- Get experience in a recording company by signing up at a temp agency that fills temporary clerical positions at recording labels.
- Send your resume and a short cover letter to the personnel directors of recording companies. Inquire about positions. If you are willing to travel or relocate to other areas, make sure you indicate these facts on your resume.
- Look for an internship program with a recording label. Contact the companies themselves or see if your college can work out a program for you.
- Many of the larger labels have minority training programs. If you qualify, take advantage of the program to get your foot in the door.
- If you can't immediately find a job with a recording label, look for a job in marketing in another field. This will provide good experience and help you hone skills.

CHAPTER 6

. . . .

Careers in Halls, Arenas, Clubs, and Other Venues

Arenas, halls, clubs, and other venues are the locations at which a great deal of live entertainment takes place. Neophyte performers often begin their careers in clubs, while amphitheaters, stadiums, and arenas are the venues for established acts to make personal appearances before their public.

The organization and operation of each venue offer a number of interesting, challenging, and lucrative career opportunities. Responsibility for the operation of these halls, clubs, and arenas lies with a number of important administrators and technicians. These individuals may control everything from booking and managing the venue to the layout, lighting, sound, traffic flow, security, and safety.

Whether the venue is a large hall or a modest-sized club, the operational pattern and the anticipated results are quite similar. The objective of those individuals responsible for operation is to provide a trouble-free atmosphere for both entertainers and audience. If problems arise, it is up to the managers and technicians to immediately cope with them so that the activity or entertainment can run smoothly.

Careers in this field require a variety of skills and experience. Space restrictions limit discussing all possible opportunities. Jobs covered in this section are:

Facility Director   Resident Sound Technician
Resident Stage Manager   Nightclub Manager

Individuals interested in careers in this area should also review entries in other sections of this book. Chapter 7, "Careers in Theater," and Chapter 8, "Careers in Orchestras, Opera, and Ballet," both discuss related opportunities.

FACILITY DIRECTOR

Job Description: Oversee activities and operations of concert hall, theater, arena, or other facility.

Earnings: $16,000–$60,000+

Recommended Education and Training: College background or degree may be preferred, but not always required.

Skills and Personality Traits: Business skills; administrative skills; knowledge of entertainment and performing arts business; ability to keep calm in a crisis.

Experience and Qualifications: Experience working in halls, clubs, theaters, arenas, or other venues helpful.

Job Description and Responsibilities

Facility directors are responsible for overseeing the activities and the operations of the venue. In this position, individuals may have varied duties depending on the size and structure of the facility. Facilities can include small to medium halls or theaters hosting plays, concerts, ballets, etc. They may also include large arenas hosting major concerts and performing arts events.

The facility director is in charge of overseeing all the financial business of the venue. One of the main functions of this individual is to make sure that the facility is booked as often as possible. Depending on the specific venue, the director may be responsible for buying the act, or may just be expected to rent the hall to promoters. As part of this function, the individual will be expected to negotiate with the performers or the promoters in order to obtain the best possible deals. The director will make sure that acts are paid on time and contracts and riders are fulfilled.

An important function of the facility director is the supervision of facility employees. These can include ushers, security, maintenance personnel, electricians, and sound and light technicians. The individual is responsible for directing the activities of the employees to insure the most efficient operation. The director is in charge of payroll, hiring and firing employees, and making sure that union regulations are enforced.

In some facilities the director is in charge of advertising, public relations, promotions, and marketing. In others the individual will work closely with the public relations firm, advertising agency, and publicists retained to promote and market the facility. The director must have a good working relationship with the media. In this way, the facility and its events will more likely be covered and publicized. The individual will usually provide the media with press and backstage passes and assist in scheduling interviews with the entertainers.

The facility director is required to keep the venue clean and in good condition, making sure repairs are made when needed. One of the most important functions of the facility director is to handle all the problems and crises that occur within the scope of the job. An individual who can solve problems quickly, calmly, and effectively will be successful in this job.

Employment Opportunities

While facility directors can find employment opportunities throughout the country, more will be available in large, culturally active cities. Individuals can work in a number of different settings including:

- Large concert halls
- Small or mid-sized halls
- Theaters
- Arenas
- Performing arts complexes
- Auditoriums
- Sports complexes

Earnings

Annual earnings for facility directors range from $16,000 to $60,000 or more. Factors affecting earnings include the type, size, location, and prestige of the specific venue as well as the experience, qualifications, and responsibilities of the individual.

Those managing smaller theaters or halls will have average earnings between $16,000 and $30,000. Individuals working for larger, more prestigious facilities can earn between $28,000 and $60,000-plus.

Advancement Opportunities

Facility directors climb the career ladder by locating similar positions at larger, more prestigious venues. This results in increased earnings and responsibilities.

Education and Training

Educational requirements vary from job to job. Some positions may only require a high school diploma. Others may require or prefer a college degree or background. Those who opt for college may consider majors in theater, music, business, or liberal arts. Courses, seminars, and workshops in accounting, bookkeeping, theater management, business, communications, public relations, marketing, and writing will be helpful.

Experience and Qualifications

Experience is required in this position. Many facility directors have a background in theater, music, dance, or the performing arts. Some started their careers as aspiring musicians, dancers, actors/actresses, or singers. Others may have worked in the business end of the performing arts in some capacity. Individuals often obtain valuable experience working as an assistant facility director.

Supervisory and business skills are mandatory for this type of position. Facility managers must be able to handle problems and crises with a cool head and be capable of developing solutions. A thorough knowledge and understanding of the performing arts as well as of facility affairs is imperative.

For Additional Information: Associations that can provide additional information regarding careers in facility management include the Musical Theaters Association (MTA) and the International Association of Auditorium Managers (IAAM).

TIPS

- Consider breaking into the field on a small scale. Get experience as a manager or assistant manager of a club.
- Jobs in this field are often advertised in the newspaper classified section under headings such as "Facility Manager," "Facility Director," "Hall Manager," "Theater Manager," "Concert Hall Manager," "Arena Director," and "Director of Hall Operations."
- Openings may also be advertised or listed in the trades or trade association newsletters.
- It is usually easier to break into this field at a smaller facility. Get some experience and apply for positions at larger, more prestigious venues.
- You might also seek out a job as an assistant facility director or manager in a small hall. There is a high employee turnover in these facilities and you will have a good chance of promotion in a shorter time span.
- Look for an internship in this field. Contact schools, colleges, facilities, and theaters to inquire about possibilities.
- Contact the Actors' Equity Association (AEA) to get lists of resident, stock, dinner, Broadway, off-Broadway, and off-off-Broadway theaters throughout the country. These will provide you with a good source of names and addresses to write to inquiring about internships or job possibilities.
- Send your resume with a short cover letter to halls, theaters, arenas, auditoriums, etc.

RESIDENT STAGE MANAGER

Job Description: Oversee and supervise activities occuring on-stage and backstage during performances.

Earnings: $12,000–$45,000+

Recommended Education and Training: No formal educational requirements.

Skills and Personality Traits: Supervisory skills; organizational skills; knowledge of lighting and sound technology.

Experience and Qualifications: Experience working backstage.

Job Description and Responsibilities

Resident stage managers supervise and oversee everything occurring on-stage and backstage during a performance. Individuals perform a vast array of duties. Depending on the size and structure of the venue, they may work alone or may supervise a staff. Individuals must attend every sound check, rehearsal, and performance scheduled. Stage managers usually do not work normal business hours. Instead, they generally work split shifts.

The resident stage manager will work closely with the crew of the artists appearing at the facility. If the performers have their own sound and light crews, the stage manager will assist and advise them. The stage manager assigns dressing rooms as well as makes sure any required amenities are available.

It is very important that the backstage area be kept as clear as possible. The stage manager must find out ahead of time who is allowed backstage. This list will usually be obtained from the performer's management or road manager. In addition to performers, singers, musicians, and crew members, others who may be included on a backstage list might include business associates, journalists, friends, and/or family members. The stage manager will issue backstage passes to each person authorized to be in that area before and during the performance. The individual will be in charge of making sure that everyone who is backstage has permission to be there.

This job has a great deal of responsibility. During a performance, the stage manager is in charge of making sure everyone does their jobs properly. The individual is expected to advise the performers about the amount of time they have before the show and exactly what time they go on-stage.

Before the show begins, the stage manager must find out the length of the show and when intermissions will be held. This information is imperative in order for the stage manager to know such things as when the curtain must be opened or closed. Additional information may also be needed to cue sound and lighting people.

The stage manager is responsible for handling all emergencies and problems occurring during a performance. Individuals are also expected to document any type of accident or injury that takes place before or during a performance.

Facilities such as concert halls, arenas, and clubs usually do not book the same entertainment night after night. Individuals, therefore, have the opportunity to see and work with a variety of performing artists. Those seeking to go on to other areas of the entertainment industry will also have opportunities to meet a great many people in the industry.

Employment Opportunities

Employment opportunities for resident stage managers can be located throughout the country. The greatest number of opportunities will usually be found in large, culturally active cities. Individuals may seek work in/on:

- Concert halls
- Clubs
- Arenas
- Theaters
- Cruise ships
- Hotels

Earnings

Annual earnings for resident stage managers can range from $12,000 to $45,000 or more. Factors affecting earnings include the size, prestige, and location of the specific facility as well as the responsibilities, qualifications, and experience of the individual. In unionized settings, stage managers will have their salaries negotiated by a union.

Advancement Opportunities

Resident stage managers can advance their careers by locating similar positions in larger, more prestigious facilities. This will result in increased earnings and responsibilities. Other individuals climb the career ladder by becoming facility managers or directors. Some resident stage managers get experience, make contacts, and go on to positions in other areas of the entertainment industry.

Education and Training

There is no formal education or training required to become a resident stage manager. Individuals often work as apprentices, interns, or assistant stage managers to obtain training. Others acquire training by watching others or by working in sound, lighting, and/or electronics.

Experience and Qualifications

Experience as an assistant stage manager is helpful. Some people obtain experience in school or local community theater and performing arts productions.

Stage managers should be well organized, detail-oriented people. Supervisory and interpersonal skills are necessary to be successful. A knowledge of lighting, sound, and electronics is important.

For Additional Information: Individuals interested in becoming resident stage managers can obtain additional information by contacting the International Alliance of Theatrical Stage Employees (IATSE) and the Actors' Equity Association (AEA).

TIPS

- Look for internships in this field to give you on-the-job training. You will also make valuable contacts.
- Positions may be advertised in the newspaper classified or display section. Look under headings such as "Resident Stage Manager," "Stage Manager," "Stage Director," "Concert Halls," "Facilities," "Arenas," and "Clubs."
- Offer to act as the stage manager in your school or community theater, music, or performing arts production.
- A summer or part-time job assisting a stage manager will also give you good hands-on experience as well as additional opportunities to make contacts.
- Send your resume and a short cover letter to the owners or managers of clubs and the personnel directors of arenas, concert halls, facilities, hotels, etc. Inquire about openings and ask that your resume be kept on file.
- Take as many workshops, seminars, and courses as you can regarding lighting, sound, electronics, and staging techniques. The more skills you have, the more marketable you will be.
- It is usually easier to get your foot in the door in smaller clubs and facilities. These venues usually experience a high employee turnover rate since people often move on quickly for career advancement.

RESIDENT SOUND TECHNICIAN

Job Description: Oversee sound requirements of facility.

Earnings: $12,000–$35,000+

Recommended Education and Training: Formal or self-taught electronic and sound training.

Skills and Personality Traits: Ability to use sound board; knowledge of electronics; dependable.

Experience and Qualifications: Experience using sound equipment and working soundboards.

Job Description and Responsibilities

A resident sound technician is responsible for overseeing the sound requirements of a specific venue. Within the scope of the job, the individual will have a multitude of responsibilities and duties.

Every facility has different sound requirements, depending on its size and structure. Different types of performances also need varying sound requirements. The individuals will oversee the setup of the sound equipment. If there are acoustical problems, the sound technician will determine what they are and how to solve them. Solutions might include moving equipment to different spots in the facility or adjusting controls on the soundboard.

One of the most important duties of the resident sound technician is operating the sound control board during performances. The individual sits at the board during a performance and makes adjustments so that the sound is properly balanced and regulated. The technician will also be responsible for adjusting the board for any special sound effects required.

In some cases, performers bring their own sound equipment. In these situations the resident sound technician will work with the performers' sound people, advising and assisting them. Sound technicians must attend rehearsals, sound checks, and performances. Working with the performers and their crew, individuals can determine the type of sound required.

The resident sound technician must be aware of and follow local ordinances and must not allow sound volume to exceed certain levels. This is especially important in venues where rock acts perform frequently.

The sound technician will be expected to keep the sound equipment in perfect working condition. Each piece of equipment must be checked after every performance to determine if there are any problems. Repairs must be attended to immediately. If something cannot be repaired, the technician must locate a replacement.

Employment Opportunities

Employment opportunities can be located throughout the country. Large, culturally active cities will offer more opportunities. Individuals may find work in a variety of settings. These include:

- All types of theaters
- Clubs
- Arenas
- Concert halls
- Cruise ships
- Hotels
- Convention centers

Earnings

Earnings for resident sound technicians can range from $12,000 to $35,000 or more annually. Factors affecting earnings include the specific facility and its size, prestige, and geographic location. Other variables include the experience and responsibilities of the individual.

Resident sound technicians working in unionized settings may have their minimum earnings negotiated by the union.

Advancement Opportunities

Advancement opportunities for resident sound technicians include locating similar positions in larger, more prestigious facilities or advancing to become the facility's stage manager. Individuals might also locate positions with major touring artists on the road.

Education and Training

Resident sound technicians must have some type of training in electronics and sound. This may be obtained through attendance at vocation and technical schools or may be self-taught. Many people pick up the skills of the trade by apprenticing or watching others.

Experience and Qualifications

Sound technicians should have a complete knowledge of electronics and sound. Experience working soundboards and other sound equipment is required.

For Additional Information: Individuals interested in this field can obtain additional information from the International Alliance of Theatrical Stage Employees (IATSE).

TIPS

• Offer to handle the sound requirements for a local musical group. It will provide good experience.
• Another way to learn skills and gain experience is by taking part in your school or local community theater productions. Volunteer to work with people handling the sound requirements.
• Look in the yellow pages of the phone book and the entertainment section of the newspaper to get leads on names and addresses of clubs, theaters, arenas, concert halls, and other facilities. Send your resume and a short cover letter inquiring about openings in this field.
• Job openings are often advertised in the newspaper classified or display section. Look under headings such as "Resident Sound Technician," "Sound Technician," "Audio Technician," "Sound Engineer," "Facility," "Hall," "Theater," "Club," and "Arena."

- Try to find an apprenticeship in this field by contacting clubs, halls, theaters, and other facilities. You might also ask a resident sound technician if you can apprentice with him or her.

NIGHTCLUB MANAGER

· ·

Job Description: Manage the operations of a club.

Earnings: $14,000–$60,000+

Recommended Education and Training: Formal or informal on-the-job training.

Skills and Personality Traits: Supervisory skills; business skills; interpersonal skills; aggressiveness.

Experience and Qualifications: Experience in clubs or entertainment industry helpful; knowledge of entertainment and music business.

Job Description and Responsibilities

Nightclub managers administer the operations of a club and handle the day-to-day running of the establishment. Individuals have varied responsibilities within the scope of the job depending on the type of establishment, its size, and structure. In some cases, the nightclub manager may also be the nightclub owner.

In many cases, the manager is responsible for determining the type of entertainment that will be used to make the club as successful as possible. The club might use live entertainment, employ DJs, or use a combination of the two. The manager must also determine the type of patrons the club wants to attract. This might include people who prefer to drink, eat, dance, listen to music, see comedy shows, or simply relax. Managers must often research other clubs in the area in order to decide the direction their clubs should take.

Responsibilities of the job include auditioning performers such as comedians, bands, singers, musicians, and DJs. In some situations, the individual may be expected to negotiate and sign contracts. In others, this function falls to the club owner. The manager is also in charge of hiring and training other key personnel including bartenders, waiters and waitresses, hosts and hostesses, chefs, security guards, and lighting and sound people.

The club manager must see to it that all state and local alcohol laws are adhered to. Clubs can be closed down if there are infractions. Depending on the size and structure of the club, the manager might also be responsible for the purchase and control of food and/or alcoholic beverages. In some clubs, the manager will just oversee this function with a food and beverage manager who handles the function.

Many of the duties of the nightclub manager are handled at night when the club is opened. The manager will usually be expected to be on hand to handle any problems that might crop up at night. He or she will usually total nightly receipts and either put cash in a safe or make a night deposit.

There are also a number of activities that the club manager may handle during the day. These include bookkeeping, checking receipts, paying bills, etc. Club managers must also determine the type of advertising campaign that will be most effective, develop a budget, and implement an advertising program.

Employment Opportunities

There are a great many employment opportunities available for nightclub managers throughout the country. Individuals may find jobs in every type of area from small college towns to culturally active cities and entertainment capitals. Employment settings range from very small clubs to large entertainment venues. Individuals may be managers of clubs specializing in a variety of types of entertainment including:

- Piano bars
- Rock-and-roll music
- Country music
- Folk music
- Comedy
- Musical productions
- Show groups

Earnings

Earnings for club managers range from $14,000 to $60,000 or more annually depending on the size, location, popularity, and type of club. Other factors include the experience and responsibilities of the individual.

Generally, the larger and more prestigious the club, the higher the earning potential of the manager. Clubs in metropolitan areas or entertainment capitals such as Las Vegas and Atlantic City will usually pay their managers salaries at the higher end of the scale.

Advancement Opportunities

Nightclub managers with experience can advance to similar jobs in larger, more prestigious clubs. This results in increased earnings and responsibilities. Other managers may move into positions managing concert halls or arenas. Many club managers strike out on their own and open up their own nightclubs.

Education and Training

There are no formal educational requirements for nightclub managers. Some positions may prefer or require training in food service or in the hospitality industry.

Others may have managers participate in either formal or informal on-the-job training programs.

Experience and Qualifications

Experience requirements vary for nightclub managers. Some positions prefer that candidates have previously worked as an assistant manager in a club. Others may accept experience in various facets of business or entertainment.

Individuals should have a basic knowledge of the entertainment and/or music business. They should be cognizant of handling contracts, negotiating, and booking talent. The ability to supervise is mandatory. Nightclub managers must be able to handle a great many projects at the same time and still keep a cool head.

For Additional Information: Additional information regarding careers in this area may be obtained by contacting the National Federation of Music Clubs (NFMC).

TIPS

- Job openings are often advertised in the newspaper classified section. Look under headings such as "Nightclub Manager," "Club Manager," "Nightclub," "Manager," "Management," "Entertainment," "Hospitality," "Music Club Manager," "Comedy Club Manager," and "Hotel Club Manager."
- Consider obtaining a short-term subscription to newspapers from geographic areas you might be considering.
- Most hotels throughout the country have nightclubs. In addition, many hotels provide training programs for club management. Contact the headquarters of major hotel chains and inquire about openings as well as training programs. You might also send your resume with a short cover letter to hotels hosting clubs.
- Similarly, send your resume and a short cover letter to other clubs in the area. Look in the yellow pages in the phone book to obtain names and addresses of nightclubs. The entertainment section of newspapers and entertainment magazines also provide names and addresses of clubs.
- There is a high turnover in these clubs since people obtain experience and move on to other jobs or are promoted. You might start out working as a host or hostess in a club, learn the ropes, and move up the career ladder to become the club manager.

CHAPTER 7

· · · · · · · · · · · · ·

Careers in Theater

The first introduction that many working in theater had with a theatrical production was when they participated in a school play as a child. Whether individuals played the lead role, portrayed a flower or a tree, or were part of a chorus, many became hooked on the mystique of theater.

No one more firmly believes the familiar line "there's no business like show business" than people who work in theater. For those who enjoy the theater, or just being around it, a career in this field can turn an avocation into a lifelong vocation.

Individuals interested in working in this area of entertainment do not necessarily have to work on Broadway to enjoy satisfying careers. Jobs in theater can be located from coast to coast and around the world. In addition to Broadway, there are opportunities in a broad spectrum of theatrical careers including stock productions, dinner theaters, regional theaters, road companies, and cabarets.

While actors and actresses are most prominent to the audience in a production, everyone involved in the process is important. In addition to performers, the theatrical industry encompasses careers for other creative people such as writers and designers as well as for those working in the business end of the industry. Behind the scenes support personnel and clerical workers also form part of the theatrical team.

A wide variety of people with different talents, skills, expertise, educational backgrounds, and experience levels are required. In order for a theatrical production to be successful, it needs support and teamwork. Participants include producers; directors; stage managers; casting directors; lighting, scenic, sound, and costume designers; electricians; lighting and sound people; stagehands; press agents; actors/actresses; hairstylists; makeup artists; dressers; property people; and more.

Space restrictions limit discussing all possible opportunities. Jobs covered in this section are:

Producer—Theater   Property Person—Theater
Director—Theater   Makeup Artist—Theater
Casting Director—Theater   Production Hairstylist—Theater
Scenic Designer—Theater   Lighting Person—Theater
Lighting Designer—Theater   Sound Person—Theater
Costume Designer—Theater   Dresser—Theater
Stage Manager—Theater   Theatrical Press Agent

Individuals interested in careers in theater should also review entries in other sections of this book. "Careers in the Business End of the Industry"; "Careers in Performing and Writing"; "Careers In Halls, Arenas, Clubs, and Other Venues"; "Careers in Orchestras, Opera, and Ballet"; and "Careers on the Road" all discuss related opportunities.

PRODUCER—THEATER

Job Description: Locate script and investors for production.

Earnings: Impossible to determine due to nature of the job.

Recommended Education and Training: No formal educational requirement.

Skills and Personality Traits: Business skills; negotiation skills; creativity.

Experience and Qualifications: Experience in theater and/or business helpful.

Job Description and Responsibilities

The producer of a theatrical production is the person that makes it all possible. The main functions of this individual are locating a good script, finding investors willing to invest in the show, and making all major decisions that have to do with the production. Within the scope of the job, there are many responsibilities.

A great deal of the responsibilities will correspond to the amount of knowledge the producer has about the business of theater. Some producers may just be business people who are interested in theater, but who don't have adequate technical knowledge to produce a show. These individuals surround themselves with others to handle more specific duties. Other producers have worked in theater for years and know it inside out. These individuals usually handle these more specific details.

Finding a good script is imperative. All the money in the world cannot turn a bad script into a good show. Scripts can be located in a number of ways. Playwrights may send them to producers. Sometimes producers might also do new versions of previous productions. In many cases, the producer may commission a playwright to write a script.

Once a script is located or written, the producer will pay the playwright for an option to use the script for a specified time period. This time is used to locate investors willing to finance the production. If financing is not located during this time, the producer may either drop the option or negotiate for a new one.

Producers must raise a great deal of money. In addition to the script, there are a multitude of start-up costs required long before a production even opens. The cast, as well as directors and production, creative, business, and administrative staff must be hired. Costumes must be designed, sets built, etc.

Investors in theater are called "angels." These people invest with hopes of earning a profit after the play opens. They take a risk that the show will not be successful and that they may lose money. It is the responsibility of the producer to negotiate terms acceptable to both parties. In many cases, the producer is one of the investors.

Other functions of the producer include hiring other staff members including the director, general manager, theatrical press agent, set and costume designer, choreographer, and casting director.

The producer may be present at auditions or actually oversee them. Depending on the situation, cast members may be chosen by the producer or by the director and casting director. However, all are usually approved by the producer.

It is ultimately up to the producer to make every major decision necessary to producing the play and making it a success.

Employment Opportunities

Producers may work in a number of settings. Those working in legitimate theater are self-employed. Some may be on staff of not-for-profit theatrical companies, regional theaters, etc. Individuals may produce a variety of productions including:

- Broadway plays
- Off-Broadway plays
- Off-off-Broadway plays
- Road company productions
- Dinner theater productions
- Cabaret theater productions
- Regional theater productions
- Stock productions

Earnings

Most producers usually do not receive a salary. These individuals are self-employed and are paid in a number of ways. Some producers receive a finder's fee for putting together a group of show investors. Others are compensated with a percentage of profits earned from the show. This is a risk because every show is not financially successful. Producers may lose time as well as money invested in putting together a show if the production does not make it commercially. However, those who are successful can earn millions of dollars during a show's run.

Producers on staff at theaters are paid a salary. Annual earnings for these individuals can range from $5,000 to $45,000. Factors affecting earnings include the responsibilities and reputation of the individual as well as the length of the theater season and the size and prestige of the theater where the producer is working.

Advancement Opportunities

Advancement in this field is to a great extent based not only on talent, but on luck as well. Producers climb the career ladder by producing shows at more prestigious theaters.

Real success can occur at any time. The ultimate goal in career advancement for every producer is to produce a successful Broadway show.

Education and Training

There are no formal educational requirements for producers. Many successful producers do not have any college background. A college degree, however, may often gain individuals a certain amount of credibility and offer greater training opportunities.

Those who choose college may find majors or classes in theater arts, arts management, communications, business, English, and liberal arts beneficial. Seminars and workshops in theater and producing will also prove useful.

Experience and Qualifications

Almost anyone with an interest in theater, money, and/or investors can become a producer. This does not mean, however, that every individual with these qualifications will be successful at the job. Experience in theater is helpful, but not always required.

Individuals striving for a career in this area need a working knowledge of the theatrical industry. They must understand and have the ability to explain to others the risks and advantages involved with investing in specific productions. Business, administration, and negotiation skills are imperative to success.

For Additional Information: There are a number of organizations that can provide aspiring producers with additional career information. These include the League of American Theatres and Producers (LATP), the League of Off-Broadway Theatres and Producers (LOBTP), and the Producers Group (PG).

TIPS

- Join professional theatrical associations and organizations. These will provide professional guidance and support to their members.
- Contacts are imperative in this career. Attend trade association meetings and conferences. These will provide you with opportunities to meet and network with others involved in the field.
- Learn as much as possible about every facet of theater. Get involved with your school and/or community theater group. Volunteer to do a variety of jobs.
- Seminars, workshops, and courses in all aspects of theater, business, and fund-raising will be useful for making important contacts as well as honing skills.
- Look for a part-time or summer job working for a producer. This will help you get experience in the industry and to make contacts.
- Contact theaters, production companies, colleges, universities, etc., to find internships, apprenticeships, and training programs in this end of the industry.
- Contact the Actors' Equity Association (AEA) to get lists of resident, stock, dinner, Broadway, off-Broadway, and off-off-Broadway theaters throughout the country. These will provide you with a good source of names and addresses to write to inquiring about internships or job possibilities.
- Offer to handle the fund-raising for your local community theater, arts council, or not-for-profit theater group. This will give you experience in raising money—a skill needed as a producer.

DIRECTOR—THEATER

Job Description: Prepare a theatrical production for opening; offer visual interpretation of a script; coordinate creative aspects of production.

Earnings: $10,000–$250,000+

Recommended Education and Training: Bachelor's degree helpful.

Skills and Personality Traits: Coordination skills; detail-oriented; patience; creativity.

Experience and Qualifications: Experience working in some facet of theater; thorough knowledge of theater and stage.

Job Description and Responsibilities

The director of a theatrical production coordinates every facet of the show. In this position, he or she has input with all creative aspects of the production.

The director begins working with the producer and the casting director to make sure that the cast chosen will be able to fulfill the individual's conception of the characters. The director also works with the costume designers, sound technicians, lighting and sound designers, production people, etc. The ultimate goal of the director is to bring the production to life on the stage.

In this position, the individual takes the words in the script and helps the cast to interpret them, adding pizazz and punch to the production. This extra sparkle is what can turn a mediocre production into a giant hit.

This is a difficult but rewarding job. The director works long hours attending rehearsals to determine how to improve the production. The individual will ascertain if lines or movements should be changed, omitted, or added. The director will also have the final say on costumes, set designs, lighting, etc. Everything must be perfect before the opening.

Much of the director's job revolves around the actors and actresses. The individual must convey to the cast his or her ideas of how the script should be interpreted, lines should be spoken, physical movements should occur, etc. To accomplish this the director will be involved in a mixture of guiding and teaching. At the end, the production should present a harmonious appearance.

Once the play is rehearsed and the production has opened, the director's job is finished. He or she will then move on to direct a new production.

Employment Opportunities

The dream of many people aspiring to work in theater is to direct a production. While employment prospects are difficult to attain, this is not impossible. Employment in this career, like many others in the entertainment industry, is to a great extent dependent not only on talent, but on luck as well. Establishing contacts, being in the right place at the right time, and perseverance will also help.

Culturally active cities such as New York, Los Angeles, Washington, D.C., Atlanta, Chicago, and Philadelphia will offer the most opportunities. Directors may obtain work in a number of different settings including:

- Broadway plays
- Off-Broadway plays
- Off-off-Broadway plays
- Road company productions
- Dinner theater productions
- Cabaret theater productions
- Regional theater productions
- Stock productions
- Production companies (staff positions)
- Theaters (staff positions)

Earnings

It is difficult to estimate annual earnings for directors working in theater. Those who are just starting out may not have any income to speak of and will have to work a second job to make ends meet. Once a director gets a foot in the door, approximate annual earnings range between $10,000 and $70,000 or more. Individuals who have a proven track record and are in demand can earn $250,000 a year.

Factors affecting earnings include the consistency of work, the experience and professional reputation of the individual, and the type and prestige of productions directed. Some directors work on a freelance basis while others are on staff at theaters or production companies.

Those on staff are usually paid a straight salary. Directors who are not on staff may be compensated in a number of ways. For example, they may be offered a set fee to direct a show or can be paid a fee plus royalties from the production.

Advancement Opportunities

Most directors usually start at the bottom of the career ladder. As they obtain experience, producers of more prestigious productions are more likely to hire them. Individuals might also advance their careers by directing a show that turns into a surprise hit. This results in the director becoming more in demand and commanding higher fees and royalties.

Some directors also advance their careers by moving on to direct television or films.

Education and Training

There is no formal educational requirement necessary to become a director. However, a college degree—bachelor's or master's—is useful for the credibility it lends and the education, experience, and opportunities it affords. Helpful majors include theater arts, drama, acting, and arts management.

Those who do not choose college often obtain training by working with and watching other directors perform their jobs or by participating in internships.

Experience and Qualifications

There is no set way to become a director. Some begin their careers acting while others work as stage managers, assistant directors, or writers. The necessary ingredient in this field is experience in theater.

Creativity is the key to this career. Individuals will be guiding actors and actresses in their roles as they (hopefully) bring productions to life. This often takes a great deal of patience.

A thorough knowledge and understanding of all aspects of theater, staging, stage jargon, and acting is mandatory. Individuals should be organized and have the ability to coordinate and handle the details of a production without becoming flustered.

For Additional Information: There are a number of organizations that can provide additional information about careers in directing. These include the Society of Stage Directors and Choreographers (SSDC), Actors' Equity Association (AEA— better known as Equity), and the American Guild of Musical Artists (AGMA).

TIPS

- Trade associations are a good source of contacts, professional guidance, and support. Contact them and inquire about membership requirements. The SSDC, for example, offers professional guidance and support to its members.
- Get experience by becoming involved with your local community theater group. Volunteer to work as an assistant to the director.
- If you are in school, make sure you are involved with your school's theater productions.
- Try to find courses and seminars in theater-related subjects. These are valuable for the education and the opportunities to make contacts and network.
- Send your resume with a cover letter to summer theaters. Inquire about a part-time or summer job to help you learn your craft and hone skills.
- Look for internships working in theater. These may be available through schools, colleges, arts councils, trade associations, theater groups, etc.
- Contact the AEA to get lists of resident, stock, dinner, Broadway, off-Broadway, and off-off-Broadway theaters throughout the country. These will provide you with a good source of names and addresses to write to inquiring about internships or job possibilities.
- Contacts are essential in this field. Learn to make them and to network.

CASTING DIRECTOR—THEATER

Job Description: Audition actors and actresses for parts in production; cast roles in theatrical productions.

Earnings: $10,000–$75,000+

Recommended Education and Training: No formal educational requirements; training may be obtained in college or through internships, apprenticeships, or on-the-job training.

Skills and Personality Traits: Communications skills; organization skills; ability to match people with roles.

Experience and Qualifications: Experience in some aspect of theater necessary.

Job Description and Responsibilities

The main function of casting directors is to cast or choose the proper actors and actresses for roles in theatrical productions. They may be hired to cast an entire show or just the major stars. Individuals may also be asked to cast road company productions of the same shows.

In order to correctly match people, casting directors read the script and then work with others in the production staff to determine their thoughts, ideas, and desires regarding the character's personality and physical appearance.

Casting directors may find the right performer in a number of ways. They develop advertisements and place them in the trades, newspapers, or other publications. These ads announce casting requirements for the production. They may also hold open auditions where hundreds or even thousands of hopeful actors and actresses come to audition for parts. Most casting directors also have a file of information on all the performers who ever auditioned for them, as well as a file on those who have sent resumes and photos but never formally auditioned.

In some cases, established actors or actresses hear about a production, are interested in a specific role, and instruct their agents to call the casting director. If these well-known actors and actresses are very successful in the industry and are right for the part, they will often get a role without auditioning. Similarly, casting directors might have a specific actor or actress in mind for a part. In these instances, they will contact the performer's agent to check out interest and availability.

Casting directors schedule casting calls and auditions. At casting calls, actors and actresses arrive with their resumes and photographs. They may be asked to read a number of lines from the script. During this process, those who are not suitable for roles in the production will be eliminated. Performers who may fit the roles will be called back for another audition, or "call back." When the casting directors have located the perfect people to fill the roles, they bring them to the attention of others, including the director, producer, and playwright. These people will then make the final decisions.

Knowing how to match people with parts is the key to success in this career. Successful casting directors try to choose actors and actresses who fit the bill and make the characters come to life during the production.

Employment Opportunities

All productions do not employ casting directors. Some utilize the services of the director or producer to handle casting responsibilities. Casting directors may work on a consulting basis, for a production company, or be on staff at theaters. Individuals may find employment in production companies or theaters, including those handling:

- Broadway plays
- Off-Broadway plays
- Off-off-Broadway plays
- Road company productions

- Dinner theater productions
- Cabaret theater productions
- Regional theater productions
- Stock productions
- Operatic productions
- Ballet productions

Earnings

It is difficult to determine annual earnings of casting directors because of the nature of the job. Determining factors include whether individuals are on staff or consultants, how many productions per year they cast, and the nature of the specific production. Earnings are also greatly dependent on the experience and professional reputation of the casting director.

Individuals may be paid a straight salary if they are on staff. Those who are consultants may receive a fee per production or a fee plus show royalties. Consultants may receive fees of $2,000 to $40,000 or more per production. Individuals on staff may have earnings ranging from $10,000 to $75,000 or more.

Advancement Opportunities

Casting directors can advance their careers in a number of ways. To some, advancement means opportunities for more work, which results in increased earnings. There are many casting directors who advance their careers by locating a staff position in a regional or dinner theater. This, in turn, offers them security and a stable income.

Another path to advancement is locating opportunities to cast more prestigious productions. Casting a Broadway play would be considered by most in this profession to be the top rung of the career ladder. Casting directors might also move up by becoming directors. Some strike out in a different direction and begin casting roles for films and television.

Education and Training

While there are no formal educational requirements necessary to become a casting director, many recommend a college degree for a number of reasons. College offers not only an education, but also opportunities for hands-on training that individuals might not normally receive. The degree also gives individuals credibility. Those who choose college might take majors in theater arts, arts management, or drama.

Many casting directors do not have a college degree. Instead, they acquire training through apprenticeships or on-the-job training by assisting casting directors, producers, and directors.

Experience and Qualifications

Casting directors generally have worked in one or more aspects of theater prior to getting jobs in casting. Some have been involved in apprenticeships or internships. Others have worked as assistant casting directors, stage managers, assistant directors, or as actors or actresses.

A thorough knowledge and understanding of theater is necessary in this career. Individuals must have an innate sense to match the right people with the right parts. Casting directors should be detail-oriented, and should have good verbal communications skills and the ability to listen and comprehend what directors are looking for. A good memory is a plus since it helps casting directors remember actors or actresses who have auditioned in the past and might be perfect for new roles.

For Additional Information: To obtain additional information regarding careers in this field contact the Casting Society of America (CSA).

TIPS

- Join the CSA. This association offers useful seminars, conferences, and information. It also provides professional guidance and support to its members.
- Look for a part-time or summer job in a theatrical agent's office. This will help you develop experience in the industry as well as make contacts.
- Contact theaters, production companies, colleges, universities, etc., to find internships, apprenticeships, or training programs in this area of the industry.
- Contact the Actors' Equity Association (AEA) to get lists of resident, stock, dinner, Broadway, off-Broadway, and off-off-Broadway theaters throughout the country. These will provide you with a good source of names and addresses to write to inquiring about internships or job possibilities.
- Offer to cast school or community theater productions. Many people do not want to volunteer for this position since they feel it might create ill will with friends.
- Consider trying out for a couple of open auditions or casting calls. This experience will help you to see the casting process from another angle. It will also offer you important insight into the demands of being a casting director.
- Become involved in all facets of your school or community theater group. This will give you valuable hands-on training in a variety of areas.
- Try to locate a mentor in theater who can help guide your career.

SCENIC DESIGNER—THEATER

∙ ∙

Job Description: Create set design for theatrical productions.

Earnings: $500–$150,000+ per production.

Recommended Education and Training: Bachelor's degree in theater arts or design.

Skills and Personality Traits: Drawing and painting skills; ability to conceptualize; creativity.

Experience and Qualifications: Experience working in theater; apprenticeships or internships.

Job Description and Responsibilities

The main function of scenic designers is creating stage sets for theatrical productions. Individuals work under the direction of the production director. Their job usually begins before the production goes into rehearsal and ends on opening night. In certain circumstances, they may be requested to design the sets for road shows in addition to the main production.

Without sets in theatrical productions, the stage would be bare and uninteresting. Sets can be elaborate or simple, depending on the specific show. Each set visually illustrates to the audience where a specific scene is taking place. In some productions, scenic designers may be required to create multiple sets. This is done in instances where the individual has to illustrate various scenes such as different rooms or different places. Sets can include backdrops, props, furniture, and lighting.

The scenic designer is responsible for defining the look and essence of the production. To accomplish this, the individual meets with the director and the lighting designer of the show. During this time, the scenic designer will determine the director's thoughts regarding sets, desired effects, the specific time period the production is set in, and any other applicable information. The individual will take this information and develop sketches and/or models to give to the director.

If the director approves the set designs, the scenic designer summarizes the information in writing, including the plans, ideas, equipment, props, and backdrops that will be required. The individual may find it necessary to create actual models of each set. The scenic designer must then solicit bids from scenery shops to build the sets.

The scenic designer is expected to make sure that sets are being built to specifications, on time, and within budget. Once they are completed, they must be checked out on-stage to make sure that the sets fit and can be changed quickly, smoothly, and easily. At this point, the scenic designer will also work with the lighting designer to make sure that the lighting is correct for each set.

Creative, artistic scenic designers can transform a stage into a set that the audience remembers long after the production has concluded.

Employment Opportunities

Scenic designers will find the most opportunities in large, culturally active cities such as New York, Los Angeles, Atlanta, Chicago, Philadelphia and Washington, D.C. All types of theatrical productions require the services of scenic designers including:

- Broadway plays
- Off-Broadway plays
- Off-off-Broadway plays
- Road shows
- Dinner theater productions
- Cabaret theater productions
- Regional theater productions
- Stock productions
- Ballet productions
- Operatic productions
- Modern dance productions

Earnings

It is impossible to determine annual earnings of scenic designers due to the nature of the job. Factors affecting earnings include the scenic designer's experience, expertise, and professional reputation. Other determining factors include the geographic location, type of theater, specific production, and number of sets required. Individuals may be paid a straight fee for each production they work on, or they may receive a percentage of profits instead of or in addition to the fee.

Those working in unionized theaters will have a minimum fee negotiated for them by the United Scenic Artists (USA) union. Scenic designers working for a Broadway multi-set musical can earn a minimum of approximately $18,000 plus royalties, as well as monies for pension and welfare funds. Talented individuals who are established in the field may earn $150,000 or more per production for Broadway shows if they have negotiated a substantial percentage of the production's profits for themselves.

Scenic designers working in nonunionized theaters may receive fees ranging from $500 to $20,000 or more for designing production sets.

Advancement Opportunities

Scenic designers who are talented, creative, determined, and lucky can advance their careers in a number of ways. Advancement opportunities for scenic designers depend to a great extent on where the designer is on the career ladder. Those entering the field are happy just to stay employed on a regular basis. Individuals working on summer stock might advance to designing sets for regional theater productions. A great achievement in this field is to design sets for Broadway shows. Some individuals may seek advancement by designing sets for films or television.

Education and Training

While a bachelor's degree will not guarantee a job in designing sets, it is recommended for a number of reasons. These reasons include opportunities to develop contacts and obtain training and hands-on experience. Good choices for majors include theater arts or design. Classes, seminars, and workshops in scenic design, art, lighting, architecture, theater arts, stagecraft, drawing, and art history will be helpful.

Experience and Qualifications

Hands-on experience is vital whether it is obtained through apprenticeships, internships, or working in theater-related situations. Those working in unionized situations must become members of the USA union. To become a member, one must pass an examination and go through an interview process.

In order to succeed in this field, scenic designers must be artistic, talented, and creative individuals with the ability to turn an idea into a stage set reality.

For Additional Information: Contact the USA union for more information about a career as a scenic designer or to learn more about membership.

TIPS

- Join the USA union. In addition to negotiating and setting minimum fees for scenic artists, the union provides professional guidance and support to its members.
- Contact theaters, opera or ballet companies, and universities or schools to locate internship or apprenticeship programs in scenic design.
- Get needed experience by volunteering to work on sets for school, college, or community theater productions.
- Theaters as well as opera and ballet companies may offer part-time or summer jobs to individuals learning their crafts and honing their skills. Send your resume with a cover letter inquiring about possibilities.
- Contact the Actors' Equity Association (AEA) to get lists of resident, stock, dinner, Broadway, off-Broadway, and off-off-Broadway theaters throughout the country. These will provide you with a good source of names and addresses to write to inquiring about internships or job possibilities.

LIGHTING DESIGNER—THEATER

Job Description: Create and coordinate all aspects of stage lighting for theatrical productions.

Earnings: $500–$150,000+ per production.

Recommended Education and Training: Bachelor's degree useful, but not required; hands-on training through apprenticeships, internships, or assisting lighting designers and electricians.

Skills and Personality Traits: Conceptualization skills; electrician's skills; creativity.

Experience and Qualifications: Experience as electrician.

Job Description and Responsibilities

The lighting designer is crucial for communicating the mood of a theatrical production to the audience. In this position, the individual will be responsible for coordinating all aspects of stage lighting for the production.

Proper lighting must be used for a number of reasons. The actors and actresses are often quite a distance from the audience. Lighting is essential for the audience to see the cast's faces, expressions, and movements. It is also often necessary to convey to the audience other types of lighting than ordinary interior stage lighting. Sometimes the director may want to illustrate a moonlit night or a foggy day. It is the responsibility of the lighting designer to produce the necessary lighting effects. These effects are produced using a variety of lights, filters, and colors, as well as by the placement of those lights.

The lighting designer meets with and gets ideas from the director and scenic designer. In this way, he or she can devise ways to achieve the results that the director and scenic designer have conceptualized.

There is quite a bit of paperwork in this job. The lighting designer must create a detailed plan documenting all lighting information, including procedures, plans, equipment, and arrangements that will be used to obtain the proper lighting effects. The individual will develop a lighting schedule for the lighting crew so that they know when each light should be turned on or off. A chart is drawn to depict which knob on the soundboard goes to which light in the theater. A map of each light and its wattage is also drawn. The lighting designer is expected to discuss and explain the implementation of lighting requirements to the people who will be handling the lightboard as well as to the electricians.

The lighting designer works closely with a master electrician on the technical end to make sure each light is the correct color and is placed and focused properly. In some instances, the lighting designer is also the master electrician.

Lighting will be checked and adjusted continually throughout the dress rehearsal. Changes will be required if the lighting does not work well with either the set or the costumes.

The lighting designer's job, like many others in theatrical productions, concludes on opening night. At that time, he or she will turn the responsibilities of lighting the production over to the individual handling the lightboard. The lighting designer is then free to go on to handle the lighting requirements of other productions.

Employment Opportunities

While the majority of people handling this position freelance, there may be some staff positions at universities, colleges, or regional theaters.

Individuals will find the largest number of employment opportunities in large, culturally active cities including New York, Los Angeles, Philadelphia, Washington, D.C., Chicago, and Atlanta.

Individuals may find employment in production companies or theaters, including those that handle:

- Broadway plays
- Off-Broadway plays
- Off-off-Broadway plays
- Road company productions
- Dinner theater productions
- Cabaret theater productions
- Regional theater productions
- Stock productions
- Ballet productions
- Operatic productions

Earnings

It is difficult to determine the annual earnings of lighting designers working in theater because of a number of variables. The most important is the amount and type of productions the lighting designer is handling. Other variables include the experience and the professional reputation of the individual.

Theatrical lighting designers are paid in several different ways. They may receive a fee for each production they work on, a percentage of the profits, or a combination of the two.

Individuals working in unionized theaters will have their minimum fee negotiated and set by the United Scenic Artists (USA) union. Minimum fees for lighting designers working on a Broadway dramatic production start at approximately $5,000. Lighting designers who have a proven track record and are in demand can earn over $150,000 per production. These individuals generally negotiate a percentage of the box office gross in addition to their set fees.

Lighting designers working in nonunionized settings may be compensated with fees ranging from $500 to $3,000 for each production.

Advancement Opportunities

There are a number of advancement opportunities for lighting designers. Some individuals advance by handling the lighting for an increased number of productions annually. Others climb the career ladder by obtaining a job designing the lighting for more prestigious shows.

Education and Training

A formal education is not required to become a lighting designer. Many individuals feel that a four-year degree is useful in obtaining training, opportunities, and experience. Those that are interested in college should consider majors in theater arts or design.

Many lighting designers obtain training through apprenticeships, internships, or assisting other lighting designers and electricians.

Experience and Qualifications

In some cases, lighting designers will act as their own master electrician. In others, they may just explain what needs to be done to an electrician. It is imperative to a career in this field that individuals have personal experience as electricians. Experience in other facets of theater will also be helpful in obtaining a job and being successful at it.

Lighting designers must have a thorough knowledge of theater, staging, and color. The ability to conceptualize as well as the ability to take the ideas developed by others and turn them into reality on-stage is also necessary.

Strong communications skills are needed to convey instructions regarding lighting to others in the crew.

For Additional Information: Aspiring lighting designers can obtain information about careers in this field by contacting the USA union. Additional information may also be obtained by contacting the International Brotherhood of Electrical Workers (IBEW) and the International Alliance of Theatrical Stage Employees (IATSE).

TIPS

- Get as much experience as possible. Offer to act as the lighting designer for a school production or a local community theater.
- Another good way to get experience is to work with a rock band that uses lighting in its show. Many bands, even those performing in bars and local clubs, use lighting to create excitement and atmosphere.
- Look for internships to help you hone skills and make important contacts. Contact schools, colleges, universities, theater groups, performing arts centers, and arts councils to inquire about possibilities.

- You might also consider an apprenticeship. These are often available through unions such as USA, the IBEW, and the IATSE.
- Contact the Actors' Equity Association (AEA) to get lists of resident, stock, dinner, Broadway, off-Broadway, and off-off-Broadway theaters throughout the country. These will provide you with a good source of names and addresses to write to inquiring about internships or job possibilities.
- Attend theatrical productions of every type, from amateur through professional. This will help you review a variety of lighting techniques and styles.
- There are many books published about theatrical lighting techniques. Read them and learn as much as you can.

COSTUME DESIGNER—THEATER

Job Description: Create costume designs for theatrical productions.

Earnings: $500–$100,000 per production.

Recommended Education and Training: College degree in costume design, fashion, or theater helpful, but not required.

Skills and Personality Traits: Design skills; sketching and fashion drawing skills; creativity.

Experience and Qualifications: Experience in clothing design required; experience in theater helpful.

Job Description and Responsibilities

Theatrical productions utilize costumes to help bring characters to life on-stage. The person who develops and creates ideas for these costumes is the costume designer. This individual plays an integral part in every production.

Costume designers have varied responsibilities depending on the specific production. These duties can range from the design and development of costumes for an elaborate musical to the location of ready-made clothing to be used as costumes in a simpler production.

Costume designers begin their jobs by reading the script and meeting with others, including the director, the scenic designer, and the lighting designer. It is necessary to explore the intricacies of the production as well as to establish the number of costumes each actor or actress will need. The designer must often research the clothing worn during a specific time period to make sure that costumes match those of the era of the production. Research may be done by visiting libraries or museums, watching television or movies, and/or going through books, periodicals, etc.

The costume designer develops ideas and creates sketches of costumes. If the director approves them, the designer goes on to the next step of making or having the costumes made. If not, he or she must go back to the drawing board and develop new ideas.

The actual responsibility of making the costumes may fall onto the shoulders of the costume designer. This may be with or without the help of assistants. It may also be handled by others working under the direction of the designer. Very elaborate productions often send the costume requirements to companies specializing in costume manufacturing.

Other duties of costume designers include designing, selecting, and locating accessories the actors and actresses will wear with each costume. These include everything from shoes and jewelry to undergarments.

A dress parade, similar to a dress rehearsal, is scheduled when all costumes are completed and ready for the production. At this time, all actors and actresses don their costumes and walk across the stage to make sure that the costumes work with the lights, sets, and movements. When everything is satisfactory, costumes are turned over to the wardrobe department and the job of the costume designer is complete.

Employment Opportunities

Costume designers may work on staff at theaters or they may freelance. Individuals will find the majority of opportunities in culturally active cities such as New York, Los Angeles, Washington, D.C., Atlanta, Philadelphia, and Chicago.

Costume designers may get a foot in the door of this profession by designing costumes for productions at stock, dinner, and regional theaters. Other opportunities include:

- Broadway plays
- Off-Broadway plays
- Off-off Broadway plays
- Road company productions
- Cabaret theater productions
- Ballets
- Operas

Earnings

It is impossible to determine annual earnings of costume designers due to the nature of the job. Factors influencing earnings include the experience, responsibilities, and professional reputation of the designer. Other variables include the type and location of the production and the frequency of work.

Costume designers working in unionized theaters have minimum fees set by the United Scenic Artists (USA) union. Those working in nonunionized settings must negotiate fees on their own.

Fees for costume designers working in nonunionized settings range from approximately $500 to $3,500 per production. Staff positions can range from $350 to $750 or more per week. Costume designers working on designs for a Broadway musical have earnings starting at approximately $15,000 per production. Those who have an outstanding reputation in costume design can command and receive $100,000 or more. These people, however, are few and far between.

Advancement Opportunities

Advancement opportunities for costume designers in theater include designing costumes for more prestigious productions. It is the dream of most costume designers working in theater to advance their careers to the point where they design costumes for a major Broadway show. Some individuals find career advancement in other areas of the entertainment industry, such as designing costumes for television or films.

Education and Training

There are no formal educational requirements for becoming a theatrical costume designer. However, college often gives one applicant an edge over another with similar talents. Helpful majors or degree programs for aspiring costume designers include costume design, theater, fashion, or a combination of these.

Individuals should take classes, workshops, and seminars in costuming, fashion, fashion design, sketching, design, drawing, art history, history, and sewing.

Experience and Qualifications

Costume designers should have experience in clothing design as well as a knowledge of theater. A thorough understanding of fashion, fabrics, color, and design is essential to success in this field. The ability to draw and sketch is mandatory.

For Additional Information: Aspiring costume designers can obtain additional information about this field by contacting the USA union and the Costume Designers Guild (CDG).

TIPS

- Consider breaking into the field on a small scale. Volunteer to act as the costume designer for your school or local community theater productions.
- Hands-on experience is necessary in this field. Look for internships in costume design or costuming. If you can't find one in theater specifically, try to locate one in fashion design.
- Contact theaters, production companies, colleges, universities, etc., to find internships, apprenticeships, or training programs in this end of the industry.

- The library can be a good source of ideas. Look through books on costuming, clothing design, and history.
- Try to find classes, seminars, and workshops in fashion design, theater, and costuming. These will give you more ideas as well as help you make contacts.
- While sewing skills are not always necessary, the ability to sew gives you an edge over others. It also might help you get your foot in the door of a job opportunity.
- Many museums throughout the country have exhibits revolving around costumes or fashions from other time periods.
- Try to attend plays, ballets, and operas. These productions often have elaborate costume designs.
- Contact the Actors' Equity Association (AEA) to get lists of resident, stock, dinner, Broadway, off-Broadway, and off-off-Broadway theaters throughout the country. These will provide you with a good source of names and addresses to write to inquiring about internships or job possibilities.

STAGE MANAGER—THEATER

Job Description: Coordinate on-stage events; block shows; call cues; act as director's representative; schedule rehearsals.

Earnings: $250–$2,000+ per week.

Recommended Education and Training: No formal educational requirements; bachelor's degree recommended; hands-on training necessary.

Skills and Personality Traits: Ability to handle many different projects at one time; detail-oriented; personable; diplomatic.

Experience and Qualifications: Experience working in all facets of theater; working knowledge of acting, directing, set design, lighting, and costuming.

Job Description and Responsibilities

Stage managers of theatrical productions have a multitude of responsibilities. Their job generally starts prior to the show's first rehearsal and ends one week after closing. During this time period, individuals act as the director's representative—the liaison with the cast, crew, and management—and coordinate occurrences on-stage.

Within the scope of the job, stage managers have varied responsibilities. Individuals may attend auditions and offer input into the casting process. They must also schedule rehearsals, informing cast and crew members of times, dates, and the like.

Stage managers are required to attend all rehearsals. As part of the job, individuals must update script changes and get new scripts to the cast. A sometimes difficult duty is making sure that cast members are performing their roles in the manner the director intended. When cast members are not, the stage manager is expected to talk to the specific actor or actress and explain the director's intentions. Individuals must continually make sure that rehearsals are running smoothly and according to schedule.

A major responsibility of stage managers is to "block" the show. Blocking illustrates where props and scenery should be placed on-stage as well as where cast members should be at specific times during the production. This can be done either verbally or with the use of tape markers.

Theatrical productions can have directors who bring plays to life by properly preparing a show for its opening. Once the show is opened, the director's job is essentially concluded. The stage manager then takes over.

The stage manager is responsible for everything that happens backstage during a performance. The individual must make sure that everyone does his/her job and performs on schedule. If actors or actresses forget a line, the stage manager will prompt them. During the performance the stage manager also "calls the show." This means calling out cues for the sound, lighting, and scenic technicians.

After a performance, before the stage manager can go home, he or she must write a report with respect to the show. This will document positive or negative activities and occurrences during the performance.

While a great deal of the day-to-day success of productions depends on the stage manager, individuals in this line of work do not often receive a great deal of public credit. They are, however, very much appreciated by the cast, crew, and director of the production.

Employment Opportunities

New York City, Los Angeles, Atlanta, Chicago, Philadelphia, and Washington, D.C.—as well as any other large, culturally active city—will offer the greatest number of employment opportunities. Individuals may find job possibilities in the following employment situations:

- Broadway theaters
- Off-Broadway theaters
- Off-off-Broadway theaters
- Road company productions
- Dinner theaters
- Cabaret theaters
- Regional theaters
- Stock productions

Earnings

Earnings for stage managers are dependent on a number of factors. These include the type of theater and production the individual is working with as well as the stage manager's experience, professional reputation, and level of responsibility. Those working in unionized theaters will have minimum salaries negotiated by the Actors' Equity Association (AEA).

Minimum earnings for stage managers working in unionized theaters can range from approximately $2,000 per week for individuals involved in a Broadway musical to $700 per week for those working on a summer stock production. Stage managers working in nonunionized settings may have weekly earnings ranging from $250 to $700 or more per week. Naturally, stage managers who have proven themselves and are in demand will earn considerably more.

Advancement Opportunities

Stage managers may advance their careers in a number of ways. Some individuals climb the career ladder by obtaining similar jobs with more prestigious productions. Others who are accomplished in their jobs may advance to become directors or producers. Stage managers may also strike out in a slightly different direction and find similar jobs in television or film.

Education and Training

While there are no formal educational requirements to become a stage manager, a bachelor's degree is often useful. A college background provides not only education, but also experience and credibility as well. Hands-on training is necessary in this profession. This practical experience can be obtained through internships, apprenticeships, or working as an assistant stage manager or in any other area of the theater.

Experience and Qualifications

Experience in all facets of theater is essential to obtaining a position and success in this job. Individuals should have a good working knowledge of every area of theater from acting and directing to set design, costuming, and lighting.

Stage managers must have the ability to handle a variety of projects at one time without getting flustered. Diplomacy, compassion, and the ability to calm people who may be tense or nervous before performances is a plus.

For Additional Information: For more information on a career in this field, contact the Actors' Equity Association (AEA).

TIPS

- Look for internship and apprenticeship programs in any area of the theater. They will provide valuable experience and help you make important contacts.

- Read books and take classes, seminars, workshops, etc., so that you can learn as much as possible about all facets of theater. The more you know, the more successful you will be in your job search (as well as in your job once one is acquired).
- Become involved with your school and/or local community theater to gain more experience.
- Another way to obtain more experience is to locate a job in summer stock. While it would be nice to work assisting a stage manager, any job will be helpful.
- Remember, the world of theater is a small one. Contacts you make at the beginning of your career will often follow you through your life.
- Contact the AEA to get lists of resident, stock, dinner, Broadway, off-Broadway, and off-off-Broadway theaters throughout the country. These will provide you with a good source of names and addresses to write to inquiring about internships or job possibilities.
- Professional contacts are helpful in this field. Attend theater-related functions and join arts councils, trade associations/organizations, and the like.

PROPERTY PERSON—THEATER

Job Description: Locate required props for sets; move props.

Earnings: $250–$1,200+ per week.

Recommended Education and Training: On-the-job training.

Skills and Personality Traits: Adept with tools; problem-solving skills; organizational skills; creativity.

Experience and Qualifications: Internship or apprenticeship useful.

Job Description and Responsibilities

Prop people are the individuals who help locate props. In a theatrical production, props are the items that make stage sets seem more authentic. Props, or properties, can include furniture, pictures, room accessories, parts of costumes, food, drinks, or anything else that helps make the stage setting appear more lifelike. In addition to being called a prop person, the individual handling this job may also be called a stagehand or a prop or property man (or woman).

Prop people work with the production's scenic designer. The designer will determine what props are needed for each set. Prop people will then be sent to find the required props. Individuals may rent props from rental companies, warehouses, or museums or may purchase them from a variety of sources.

Props are not always easy to locate, especially if the production is set in an earlier time period. Property people do a great deal of shopping. One day they might be rummaging through a secondhand store and another through antique shops. Those successful in their jobs usually keep detailed lists and records of where items can be found.

Sometimes property people cannot find a prop that will fit the requirements of the scenic director. The prop person will then be responsible for having it built. Construction may be done personally by, or under the supervision of, the property person, depending on the individual's skills. The prop person will handle every aspect of getting props together for use in various scenes. For example, they may mix liquids that resemble alcoholic beverages or prepare the food used during a scene.

Once all the props are gathered, prop people are responsible for moving them to the correct place on stage. If the production has several sets, which many do, the individual must move the props every time there is a scene change. Prop people are also expected to physically hand actors and actresses the props they need during a scene before they walk on-stage.

Other functions of prop people include making sure that all props are clean and in good condition. Individuals may handle this personally or, when necessary, find experts to take care of repairs. Every prop must be checked after a show to make sure that it is ready for the next performance.

Employment Opportunities

The greatest number of employment opportunities for property people can be located in large, culturally active cities such as New York, Los Angeles, Philadelphia, Atlanta, Washington, D.C., and Chicago. Every production has at least one property person; most have more. Opportunities can be located in:

- Broadway plays
- Off-Broadway plays
- Off-off-Broadway plays
- Road company productions
- Dinner theater productions
- Cabaret theater productions
- Regional theater productions
- Stock productions
- Ballet productions
- Operatic productions

Earnings

Property people working in unionized settings will have minimum earnings set by the International Alliance of Theatrical Stage Employees (IATSE). Individuals working in nonunionized settings will have to negotiate their own salaries.

Earnings for property people range from approximately $250 to $1,200 per week or more. Variables affecting earnings include the experience, skills, responsibilities, and professional reputation of the individual as well as the type of production and theater he or she works in.

Advancement Opportunities

There are a number of paths property people can take towards career advancement. Individuals may advance their careers by locating similar positions with more prestigious productions. Some property people advance to become property masters. Others find more secure work handling similar responsibilities in television and film.

Education and Training

On-the-job training is necessary in this field. This can be obtained through internships, apprenticeships, or working in local community theaters.

While a college degree is not required in this position, many feel that it is useful. A formal education can often provide experience, opportunities, and credibility that others may lack. Those opting for college should consider a degree in theater arts.

Experience and Qualifications

An aspiring property person should get as much experience as possible working in theaters, especially backstage. This can be acquired at school and community theater productions as well as by participating in apprenticeship and internship programs.

The ability to use tools effectively will make individuals more marketable. A working knowledge of theater and stagecraft is helpful.

For Additional Information: The IATSE, as well as many local arts councils, can provide additional information on careers in this field.

TIPS

- Look for classes, workshops, and seminars related to all facets of the theater. These are useful in honing skills, learning your craft, and making important contacts.
- Become involved in school and community theater groups. Volunteer to build sets and scenery, locate props, etc. This will give you valuable hands-on training.
- Contact the Actors' Equity Association (AEA) to get lists of resident, stock, dinner, Broadway, off-Broadway, and off-off Broadway theaters throughout the country. These will provide you with a good source of names and addresses to write to inquiring about internships or job possibilities.
- Contact theaters, production companies, colleges, universities, etc., to find internships, apprenticeships, or training programs in this end of the industry. If

you can't find one in the prop or scenic design department, take anything that is open to get your foot in the door.

- Send your resume to opera and ballet companies and to not-for-profit as well as commercial theaters. Include a short cover letter inquiring about openings in the prop or scenic design departments.
- Consider a part-time or summer job in a dinner theater, summer stock theater, resident theater, etc., to learn new skills, obtain experience, and make contacts.

MAKEUP ARTIST—THEATER

Job Description: Create the appearances of actors and actresses through the utilization of makeup.

Earnings: $13,000–$75,000+

Recommended Education and Training: Requirements vary from formal training to hands-on training or practical experience.

Skills and Personality Traits: Cosmetology, theatrical makeup, and hairstyling skills; creativity.

Experience and Qualifications: Experience working with theatrical makeup.

Job Description and Responsibilities

Theatrical makeup artists create the appearances of actors and actresses through the utilization of makeup. Responsibilities of the individual will depend on the specific production.

In its simplest form, theatrical makeup is used to help convey to the audience the personality of the characters in a production. Makeup is often required for the audience to clearly view the faces and expressions of actors and actresses on-stage. When applying makeup, the makeup artist must keep the size and lighting of the theater and the stage in mind. Theatrical makeup is heavier and more pronounced than street makeup.

Makeup artists may be expected to totally change the look and appearance of a character. Skillfully applied, makeup can age characters or make them appear ugly or attractive.

Knowledge of theater, lighting, staging, and costume design is imperative to success in this job. Before they get started, makeup artists must determine the type of "look" the director wants the character to have. Individuals will work closely with the costume designers and the production hairstylists to try and capture that look. To accomplish this, makeup artists coordinate colors of makeup with the character's costumes, hair color, and style. Makeup artists may also function as production hairstylists as well.

Depending on the complexity of the makeup, makeup artists must usually get to the theater a couple of hours before each performance in order to apply the required makeup to the actors and actresses. They may also be required to reapply makeup, make changes, or do touch-ups between acts during the performance.

Employment Opportunities

The greatest number of employment opportunities for theatrical makeup artists can be located in large, culturally active cities such as New York, Los Angeles, Philadelphia, Washington, D.C., Chicago, and Atlanta. Individuals often work in cosmetology or hairstyling in other industries outside theater to enhance employment opportunities and income. Theatrical makeup artists can work in a variety of employment situations including:

- Broadway plays
- Off-Broadway plays
- Off-off-Broadway plays
- Road company productions
- Dinner theater productions
- Cabaret theater productions
- Regional theater productions
- Stock productions
- Ballet productions
- Operatic productions

Earnings

Earnings for makeup artists working in theater vary greatly. Approximate annual earnings range from $13,000 to $75,000 or more. Factors affecting earnings include the experience, expertise, responsibilities, and professional reputation of the makeup artist. Other variables include the specific type of production an individual is working on as well as the amount of work he or she does annually.

Makeup artists working in Broadway productions are required to be members of the International Alliance of Theatrical Stage Employees (IATSE) local. This union negotiates and sets the minimum earnings for makeup artists. Minimum weekly earnings for makeup artists working in Broadway productions are approximately $700. Makeup artists with proven track records and good professional reputations can earn considerably more.

Individuals working in nonunionized settings may be paid weekly salaries or by the performance. Makeup artists in these situations may earn between $300 and $700 per week or more.

Advancement Opportunities

Makeup artists who develop a good professional reputation can advance their careers by working on larger, more prestigious productions. The top rung of the career ladder in theater for a makeup artist is handling the makeup for a successful Broadway show.

Many individuals also advance their careers by becoming makeup artists for television or film artists.

Education and Training

Educational and training requirements vary from on-the-job training to a college degree with a major in theater arts. Individuals opting for a college degree will find classes in theatrical makeup, hairstyling, staging, lighting, and costuming useful. Workshops and seminars in theatrical makeup techniques will also be beneficial.

On-the-job training may be obtained through internships and apprenticeships. Some individuals may also attend a licensed school of cosmetology and hairstyling in order to obtain basic training.

Experience and Qualifications

Makeup artists striving to work in theater need experience working in theatrical situations. This can be obtained through volunteer work in local community theaters or school productions, or by internships or apprenticeships.

Many areas of the country require makeup artists to hold state licenses. These are usually obtained by attending a licensed school of cosmetology and hairstyling as well as by taking and passing a written and practical state exam.

Makeup artists working in unionized theater situations may also be required to be members of the IATSE. To become a member, one must pass a practical exam illustrating competence with various theatrical makeup techniques.

For Additional Information: Aspiring makeup artists may obtain additional information regarding careers in this field by contacting IATSE and the National Hairdressers and Cosmetologists Association (NHCA).

TIPS

- Classes, seminars, and workshops in theatrical makeup, lighting, staging, and costume design will be useful in honing skills and making necessary contacts.
- Offer to do the makeup for the cast of your school or local community theater production. This will provide good hands-on experience.
- Try to locate a theatrical makeup artist who will let you apprentice with him or her. The best way to learn is by watching and working with a pro.
- Internships are another method of learning this craft. Contact community, regional, dinner, and stock theaters to inquire about internship programs.
- Contact the Actors' Equity Association (AEA) to get lists of resident, stock, dinner, Broadway, off-Broadway, and off-off-Broadway theaters throughout the

country. These will provide you with a good source of names and addresses to write to inquiring about internships or job possibilities.

- Contact the local affiliate of the IATSE and the NHCA to find out about membership requirements. These groups offer useful seminars, conferences, and information, as well as provide professional guidance and support to their members.
- Attend a variety of theatrical productions, operas, and ballets to study the makeup and appearance of actors and actresses. The Broadway production of *Cats,* for example, is a wonderful illustration of how makeup is used to create characters.
- Visit the library to find books on theatrical makeup. Learn as much as you can by reading about the subject.

PRODUCTION HAIRSTYLIST—THEATER

Job Description: Create hairstyles for cast members in theatrical productions.

Earnings: $14,000–$75,000+

Recommended Education and Training: Requirements vary from classes in theatrical hairstyling to completion of a cosmetology/hairstyling course.

Skills and Personality Traits: Hairstyling skills; knowledge of theatrical lighting and makeup.

Experience and Qualifications: Experience in hairstyling and theatrical hairstyling; licensing may be required in some states.

Job Description and Responsibilities

Production hairstylists are responsible for styling the hair, wigs, hairpieces, and facial hair of actors and actresses in a theatrical production. Individuals work with costume designers and makeup artists to develop the "look" of the characters in the play. Production hairstylists often work in the preproduction period, developing and designing the perfect hairstyles for each character.

Responsibilities of production hairstylists will vary depending on the specific production. The first thing the individual must do is determine how the director wants the character to appear. If the production is set in a different time frame, the hairstylist must research the specific era to determine what styles were in vogue. Production hairstylists are expected to wash, cut, color, and style the hair of the actors and actresses in the production so that it fits the specific role. The hairstylist is also responsible for styling the mustaches, sideburns, and beards of performers.

Individuals must be adept at working with wigs, since these items are frequently used in theatrical productions. Wigs may be purchased from a wig shop or may be custom-designed by a wigmaker. After the initial fitting at the wig shop, production hairstylists are required to cut and style the wigs.

Production hairstylists may have additional responsibilities including determining what equipment and supplies will be needed, as well as ordering and purchasing them. In some cases, the production hairstylist may also be the makeup artist.

Depending on the specific production, stylists may be expected to style all the cast members' hair or just the hair of one or two of the show's stars.

Employment Opportunities

Production hairstylists can work either full- or part-time. The largest number of employment opportunities will be found in culturally active cities. Individuals may find work in the following settings:

- Broadway plays
- Off-Broadway plays
- Off-off-Broadway plays
- Road company productions
- Dinner theater productions
- Cabaret theater productions
- Regional theater productions
- Stock productions
- Ballet productions
- Operatic productions

Earnings

Annual earnings for production hairstylists can range from $14,000 to $75,000 or more. Factors affecting earnings include the experience, responsibilities, and professional reputation of the hairstylist as well as the specific production. Individuals may be paid by the performance or by the week, depending on the production.

Those working in Broadway productions will have minimum salaries negotiated and set by the International Alliance of Theatrical Stage Employees (IATSE) local for Makeup Artists and Hairstylists. Minimum weekly salaries are over $700. Individuals working in other situations must negotiate their own salaries. Earnings can range from $250 to $700 per week or more.

Advancement Opportunities

Production hairstylists who make people feel comfortable and are skilled at their job will be requested on a more consistent basis. Individuals can advance their careers by doing similar work in more prestigious productions. The highest level of career advancement in theatrical hairstyling is working for a star in a successful Broadway production.

Some hairstylists climb the career ladder by locating similar jobs in television, commercials, or films.

Education and Training

Education requirements vary for production hairstylists, depending on the state in which they work and the specific production. Some positions do not require any education or training and just want the hairstylist to know how to work with hair and wigs. Others require graduation from a licensed school of cosmetology and hairstyling.

Another option is a college degree with a major in theater arts. Courses, seminars, and workshops in theatrical hairstyling and makeup are helpful in learning and honing skills.

Experience and Qualifications

Many states require production hairstylists, like all hairstylists, to hold a state cosmetology or hairstyling license. This is acquired by attending and graduating a licensed school of cosmetology and hairstyling. Individuals must also pass a written and practical state exam.

A practical exam is also required in order to become a member of the IATSE. During this examination, the applicant must illustrate hair techniques and stylings for different time eras.

Experience in theatrical hairstyling can often be obtained through internships or apprenticeships. A thorough understanding of lighting, staging, and costume design is needed.

For Additional Information: Individuals interested in becoming a production hairstyist can learn more about careers in this field by contacting the IATSE and the National Hairdressers and Cosmetologists Association (NHCA).

TIPS

- Contact theaters, production companies, colleges, universities, etc., to find internship, apprenticeship, or training programs in this area of the industry.
- Contact the Actors' Equity Association (AEA) to get lists of resident, stock, dinner, Broadway, off-Broadway, and off-off-Broadway theaters throughout the country. These will provide you with a good source of names and addresses to write to inquiring about internships or job possibilities.
- You can get experience in theatrical hairstyling by volunteering to be the production hairstylist for your school and community theater productions.
- If you can, become a licensed hairstylist. It may not always be necessary to

have a license, but it makes you more marketable. You also will have the ability to earn extra income in between theater jobs.

• Learn as much as you can by taking classes, seminars, and workshops in theatrical hairstyling and makeup.

• Go to the library to find books that have pictures of hairstyles from different eras.

LIGHTING PERSON—THEATER

Job Description: Work lightboard during performances.

Earnings: $300–$1,500+ weekly.

Recommended Education and Training: No formal educational requirements; training through internships, apprenticeships, or hands-on training as assistant.

Skills and Personality Traits: Electronics skills; communications skills; reliability.

Experience and Qualifications: Experience working with lighting.

Job Description and Responsibilities

Lighting people handle the lighting requirements during the performance of a theatrical production. Individuals follow instructions that have been developed and documented by the production's lighting designer.

The documentation describes exactly what the lighting person must do in order to duplicate the lighting effects that were developed by the lighting designer. Various lights, filters, and colors will be utilized to create an array of lighting effects.

The lighting person is responsible for working the lighting control board during the performance. The individual follows a schedule that contains cues provided by the lighting designer. These cues alert the lighting person to which lights are to be used at specific times during the performance.

Other responsibilities of the lighting person include making sure that all lights and equipment are working properly. This is usually done an hour before each performance. The individual is expected to check that all lights are in the proper positions, bulbs are ready, and filters are in place.

The lighting person must be at each performance. In smaller productions, the lighting person might also be the lighting designer.

Employment Opportunities

Almost every theatrical production employs one or more lighting people. Large, culturally active cities such as New York, Los Angeles, Atlanta, Washington, D.C., Philadelphia, and Chicago offer the most employment opportunities. Positions may be located in all types of theatrical productions including:

- Broadway plays
- Off-Broadway plays
- Off-off-Broadway plays
- Road company productions
- Dinner theater productions
- Cabaret theater productions
- Regional theater productions
- Stock productions
- Ballet productions
- Operatic productions

Earnings

Earnings for lighting people can range from $300 to $1,500 or more weekly. Depending on the specific situation, those working in unionized settings will have their minimum weekly earnings negotiated and set by either the International Alliance of Theatrical Stage Employees (IATSE), the United Scenic Artists (USA) union, or the International Brotherhood of Electrical Workers (IBEW). Individuals working in nonunionized settings negotiate their own salaries.

Factors affecting earnings include the specific production the lighting person is working with, the type of theater, and its geographic location. Other factors include the specific responsibilities, experience, and professional reputation of the individual.

Advancement Opportunities

Lighting people can advance their careers in several ways. Individuals may either locate a greater number of jobs, do similar work for more prestigious productions, or advance to become lighting designers.

Education and Training

There are no educational requirements necessary to become a lighting person. However, many individuals interested in a career in theater opt for a college degree. This is often because the education, opportunities, and experience obtained in school may not be available elsewhere.

Training is necessary and can be acquired through apprenticeships, internships, or working as an assistant to other lighting people or lighting designers. Other valuable training includes classes in lighting and electronics. These are often offered in school or through vocational programs.

Experience and Qualifications

Experience in lighting is necessary in this job. As noted previously, experience can be obtained through apprenticeships, internships, or working as an assistant to a lighting person or designer. Other experience may be acquired by observing and assisting lighting people as they handle lights in school or community theater productions.

A background in theater is helpful. Knowledge of lighting, staging, and electronics is imperative. The lighting person must have the ability to follow written directions developed by the lighting designer.

For Additional Information: Individuals interested in becoming a lighting person can obtain additional information by contacting the IATSE, the USA union, and the IBEW.

TIPS

- Consider breaking into the field on a small scale. Get experience working the lights in a local club.
- You might also consider a short stint handling lights for a local rock group.
- Another way to obtain experience is by volunteering to handle the lighting for school and community theater productions.
- Contact the various unions to learn about membership requirements. Join as soon as you can.
- Look for and take workshops and seminars in theatrical lighting, staging, etc. These are helpful in honing old skills, learning new ones, and making valuable contacts.
- Learn as much as you can from as many sources as possible. Watch other lighting people, take classes, read books, etc. The more you know, the more marketable you will be.
- If you know someone who already has this job, tell him or her about your aspirations and ask for help. Most people are flattered and are willing to be a mentor.
- Contact theaters, production companies, colleges, universities, etc., to find internship, apprenticeship, or training programs in this area of the industry.
- Contact the Actors' Equity Association (AEA) to get lists of resident, stock, dinner, Broadway, off-Broadway, and off-off-Broadway theaters throughout the country. These will provide you with a good source of names and addresses to write to inquiring about internships or job possibilities.
- Jobs may be advertised in trade papers or local newspapers. Look under headings such as "Theater," "Lighting," "Lighting Person," and "Lightman/woman."

SOUND PERSON—THEATER

• •

Job Description: Handle sound requirements during a theatrical production.

Earnings: $250–$1,250+ weekly.

Recommended Education and Training: Training in electronics and sound technology through apprenticeships, internships, vocational school, college, or on-the-job training.

Skills and Personality Traits: Skilled using soundboard; ability to follow written instructions; electronics skills.

Experience and Qualifications: Experience working with sound; apprenticeship may be required.

Job Description and Responsibilities

Every theater is different. The size of a theater can range from small to very large, and acoustics can vary accordingly. The major responsibility of a sound person working in a theatrical situation is to make sure that the entire audience can hear everything that is said on-stage.

Before the production opens, a sound designer develops methods for handling the sound requirements for the particular theater. The designer documents the sound information in writing. The sound person follows the instructions of the sound designer. The individual will know exactly what equipment to use, where it should be placed in the theater, and how and when to adjust the controls on the soundboard.

The sound person makes sure that the voices of the actors and actresses are audible without them having to scream or speak too loudly. This is done by mixing together and blending the sounds from all microphone sources. Sound is then amplified to the correct decibel level.

During the production the sound person works at a control or soundboard, adjusting the sound until it is perfect. This board can be situated in either the house (where the audience is) or the stage (where the actors and actresses are). The sound person will follow the schedule written by the sound designer. The individual will also get cues from the stage manager when it is time to use special sound effects or play recorded music.

The sound person is expected to place microphones and speakers in locations and angles that will create the best sound. The individual may personally place the sound equipment or may oversee the installation by others. Before each performance, the sound person is responsible for performing sound checks to make sure everything is working and the sound is ready.

Employment Opportunities

Almost every theatrical production requires the services of one or more sound people. Large, culturally active cities such as New York, Los Angeles, Washington, D.C., Atlanta, Philadelphia, and Chicago offer the most employment opportunities. Positions may be located in all types of theatrical productions including:

- Broadway plays
- Off-Broadway plays
- Off-off Broadway plays
- Road company productions
- Dinner theater productions
- Cabaret theater productions
- Regional theater productions
- Stock productions
- Ballet productions
- Operatic productions

Earnings

Sound people working in the theater earn approximately $250 to $1,250 or more weekly. Earnings vary depending on a number of factors including the size, type, and location of the theater that the sound person is working in as well as his or her responsibilities and experience.

Sound people working in unionized theaters will have their minimum weekly earnings negotiated and set by the International Alliance of Theatrical Stage Employees (IATSE).

Advancement Opportunities

There are a number of advancement opportunities available to sound people working in the theater. Individuals may climb the career ladder by handling sound requirements for larger, more prestigious productions or by becoming sound designers.

Education and Training

There is no single method of training for sound people. Some individuals get a college degree or background in theater arts and take classes in sound, electronics, and staging. Others attend vocational schools. A great many people acquire on-the-job training through internships, apprenticeships, or working as an assistant to another sound person or sound designer.

Experience and Qualifications

Individuals who will be working in unionized theaters must be members of the IATSE. To become a member, sound people are required to go through an apprenticeship program. Other sound people may acquire experience through interning, handling sound for school or community theater groups, or working soundboards in nightclubs.

A thorough working knowledge of electronics, the soundboard, and other sound equipment is required. The ability to follow written and verbal instructions is imperative.

For Additional Information: Individuals interested in a career as a theatrical sound person should contact the IATSE for additional information.

TIPS

- There are a number of ways to get the required experience in this field. Consider a short stint handling the sound at a local club.
- Many local rock groups and other musical acts require the services of a sound person. Put an ad in the local paper advertising your expertise.
- Positions in this field may be advertised in the trades or newspaper classified sections. Look under headings such as "Sound," "Theater," "Sound Person," and "Soundman/woman."
- Contact the IATSE and inquire about membership requirements. If you want to be a professional in this field, you should be a member.
- Offer to handle the sound requirements for your school and local community theater productions.
- Look for classes, seminars, and workshops in sound, electronics, theater, staging, and related areas. You will learn valuable new skills, hone the ones you already have, and make important contacts.
- Learn as much as you can from as many sources as possible. Take classes, read books, watch other sound people, etc. The more knowledge you obtain, the more marketable you will be.
- If you know someone who already works in this field, tell him or her about your aspirations and ask for assistance. Most people are flattered and willing to help in your career quest.
- Contact theaters, production companies, colleges, universities, and the union to find internship, apprenticeship, or training programs in this area of the industry.
- Contact the Actors' Equity Association (AEA) to get lists of resident, stock, dinner, Broadway, off-Broadway, and off-off-Broadway theaters throughout the country. These will provide you with a good source of names and addresses to write to inquiring about internships or job possibilities.

DRESSER—THEATER

Job Description: Assist actors and actresses into costume; keep costumes in good condition.

Earnings: $23,000–$75,000+

Recommended Education and Training: No formal educational requirements.

Skills and Personality Traits: Sewing skills; laundering skills; personable.

Experience and Qualifications: Experience in some facet of theater.

Job Description and Responsibilities

Dressers working in theater are responsible for keeping costumes used in productions in perfect condition. Individuals perform a multitude of responsibilities. They may also be referred to in theatrical circles as wardrobe dressers, personal dressers, or day workers.

Dressers maintain the costumes that the actors and actresses wear during the performance. These include everything from the main costume to accessories, jewelry, and undergarments. Before and after every performance, the dresser will check each piece of the costume. If anything is in need of repair, the individual will be expected to fix it. This includes repairing hems, seams, buttons, or sequins that have come loose. Major problems are reported to the wardrobe supervisor. The dresser must follow up to make sure that repairs are done and that the costume is ready for the next performance.

Dressers are required to spot clean or launder costumes as well as bring other soiled items to laundromats or dry cleaners to be taken care of.

Another major function of the dresser is to help the actors and actresses into their costumes. The dresser will usually be familiar with the script so that he or she knows when the actor or actress has to change costumes. Changing must often be done quickly. To accomplish this, the dresser will lay out clothing in the order in which it will be put on and used in the different acts of the play.

Day workers are dressers who work during the day before a performance. Other dressers may work immediately before and during the performance. Many individuals work both shifts, thereby increasing their earnings.

As dressers often spend a great deal of time with the actors and actresses they are assigned to work with, they often become very close to them. In many situations, stars request certain dressers who have the ability not only to take care of their costuming needs but also make them feel comfortable. These dressers are called personal dressers and may have additional responsibilities, including receiving, tending, and caring for flowers, telegrams, or other gifts the star receives from friends and other well-wishers. In some instances, the personal dresser will also be expected to write thank-you notes. Personal dressers may work with the same star for years in every production in which he or she appears.

Employment Opportunities

The greatest number of employment opportunities will be located in large, culturally active cities hosting many theaters. Individuals may find employment in the following settings:

- Broadway plays
- Off-Broadway plays
- Off-off Broadway plays
- Road company productions
- Dinner theater productions
- Cabaret theater productions
- Regional theater productions
- Stock productions
- Ballet productions
- Operatic productions

Earnings

Earnings for dressers range from $23,000 to $75,000 or more annually for those who are employed on a full-time basis. Earnings depend on the number of weeks individuals work, the type of production and theater that work is performed in, and the specific local affiliation. Other factors affecting earnings include the responsibilities, experience, and professional reputation of the dresser.

Dressers working in unionized situations will have minimum salaries set by the International Alliance of Theatrical Stage Employees (IATSE) local. Dressers may be paid by the week or by the hour. Minimum weekly earnings for an individual working in a Broadway theater are approximately $550, but dressers who are in demand can command and receive more. Individuals working as personal dressers for major stars can have annual earnings of $75,000 or more.

Advancement Opportunities

There are a number of paths towards career advancement for dressers. Advancement in this area is determined not only by the skills of individuals, but by their personalities as well. If dressers have the ability to make actors and actresses feel comfortable, they will be requested on a more frequent basis.

Individuals may climb the career ladder to the position of wardrobe supervisor or become a personal dresser to the star of a production. Dressers may also find advancement opportunities doing similar work in television, commercials, and films.

Education and Training

There are no educational requirements to become a dresser. Individuals must have some type of training in basic sewing, laundering, and pressing. For many, these are basic skills acquired at home. Others may pick up these skills by watching others or go through apprenticeship or internship programs.

Experience and Qualifications

Most dressers have worked in theater in some other capacity prior to their current positions. Many were actors or actresses. Others worked in any of various positions behind the scenes.

To be qualified for this job, individuals must have the basic sewing skills necessary to make minor repairs on costumes. Dressers must also be able to launder and press costumes. The ability to get along well with others and make them feel comfortable is essential to success in this job.

For Additional Information: Individuals aspiring to become dressers should contact the IATSE for more information.

TIPS

- Call or write to the IATSE local to find out about membership requirements. If you plan on working in a unionized theater, you must either be a union member or be in the process of becoming one.
- Take classes in basic sewing. The more you are capable of doing, the more marketable you will be.
- Try to locate a mentor in this facet of theater who can help guide your career.
- Get hands-on experience wherever you can. Offer to be the dresser in school plays and local community theater productions.
- A summer or part-time job with a dressmaker or tailor will also provide good experience.
- Contact theaters, production companies, colleges, universities, etc., to find internship, apprenticeship, or training programs in this area of the industry.
- Contact the Actors' Equity Association (AEA) to get lists of resident, stock, dinner, Broadway, off-Broadway, and off-off-Broadway theaters throughout the country. These will provide you with a good source of names and addresses to write to inquiring about internships or job possibilities.
- Look for seminars, courses, and workshops in theater arts, theatrical costuming, and other related subjects. These will be helpful in learning new skills, honing old ones, and making important contacts.

THEATRICAL PRESS AGENT
....

Job Description: Publicize theater productions; develop publicity campaigns.

Earnings: $600–$1,600+ per week.

Recommended Education and Training: Three-year apprenticeship required.

Skills and Personality Traits: Verbal and written communications skills; creative; detail-oriented; aggressive.

Experience and Qualifications: Experience in publicity, promotion, or public relations.

Job Description and Responsibilities

Theatrical press agents handle the publicity for Broadway shows, off-Broadway shows, and regional theater group productions. Publicity is essential to the success of theatrical productions because of the exposure and ticket sales it generates.

Theatrical press agents have varied responsibilities, some of which are tackled prior to the opening and others handled afterward. Theatrical press agents develop publicity campaigns that will help attract audiences and make people aware of the production. To do this, they must create and implement ideas that attract media attention. This may include compiling press kits, preparing biographies, writing press releases, dealing with the media, and arranging interviews and personal appearances for stars of the show.

Media contacts are critical in this job. Individuals must compile media lists, making sure that names, addresses, and fax and phone numbers are accurate. This is important when sending and delivering ideas or calling the media with press releases, opening night invitations, press passes, etc.

Press agents also plan and stage special media events and press conferences that help generate as much publicity and interest in the production as possible. There is a great deal happening in the entertainment world, and there is also a tremendous amount of competition. Theatrical press agents must be creative in developing ideas and angles for feature, entertainment, and assignment editors, reporters, columnists, etc. Successful theatrical press agents explore every possible angle to obtain press coverage.

A great deal of the theatrical press agent's job is centered around the opening night of a show. The individual must schedule and implement opening night parties or other media events that will put the show in the public eye. The day of the opening, the theatrical press agent must call critics and reviewers to make sure they are attending the show. They will also be on hand at the opening to deal with the media, answer questions, and pass out press kits and other information.

Some theatrical press agents work alone. Others have apprentices who work with them, assisting on projects.

Employment Opportunities

Theatrical press agents will find the largest number of employment opportunities in large, culturally active cities. These include:

- New York
- Los Angeles
- Hollywood
- Washington, D.C.
- Chicago
- Philadelphia
- Atlanta

Earnings

It is difficult to determine annual earnings for theatrical press agents. Individuals are usually hired for specific productions. Factors affecting earnings include the number of projects per year that theatrical press agents are hired for, how long each specific production lasts, and the type and size of theater the production is in.

Minimum earnings are negotiated by the Association of Theatrical Press Agents and Managers (ATPAM), an AFL-CIO union. Earnings include a minimum weekly salary plus a percentage for vacation pay, pension, and a specific amount for a welfare fund.

The minimum weekly salary for theatrical press agents working on Broadway shows is approximately $1,600. The salary for those working on off-Broadway productions is determined by the seating capacity of the theater. Individuals handling this job in a small-theater production will earn a minimum of approximately $600 per week. Theatrical press agents that have built up their professional reputation can command and receive weekly salaries that are much higher.

Advancement Opportunities

Theatrical press agents advance their careers by creating a great deal of excitement for the theatrical productions they promote. Individuals may climb the career ladder by finding more prestigious jobs. Those who work in regional theater may handle off-Broadway productions. Theatrical press agents for off-Broadway may advance by publicizing Broadway shows.

Education and Training

In order to become bona fide theatrical press agents, individuals must go through a three-year apprenticeship with a member of ATPAM.

While a college degree is not a requirement, many feel that it is the best course of action. Good choices for majors and other courses include public relations, communications, writing, English, advertising, marketing, business, and theater arts.

Experience and Qualifications

As noted, individuals must have participated in a three-year apprenticeship. Any experience in publicity, theater, or the entertainment business will also be useful.

Those who are successful in this field should be creative individuals with good verbal and written communications skills.

For Additional Information: To learn more about careers as theatrical press agents contact ATPAM. This organization negotiates minimum earnings for individuals in the field as well as sets standards for the profession. Individuals aspiring to become theatrical press agents might also obtain additional information by contacting the Public Relations Society of America (PRSA).

TIPS

- Get experience handling the publicity and promotion for school, college, or community theater productions.
- To obtain a fuller understanding of the theater industry and to make important contacts, consider getting a summer or part-time job with a local theater company.
- As soon as you decide to get into this career, contact ATPAM. They will provide professional guidance.
- You must go through an apprenticeship program to become a theatrical press agent. Call or write ATPAM to locate a branch office near you and to get specifics on apprenticeship applications.
- In order to get into the required apprenticeship program, you must also have a sponsoring member from ATPAM. If you do not know anyone in the union, ATPAM will help you find a sponsor to work with.
- Do not take the easy way out. Learn as much as you can from your sponsor. He or she will teach you the techniques of the profession so that one day, you will have the ability and the experience to do it on your own.
- Look for seminars, workshops, and classes in publicity, promotion, writing, and theater. These will help you hone your skills as well as give you additional opportunities to make contacts.

CHAPTER 8
· · · · · · · · · · · · ·

Careers in Orchestras, Opera, and Ballet

Operas, ballets, and orchestras provide a musical channel for stories about life, real and fancied. The stories are conveyed to the listening and viewing audience from the dancers and actors on the stage or from the instruments of the musicians in the orchestra pit.

The path for developing and transmitting the story from actor, dancer, or musician to audience requires a great many talented support professionals.

An orchestra or a ballet or theater company requires funding to maintain its operation. Money comes from the sale of show tickets and other sources, but generally, there is a funding shortfall. To remedy this situation and to keep the company operational, a director of fund-raising and development is a necessary part of the support system.

There is also a need for professionals with the talent for guiding the business operations of an opera, ballet, or orchestra to insure that the company remains in the black. Other people may be required to handle the many managerial details that go into the makeup of an opera, ballet, or musical company. Consider, for example, the need for a music librarian or a public relations director to insure that the company is consistently kept in the public's eye.

Each of these support functions represents a career opportunity for those interested in becoming an integral part of this entertainment field. This support contributes to the success of the individual entertainer as well as to the company in which he or she is appearing.

Space restrictions limit discussing all possible opportunities. Careers covered in this section include:

Business Manager—Orchestra/
Opera or Ballet Company/
Not-For-Profit Theater
Director of Fund-raising & Devel-
opment—Orchestra/Opera or
Ballet Company/Not-for-Profit
Theater/Performing Arts
Center

Director of Educational Activi-
ties—Performing Arts
Company
Public Relations Director—Or-
chestra/Opera or Ballet
Company
Music Librarian—Orchestra/
Opera or Ballet Company

Individuals interested in careers in this field should also review entries in Chapter 7, "Careers in Theater," for related opportunities.

BUSINESS MANAGER—ORCHESTRA/OPERA OR BALLET COMPANY/NOT-FOR-PROFIT THEATER

· ·

Job Description: Supervise financial affairs of an orchestra or of an opera or ballet company.

Earnings: $16,000–$60,000+

Recommended Education and Training: Bachelor's degree preferred, but not required for all positions.

Skills and Personality Traits: Accounting and bookkeeping skills; ability to work well with numbers; accurate.

Experience and Qualifications: Bookkeeping and/or accounting experience useful.

Job Description and Responsibilities

The business manager of an orchestra or of an opera or ballet company supervises the organization's financial affairs. The individual's responsibilities can differ depending on how large the organization is and how many people are working in the department. Duties include keeping records of all expenditures, checking bills for accuracy, issuing checks for payment of bills, and preparing payroll in accordance with union and governmental regulations.

Another important responsibility of the business manager is working with the company's managing director to develop an annual budget. Once the budget is approved, the individual will be responsible for keeping the operating costs of the company within its allocations.

Other duties of the business manager of an orchestra or of a ballet or opera company include working with the director of development. In this capacity, the individual will be responsible for keeping tabs on all monies raised through fund-raising efforts.

The business manager will often be required to bid out projects to find the most economical prices on items that are needed by the company, such as travel accommodations when on tour and various other expenditures.

Depending on the specific company, the business manager can be responsible to the company's board of directors or its general manager.

Employment Opportunities

The greatest number of opportunities for those interested in this type of career will be found in large, culturally active cities such as New York, Washington, D.C., Boston, Philadelphia, and Chicago. Smaller, less culturally active areas with fewer companies will have less opportunity for this type of position. Depending on the size and budget of the specific company, this position may be full- or part-time. Individuals may find opportunities in the following settings:

- Orchestras
- Opera companies
- Ballet companies
- Not-for-profit theaters
- Not-for-profit performing arts centers

Earnings

The range of annual earnings for business managers in these situations can run from $16,000 to $60,000 or more for a full-time position. Variables affecting earnings include the size, prestige, classification, and budget of the company as well as the responsibilities, experience, and qualifications of the business manager.

Salaries of part-time business managers will be dependent on the time required to handle the job as well as the responsibilities of the individual.

Advancement Opportunities

There are a number of methods of advancement for business managers working in this field. The most common is to locate a similar position with a larger or more prestigious company. Another method of climbing the career ladder is to find a position as a company manager.

Education and Training

While a bachelor's degree is not mandatory for all positions, it is usually preferred. Good majors to choose when preparing for this type of job include accounting, business, finance, theater arts, and arts management.

Experience and Qualifications

Any type of bookkeeping or accounting experience will be useful in obtaining a job in this field. Experience working in any type of not-for-profit, arts-related company will also be helpful. A basic knowledge of the workings of orchestras or of ballet or opera companies is beneficial.

Business managers should be comfortable working with numbers and should be able to do so accurately. The abilities to set up a payroll, develop a budget, and negotiate are also necessary.

For Additional Information: Associations and organizations that can provide additional information about this job include the American Symphony Orchestra League (ASOL), the Ballet Theater Foundation (BTF), Opera America (OA), the Central Opera Service (COS), the Metropolitan Opera Association (MOA), and the National Opera Association (NOA). Information may also be obtained by contacting local arts councils.

TIPS

- Send your resume and a short cover letter to all the orchestras and to all the opera and ballet companies in the geographic area you are considering. You might also send them to performing arts companies, not-for-profit theater groups, and the like.
- It is often easier to break into this field by locating a job in a small local or regional company. After you get some experience under your belt, you can move up to a larger or more prestigious company.
- Jobs are often advertised in the newspaper classified sections. Look under headings such as "Symphony," "Orchestra," "Opera Company," "Ballet Company," "Business Manager," "Arts," "Music," "Dance," and "Business."
- Positions may also be advertised in organization, union, and/or trade association newsletters. These jobs are most often vacant at the end of one season or at the beginning of a new one.
- Contact trade associations, local arts councils, orchestras, and opera, ballet, theater, or performing arts companies to inquire about internships.

DIRECTOR OF FUND-RAISING & DEVELOPMENT— ORCHESTRA/OPERA OR BALLET COMPANY/NOT-FOR-PROFIT THEATER/PERFORMING ARTS CENTER

Job Description: Raise money for ballet or opera company, orchestra, not-for-profit theater, or performing arts center; develop, coordinate and implement fund-raising programs.

Earnings: $12,000–$80,000+

Recommended Education and Training: College degree preferred, but not required for all positions.

Skills and Personality Traits: Organization; communications skills; sales ability; aggressiveness; creativity; interpersonal skills; detail-oriented.

Experience and Qualifications: Experience in fund-raising, development, or public relations necessary; knowledge of grant writing; understanding of performing arts industry.

Job Description and Responsibilities

The director of development for an orchestra, a ballet or opera company, a not-for-profit theater, or a performing arts center has an extremely important and difficult task to accomplish. These organizations are run under a not-for-profit status. In order to remain solvent under their not-for-profit status, these organizations require the financial support generated by a combination of grants, ticket sales, contributions, and donations.

The director of development is in charge of the fund-raising department. Depending on the specific company, this means that the director will supervise and oversee other employees and volunteers working on fund-raising activities.

Responsibilities include the development, coordination, and implementation of strategies for raising monies. These strategies can include capital campaigns, annual donating activities, and deferred donating opportunities.

As part of this function, the director of development will formulate a variety of special events designed to provide financial support for the company. These can include cocktail parties, galas, luncheons, fashion shows, auctions, and dinner dances. Other fund-raising efforts might include the development and implementation of century clubs, direct mail campaigns, telephone fund raisers, and telethons. The director of development may also be expected to find ways to increase attendance at the company's performances, thereby increasing ticket sales.

A great deal of coordination is necessary in order to fulfill this position effectively. The director of development will work closely with the company manager and with other departments, including public relations, subscription and ticket services, and educational activities.

One aspect of the job encompasses locating and cultivating potential supporters. This may be accomplished through the use of questionnaires, research, and surveys. The director of development will also be expected to have a strong and positive public image. Many potential donors are uncovered when the director of development of an organization gives speeches or appears at functions on behalf of the organization.

Volunteers are often recruited from the community to help with fund-raising efforts. In addition to helping recruit volunteers, the director of development must find ways to effectively utilize the services of these people.

There is a great deal of writing involved in this job: speeches, press releases, reports, fliers, newsletters, letters and other fund-raising literature, brochures, pamphlets, and booklets. Another important writing function includes the development of proposals for grants as well as requests for corporate gifts, monies from foundations, and endowments for the arts.

Other responsibilities of the director of development can include attending functions, meetings, and special events on behalf of the company; keeping accurate records on fund-raising and donor activities; and acting as a liaison between the company and donors as well as between the company management and the board of directors.

The director of development can be responsible to either the company manager, managing director, and/or the board of directors, depending on the structure of the company.

Employment Opportunities

The director of development is integral to the success of not-for-profit companies. Enthusiastic individuals who are dedicated and who can produce results are always in demand. More opportunities can usually be located in large, culturally active cities with a greater number of performing arts companies. Individuals can work in a variety of settings including:

- Orchestras
- Opera companies
- Ballet companies
- Not-for-profit theaters
- Not-for-profit performing arts centers

Earnings

The director of development for a not-for-profit performing arts company can have annual earnings ranging between $12,000 and $80,000 or more. Variables include the individual's experience, responsibilities, and track record for raising funds. Other factors affecting salary include the size, budget, geographic location, and prestige of the specific company. Generally, individuals with less experience or those working in smaller, lesser-known companies will have earnings at the bottom quarter of the pay scale. Directors of development for large, prestigious companies located in major cities will have earnings in the top half of the pay scale.

Advancement Opportunities

The most common path for career advancement for the director of development of a not-for-profit performing arts company is locating a similar position in a larger or more prestigious organization. This will result in increased earnings and responsibilities.

Education and Training

The minimum educational requirement for a position in this field is a high school diploma. However, educational requirements vary from job to job. Some organizations require or prefer a college background or degree.

The best educational preparation for the job as well as for career advancement is a bachelor's degree. There are a number of options for majors that will be helpful in pursuing careers in this field. They include marketing, public relations, arts administration, arts management, and liberal arts.

Courses and seminars in fund-raising, development, grant proposal writing, public relations, marketing, and arts administration will also be valuable.

Experience and Qualifications

Experience in fund-raising, development, marketing, or public relations is necessary in order to obtain this job. To gain experience, many work as assistants or in other staff positions in the fund-raising and development office of a not-for-profit organization. While it is helpful to work in the performing arts, experience with any type of not-for-profit organization is usually acceptable.

Individuals should have the ability to write well, communicate articulately, handle a great many details, and deal well with people on all levels. Creativity, aggressiveness, and an understanding and dedication to the performing arts are required for success in this field.

For Additional Information: Associations and organizations that can provide additional information about careers in this area include the Associated Council of the Arts (ACA), the Public Relations Society of America (PRSA), the American Symphony Orchestra League (ASOL), the Ballet Theater Foundation (BTF), Opera America (OA), the National Opera Association (NOA), the Metropolitan Opera Association (MOA), Central Opera Services (COS), and local arts councils.

TIPS

- Openings may be advertised in trade papers, journals, and newsletters from trade associations and arts councils.
- Positions are also advertised in the newspaper classified section under headings such as "Development," "Fund-Raising," "Director of Development," "Director of Fund-Raising," "Performing Arts," "Opera," "Ballet," "Symphony," "Orchestra," "Theater," "Performing Arts Center," and "Not-For-Profit."
- There is a high turnover in this field. Contact orchestras, ballet and opera companies, not-for-profit theater groups, and performing arts centers. Send your resume with a short cover letter inquiring about openings. Ask that your resume be kept on file if there are no current openings.
- Locate an internship program in the development office of a not-for-profit performing arts organization. These are often available through the companies themselves or through colleges, universities, or trade associations.
- Look for seminars and workshops in development, fund-raising, grant proposal writing, and other topics of interest in the performing arts field. These offer valuable information and training as well as provide an environment to make important contacts.

DIRECTOR OF EDUCATIONAL ACTIVITIES— PERFORMING ARTS COMPANY

Job Description: Develop concert series, ballets, or theatrical productions for young people; plan and coordinate activities related to the performing arts for youth.

Earnings: $12,000–$35,000+

Recommended Education and Training: Bachelor's degree preferred, but not always required.

Skills and Personality Traits: Written and verbal communications skills; knowledge of performing arts; administrative and business skills; ability to get along well with young people.

Experience and Qualifications: Experience working in some facet of performing arts.

Job Description and Responsibilities

The director of educational activities for an orchestra, an opera or ballet company, or a not-for-profit theater has an important job. The individual is responsible for developing and coordinating activities related to the performing arts for young people in the community.

The director of educational activities works with supervisors, administrators, department heads, and teachers in the schools surrounding the company's base of operations. The individual meets and talks to these people to see what types of programs are needed. The director of educational activities will then develop and offer various programs to the schools. These might include presenting special performances in the schools such as plays, ballets, or concerts.

In addition to bringing events into the schools, the director of educational activities might also work with others in the company to develop a concert, dance, or theater series aimed at young people in the venue where the company normally performs. Wherever events take place, the director attempts to develop extra and related activities. These could include question-and-answer sessions, competitions, etc. The purpose of these activities and events is to interest young people in the performing arts and help them learn more about them.

The individual is expected to counsel students interested in careers in the performing arts, develop pamphlets and booklets related to careers in the specific field, orchestrate career days for those interested in performing arts, and cultivate scholarships and internship programs related to the specific performing arts company.

As part of the job, the director of educational activities will develop and recommend a price structure for student tickets. They will also be required to make sure that students, parents, and others are aware of the scheduled special events and activities. This may be accomplished through the use of press releases, brochures, posters, and mailings.

Individuals with a deep interest in the performing arts as well as in young people will find this job especially fulfilling.

Employment Opportunities

Generally, this type of position is only located in not-for-profit performing arts companies. Individuals will find the greatest number of opportunities in large, culturally active cities.

The position of director of educational activities can be located in the following areas:

- Orchestras
- Ballet companies
- Opera companies

- Symphonies
- Not-for-profit theater groups
- Modern dance companies

Earnings

Earnings for the director of educational activities can range from $12,000 to $35,000 annually. Factors affecting earnings include the size, location, prestige, and budget of the performing arts company. Other variables include the responsibilities and experience of the individual.

Advancement Opportunities

There are a number of paths to career advancement for the director of activities in a not-for-profit performing arts company. Individuals may locate similar positions in larger, more prestigious companies, resulting in increased responsibilities and earnings. Other advancement opportunities include taking positions as the director of either the public relations, fund-raising, or development department for similar types of organizations.

Education and Training

While there are some positions requiring only a high school diploma, a four-year college degree is recommended. Individuals might opt for majors in theater arts, public relations, communications, education, or liberal arts.

Experience and Qualifications

Experience working in some facet of performing arts will be useful. This may be acquired through internships or through summer or part-time jobs. Many individuals obtain experience and a basic knowledge of the performing arts industry by working in a different capacity in theater or the other arts as administrative, public relations, or fund-raising assistants. Other individuals have been dancers, musicians, or actors/actresses.

To be successful in this field, individuals must have the ability to get along well with young people and understand their needs. Excellent written and verbal communications skills are mandatory. The director of educational activities should have a thorough understanding of the specific performing art they are working with, whether it be theater, opera, ballet, or orchestra.

For Additional Information: There are a number of organizations that will provide additional information on a career in this field. These include the Metropolitan Opera Association (MOA), Ballet Theater Foundation (BTF), the Public Relations Society of America (PRSA), the American Symphony Orchestra League (ASOL), the Central Opera Service (COS), the Metropolitan Opera Guild (MOG), Opera America (OA), and the National Opera Association (NOA).

TIPS

- Contact the personnel director of orchestras and of opera, ballet, and theatrical companies. Send your resume and a cover letter inquiring about openings. Request that your resume be kept on file.

- Positions in this field may be advertised in the newspaper classified or display sections. Look under headings such as "Director of Educational Activities," "Symphony," "Orchestra," "Opera," "Ballet," "Education," "Theater," "Education Director," "Not-For-Profit," "Dance," and "Music."
- Openings may also be advertised or listed in trade association newsletters, arts council newsletters, and the trades.
- Contact the trade associations and organizations in the field you are interested in and find out about the membership requirements. Join if you can.
- Look for internships with orchestras or with opera, ballet, or not-for-profit theater companies. Internships will provide you with an opportunity to learn new skills, obtain experience, and make valuable contacts.
- Take classes, seminars, and workshops offered by ballet, opera, and theatrical companies, orchestras, arts councils, colleges, schools, etc., on arts management and administration, public relations, writing, theater, performing arts, and the like. These will be useful for their educational value, and they will provide another opportunity to make important contacts.

PUBLIC RELATIONS DIRECTOR—ORCHESTRA/ OPERA OR BALLET COMPANY

Job Description: Plan and implement publicity, promotion, and public relations for orchestra or for opera or ballet company.

Earnings: $16,000–$60,000+

Recommended Education and Training: Bachelor's degree preferred.

Skills and Personality Traits: Excellent verbal and written communications skills; creativity; interest in performing arts.

Experience and Qualifications: Experience in public relations, promotion, publicity, or journalism. Knowledge of performing arts industry helpful.

Job Description and Responsibilities

The public relations director of an orchestra or of an opera or ballet company is responsible for handling the publicity, promotions, and public relations needs of the company. The individual will have varied responsibilities depending on the specific company and the size of the department.

The director will supervise other employees on staff in the department. This includes delegating responsibilities and overseeing all that occurs in the department. In smaller companies with lower budgets, the public relations director may be the only employee in the department.

Operas, ballets, and orchestras do not have performances continuously throughout the year. Instead, each has a specific season during which it performs. It is the function of the public relations director to plan, develop, and implement a public relations campaign geared towards ensuring that the community is aware of the company's performances, special activities, news, and events.

This may be accomplished in a number of ways. The p.r. director must see to it that press releases regarding all company events are written and sent to area media regularly. These include scheduled performances, holiday shows, and the appointment of new or guest dancers, soloists, musicians, conductors, etc. The individual may also develop media kits, book interviews, arrange for feature stories, schedule press conferences, and coordinate opening-night parties. Depending on the structure of the company, the public relations department might be directly responsible for the advertising needs or may work with an advertising agency to advertise performances and other events.

The individual will often be expected to develop a company newsletter or other written materials. In addition to acting as the company spokesperson, the p.r. director will also frequently be asked to speak to various groups about the company and its goals, efforts, and achievements.

The public relations director will also handle the publicity and promotion for events of other departments in the company. These might include the fund-raising and development departments, educational activities department, and the like.

The public relations director might be responsible to the company manager, managing director, or board of directors.

Employment Opportunities

The good news about this position is that most companies employ at least one person in their public relations department. However, smaller companies may hire only a part-timer. While opportunities are available throughout the country, individuals interested in working in this field will find the most opportunities in large, culturally active cities hosting a greater number of orchestras and ballet and opera companies. These cities include:.

- New York
- Boston
- Memphis
- Philadelphia
- Washington, D.C.

- Phoenix
- Pittsburgh
- Atlanta
- Los Angeles

Earnings

Earnings for p.r. directors working in orchestras and in opera and ballet companies vary depending on their experience and responsibilities, as well as on the size, location, budget, and prestige of the specific company.

Annual salaries for full-time p.r. directors in this field start at approximately $16,000. Those with a great deal of experience working in large, prestigious companies with big budgets can earn $60,000 or more annually. Individuals working in mid-sized regional companies can earn between $20,000 and $35,000 a year.

Advancement Opportunities

One road to advancement is to locate a similar position in a larger or more prestigious company, resulting in increased responsibilities and earnings. Another is for the individual to become a director of development for an orchestra or for a ballet or opera company.

Others find higher paying public relations jobs in an unrelated field. Some aspire to open up their own p.r. or publicity firms or to become press agents for entertainers.

Education and Training

Educational and training requirements vary depending on the specific job. Smaller companies may not require any college; however, a bachelor's degree is always preferred. Larger, more prestigious companies will usually demand a four-year degree. Good choices for majors include public relations, journalism, communications, English, liberal arts, theater arts management, and music business and administration.

Courses, seminars, and workshops in writing, communications, public relations, publicity, etc., are always useful.

Experience and Qualifications

Most public relations directors of orchestras or of ballet or opera companies have had some type of public relations or promotional experience prior to obtaining their positions. Experience may include working in a similar position in a related or unrelated field, or working as an assistant to a p.r. director in an orchestra or in an opera or ballet company. Other experience may be obtained by working in the marketing or development department of a company, or by working as a journalist in any field.

There is a great deal of writing and speaking necessary in this position. To be successful, individuals should have excellent written as well as verbal communications skills.

For Additional Information: Trade associations and organizations will provide professional guidance and support as well as offer useful seminars and workshops. One of the most prominent organizations in the public relations field is the Public

Relations Society of America (PRSA). Other groups that can provide additional information include the American Symphony Orchestra League (ASOL), the Central Opera Service (COS), the Metropolitan Opera Guild (MOG), the National Opera Association (NOA), Opera America (OA), the Metropolitan Opera Association (MOA), and the Ballet Theater Foundation (BTF).

TIPS

- Job openings are often advertised in the newspaper classified section under such headings as "Public Relations," "P.R.," "Publicity," "Marketing," "Development," "Orchestra," "Opera," "Ballet," "Symphony," "Entertainment," "Performing Arts," "Music," and "Dance."
- Look for openings in Sunday newspapers from culturally active cities. Many libraries receive newspapers from other cities. Specialty newsstands may also be able to get newspapers from various locations. If you can't locate newspapers from other areas in either your library or newsstand, consider a short-term subscription to a few papers from cities that host orchestras and opera and ballet companies.
- Positions may also be listed or advertised in trade papers, association newsletters, and regional arts council publications.
- You might find it easier to enter the field by locating a job with a small or regional company.
- There are publications listing the names and addresses of orchestras and opera and ballet companies throughout the country. Send your resume with a cover letter inquiring about openings to the personnel directors of some of these companies.
- An internship with a company is an excellent way to obtain experience and to make contacts in the field.

MUSIC LIBRARIAN—
ORCHESTRA/OPERA OR BALLET COMPANY

Job Description: Catalog and order music for company; hand out and collect sheet music prior to and following rehearsals and performances.

Earnings: $13,000–$35,000

Recommended Education and Training: Bachelor's degree in library science, music history, theory, and/or theater; graduate degree may be preferred.

Skills and Personality Traits: Communications skills; organized; ability to copy music scores.

Experience and Qualifications: Internship or experience as music librarian assistant; comprehensive knowledge of music; enjoyment of music and other performing arts.

Job Description and Responsibilities

The job of a music librarian in an orchestra or in an opera or ballet company is similar to that of a librarian working in a traditional library. However, librarians in this area deal mainly with music instead of books. Individuals choosing this field are able to combine a career as a librarian with one in music and the other performing arts.

Music librarians have a number of responsibilities. One of the main functions of this individual is keeping track of and cataloging the company's printed sheet music. When the conductor determines new music is required, the music librarian is in charge of either buying or renting it. In the event that the music is rented, the music librarian will also be responsible for making sure that it is returned when it is no longer needed.

In this capacity, the music librarian will work closely with the conductor. Part of this job includes copying music markings and parts for the various section members. Another duty is to contact any guest conductors or soloists to determine their musical requirements.

The music librarian is expected to attend every rehearsal and performance of the company, whether they are at their home base or on tour. During these periods, the music librarian is responsible for handing out music to section members prior to each rehearsal and performance as well as collecting it after the performance is completed.

This is an ideal career for those who have the skills of a librarian and enjoy music, the performing arts, and travel.

Employment Opportunities

The greatest number of jobs in this area are in large, culturally active cities hosting opera and ballet companies, symphonies, and orchestras. Individuals may locate positions with:

- Major or regional orchestras or symphonies
- Major or regional ballet or other dance companies
- Major or regional opera companies
- Theatrical companies producing musicals

Earnings

Earnings for music librarians working for orchestras or for opera or ballet companies can range from approximately $13,000 to $35,000 annually. Salaries are dependent on a number of variables including the size, prestige, and geographic location of the specific company as well as the individual responsibilities and experience of the music librarian.

Advancement Opportunities

Advancement opportunities for music librarians seeking to stay with an orchestra or with an opera or ballet company are limited to locating a similar position in a larger or more prestigious company. Individuals may also locate positions at universities or colleges.

Education and Training

A minimum of a bachelor's degree is usually mandatory for music librarians. A dual major in music and library sciences may be the best choice in order to be prepared for available jobs. Other appropriate majors include music theory, history, and theater. Many companies may prefer or require a graduate degree in either library science or music.

Training in copying musical parts and scores is imperative for this position.

Experience and Qualifications

Experience is usually required for this job in larger orchestras and opera and ballet companies. This can be obtained by locating a position as an assistant to a company's music librarian. Other useful experience can be procured by working as a music librarian at a radio station. Smaller companies may not require any experience and may hire people right out of college.

Music librarians working in orchestras or in opera or ballet companies need the ability to copy the conductor's markings on scores neatly and legibly. They should also have an interest in music and be extremely well organized and detail-oriented. Strong interpersonal skills are necessary.

For Additional Information: There are a number of associations and organizations that can provide additional information to those interested in a career in this field. These include the American Symphony Orchestra League (ASOL), the Central Opera Services (COS), the Metropolitan Opera Association (MOA), the Metropolitan Opera Guild (MOG), the National Opera Association (NOA), the Ballet Theater Foundation (BTF), Opera America (OA), the American Library Association (ALA), and the Special Libraries Association (SLA).

TIPS

- Openings are often listed in association and organization trade journals.
- Positions may be advertised in the newspaper classified or display sections under the headings of "Music Librarian," "Orchestra," "Opera," "Ballet," "Music," "Performing Arts," "Theater Arts," and "Library." If you are seeking a position in a geographic area other than the one you live in, get a short-term subscription to a newspaper from that area.

- Contact trade associations and organizations to locate an internship.
- Send your resume and a short cover letter inquiring about openings as assistant to the company's music librarian to major orchestras and ballet and opera companies.
- You might also send your resume to smaller regional companies and inquire if they have an opening for a music librarian.

CHAPTER 9

· · · · · · · · · · · ·

Careers on the Road

In order for recording artists to tout their music to fans live and in concert, they must go on tour. Orchestras, operas, and ballets also often hit the road in order to bring their unique performances to people throughout the country and the world. Theatrical road companies and circuses earn their keep by touring.

While television and radio appearances can bring the message to the most people at one time, nothing beats personal appearances for building a following. Some entertainers tour only when they have to, finding road life an experience that they would rather not tolerate on a consistent basis. Others have a genuine love for the road and stay on tour for a majority of the year.

There are numerous individuals whose job it is to support the entertainers and make their lives easier while touring. These people go on tour to handle details so that all the entertainers have to do is perform.

Road jobs require an array of people with different talents, skills, educational backgrounds, training, and experience levels. There is a wide variety of opportunities on the road, depending on how elaborate the tour. There may be tour coordinators, tour managers, roadies, electricians, lighting and sound technicians, bodyguards, security, publicists, advance people, accountants, set designers, backup singers and musicians, secretaries, accountants, drivers, and/or chefs.

A tremendous love of the road and of the entertainment business is necessary for a career in this field. Most people who are successful in this area are happiest on the road. They find that the opportunities to travel, meet new people, and work in the entertainment industry make for an exciting career.

Space restrictions limit discussing all possible opportunities. Careers covered in this section are:

Tour Coordinator   Tour Publicist
Road Manager   Advance Person

Individuals interested in careers in theater should also review entries in other sections of this book. Chapter 1, "Careers in the Business End of the Industry," and Chapter 8, "Careers in Orchestras, Opera, and Ballet," both discuss related opportunities.

TOUR COORDINATOR

Job Description: Coordinate all facets of entertainer's tour.

Earnings: $30,000–$95,000+

Recommended Education and Training: No formal educational requirements.

Skills and Personality Traits: Coordination skills; detail-oriented; organization; supervisory skills; responsibility; ability to travel.

Experience and Qualifications: Experience traveling with entertainers as road manager or tour publicist.

Job Description and Responsibilities

Tours are an important part of many entertainers' careers. Many musical groups spend months on the road touring throughout the country and sometimes the world. Touring can be grueling. Tour coordinators are responsible for coordinating and overseeing all facets of an entertainer's or artist's tour.

Individuals in this position work closely with the act's support team, planning the tour day-by-day. This is done to use time as effectively as possible. Tour coordinators must make sure that everyone on the tour is where they are supposed to be, and to do this with the least amount of effort.

Tour coordinators begin working before the tours begin. They meet with the act's management, agents, and publicists to determine the times and dates of personal appearances, concerts, media appearances, interviews, etc. All times, dates, and events should be prescheduled.

Tour coordinators determine the best transportation and routing to use for entertainers and equipment. These might include private buses, chartered jets, limos, cars, trains, and planes. Sometimes, some of the featured entertainers might travel by plane, while back-up singers and musicians tour by private bus or car. Equipment may be transported by truck or van.

The tour coordinator may make reservations for travel and accommodations personally, or work with a travel agent on this task. Arrangements must be made as economically and efficiently as possible. It is imperative that acts not get so bogged down traveling that they arrive too exhausted to perform well.

Tour coordinators work closely with other tour personnel, especially the road manager. In some cases, the tour coordinator is the road manager. The individual must also keep in constant contact with the artist's management, agents, and publicists. The tour coordinator will be responsible for supervising and overseeing the jobs of the others on the tour.

As crises will occur on the road, the individual must have the ability to handle them effectively. Whether it is a bus breaking down, a plane arriving late, a musician quitting, or an entertainer becoming emotionally and physically exhausted from touring, the tour coordinator must find a solution quickly and calmly.

Tours average 6 to 12 weeks, although there are both shorter and much longer ones scheduled. The tour coordinator is on call every hour of every day that the tour is on the road. The individual must deal with the entertainers, the entourage, management, agents, and even the artists' families and friends.

For those who love the road and the entertainment industry, this is a perfect job.

Employment Opportunities

Tour coordinators may work on staff at record companies or management companies. They may also work for entertainers personally or may freelance. Employment opportunities include:

- Record companies
- Management companies
- Recording artists
- Entertainers
- Musical shows
- Dance companies
- Orchestras
- Booking agencies
- Theatrical road companies

Earnings

Tour coordinators are on call 24 hours a day when on tour. As a result, salaries are usually high. Annual earnings of tour coordinators range from approximately $30,000 to $95,000 or more. In addition to a salary, individuals may receive a bonus at the end of a tour. As a rule, expenses are reimbursed or picked up by the tour.

As acts do not usually go on the road 52 weeks a year, tour coordinators may be paid a reduced fee when the act they work with is not touring.

Advancement Opportunities

There are a number of paths tour coordinators may take toward career advancement. Some individuals locate positions with better-known or more prestigious acts. Others are retained by major tours. Some move into the field of personal management or booking.

Education and Training

There are no formal educational requirements to become a tour coordinator. Many individuals, however, do have a college background or degree. Courses that may prove useful include bookkeeping, accounting, psychology, publicity, and promotion. Additional classes, seminars, or workshops in the music or travel industry are helpful.

Experience and Qualifications

Tour coordinators usually have some type of experience working on the road or in the travel industry, or handling publicity. Some began their careers as roadies or road managers. Others worked as touring or traveling performers themselves. Individuals may also have worked as travel agents, travel escorts, or publicists in the entertainment industry.

It is imperative that tour coordinators not only enjoy traveling, but love the road as well. This job is not a vacation. There is a tremendous amount of organization and responsibility associated with the job. Individuals must have the ability to handle crises quickly and effectively with a cool head. Supervisory skills are a necessity.

For Additional Information: The Touring Entertainment Industry Association (TEIA) can provide additional information about careers on the road.

TIPS

- Consider breaking into the field on a small scale to obtain experience. Offer to handle the details of a small tour for a regional act.
- Positions are often advertised or listed in the trades.
- Not everyone enjoys going on the road. Therefore, companies may not have people on staff to handle this position. Send your resume and a cover letter to record companies, booking agencies, and management companies. Follow up periodically to inquire about new tours going out.
- Consider placing a small ad in one or more of the trades advertising your specialty.
- Contacts in the music industry help. If you have any, use them. Tell everyone about your career aspirations.
- The more skills you have, the more marketable you are. If you can handle publicity on the road in addition to tour work, you will be even more valuable. If you are good at making travel arrangements, be sure to list those skills on your resume.

ROAD MANAGER

. . . .

Job Description: Coordinate activities of entertainers and whereabouts of equipment to make sure they arrive at performances as scheduled; supervise equipment, sound and light requirements, and personnel on the road; handle problems and situations that occur while act is traveling and touring.

Earnings: $15,000–$100,000+

Recommended Education and Training: No formal educational requirements.

Skills and Personality Traits: Supervisory skills; interpersonal skills; communications skills; reliability; dependability; enjoys traveling.

Experience and Qualifications: Experience as roadie or equipment manager helpful, but not always required; free to travel.

Job Description and Responsibilities

A road manager plays an extremely important role in the success of a tour. The main function of the individual is to make sure that the entertainers as well as all the equipment needed for a performance get where they are going when they are supposed to be there. To accomplish this, the road manager has a myriad of responsibilities and duties.

Responsibilities vary widely depending on the type of entertainer or act that is on tour, as well as its popularity, prestige, and success. Road managers are expected to handle problems that can occur on the road regarding transportation, accommodations, meals, sound, lights, and equipment.

Road managers touring with acts that are just starting out and are short of personnel may have to handle the functions of a roadie. In these instances, the individual may have to physically move equipment, or set up and run sound and lights. The road manager will act in a supervisory capacity when the entertainer has roadies and sound and light personnel. He or she will also be expected to deal with unions that handle these functions in unionized theaters, halls, and clubs.

The road manager must make sure that the entertainers, support personnel, and any necessary equipment get to rehearsals, performances, public appearances, interviews, and television and radio appearances on time. Each hall and club has different acoustic dimensions. In order to insure the quality of the performance, the road manager will supervise the setup of equipment and instruments, as well as supervise sound and light checks for each performance.

Another duty of the road manager is to act as a liaison between an act and either the promoter or club manager. The individual will make sure that all contractual responsibilities have been fulfilled. In this capacity, the road manager will be responsible for collecting monies owed to the act. Other financial functions of the road manager include handling the payroll of support personnel and employees while on tour; paying bills for accommodations, travel, meals, and other miscellaneous expenses; keeping track of receipts; and accounting for all monies.

If there is no tour coordinator, the road manager will have additional responsibilities. These might include supervising all tour personnel, reporting on a regular basis to the management company, and coordinating every facet of a tour.

Road managers do not work an eight-hour day. While on tour, they are always on call to handle problems that can and often do crop up. Calmness, even in the eye of a storm, is essential for success in this type of job.

Employment Opportunities

Road managers may work with any type of musical group or solo performer. They can also work with a variety of other types of entertainers who tour. These include:

- Comedians
- Magicians
- Dance troupes
- Ventriloquists
- Speakers

Earnings

Earnings of road managers can vary greatly, depending on a number of factors. These include the type of act that the road manager is working with as well as the act's popularity. Other variables include the responsibilities and experience of the road manager and the number of weeks per year that the individual works.

Road managers, as a rule, are paid weekly salaries. They may also be paid a flat fee for working a tour. In some cases, individuals may be paid a specific salary when an act is touring and receive a lower salary when the act is not on the road. Using this system, the act maintains the individual on salary. This is usually done when acts stay on the road for a good portion of the year. In other situations, when the road manager is not on salary, the individual may work for a number of different acts during the year.

Salaries can start at approximately $300 per week for those with little experience or those working for less popular acts. Road managers working with popular solo acts outside of the music business will have earnings ranging between $500 and $1,000 per week. Earnings can go up to $2,000 or more per week for road managers working with a top recording group.

It should be noted that road managers have most of their expenses paid while on the road. Expenses usually include accommodations and transportation and may or may not include meals. They may be paid directly by the act or the road manager may receive a per diem.

Advancement Opportunities

Road managers can advance their careers in a number of ways. Individuals may find similar positions with more successful, prestigious, and popular acts. This will result in increased responsibilities and higher salaries. Road managers may also climb the career ladder by locating a position as a tour coordinator. Some road managers get "off the road" completely and go into another facet of the entertainment business, such as management or booking.

Education and Training

There is no formal education or training that can help a person become a road manager. Individuals who have become successful in this field come from all different walks of life. Some have college degrees, others don't even have high school diplomas.

Experience and Qualifications

Experience requirements for road managers vary depending on the specific act. Up-and-coming acts often ask family members or friends to fill this position. Some road managers began as roadies, carrying equipment. Others handled the sounds or light for a group, theater, or hall. Every road manager has a different story on how he or she entered the business. Many road managers started out as entertainers themselves.

Individuals must possess certain traits to be successful at this type of career. These include reliability, dependability, and responsibility. Road managers must be patient, personable, and easy to get along with. Good interpersonal skills are mandatory. Life on the road is difficult and tempers are often short. The ability to be a problem-solver is imperative. Things do go wrong, and the road manager must find a way to make them right quickly, without panicking.

For Additional Information: Individuals interested in becoming road managers may contact the Touring Entertainment Industry Association (TEIA). This organization provides support and guidance for those in the industry.

TIPS

- Send a short cover letter inquiring about openings along with your resume to record companies, entertainment and music public relations companies, management firms, booking agencies, and lighting and sound companies.
- Make sure that when you develop a resume for this type of job or apply for a position, you include all experience that may be relevant. Can you handle sound? Do you know about lighting? Have you worked in publicity? The more talents you have, the more you will be in demand.

- When you do apply for positions, or send out resumes, check back often. Many people find that once they have been on the road for a while, they really don't like the lifestyle.
- Place an advertisement in either the classified or display section of entertainment trades.
- Positions may also be advertised in the trades. However, even if no position is advertised, the trades can be very helpful. Read through them on a consistent basis to find out what tours are being planned. Follow up and contact the personal manager, management firm, or booking agency handling the act.
- If you have contacts, use them. Tell everyone what you do (or would like to do).
- Start out by working with an up-and-coming act. This will give you good experience, help you make contacts, and get your foot in the door.

TOUR PUBLICIST
· ·

Job Description: Go on tour with entertainers to publicize the tour, artist, and records.

Earnings: $20,000–$90,000+

Recommended Education and Training: Bachelor's degree in public relations, communications, journalism, music business, music merchandising, or related field.

Skills and Personality Traits: Written and verbal communications skills; interpersonal skills; creative; aggressive; enjoys traveling.

Experience and Qualifications: Prior publicity or public relations experience.

Job Description and Responsibilities

Tour publicists have a very exciting job. In this position, individuals go on tour with recording artists and other entertainers and handle their publicity requirements.

There is a great deal of work involving publicity that must be done prior to a tour. Media interviews must be arranged with television, radio, newspapers, and magazines in cities where concerts are scheduled to take place. Press kits must be compiled and news releases must be developed. Press conferences and parties will be scheduled and other details worked out. Depending on the specific situation, either the tour publicist or another staff publicist will handle these functions.

After the pre-tour arrangements have been concluded, the major responsibilities of the tour publicist begin as soon as the artist leaves on tour. The tour publicist is expected to be part of the tour's entourage. In this position, the individual is responsible for every aspect of publicity that involves the act.

The tour publicist arranges for interviews, photography sessions, press conferences, television, radio, and other personal appearances, etc., that have not been scheduled prior to the tour. As the tour publicist, the individual must accompany the artists to all appearances, concerts, interviews, etc. The publicist may meet with show producers and talent coordinators before interviews to talk about the direction of the interview.

Tour publicists take advantage of every opportunity that can provide positive media exposure. On the road, unexpected situations can occur at any time that could generate positive publicity, such as sold-out performances or other superstars attending shows of the touring artist. In other circumstances, difficulties, dilemmas, and problems may occur while an artist is on tour that may cause negative publicity. The tour publicist will attempt to block negative publicity and turn it into a positive situation or event.

Other functions of the tour publicist include issuing and determining who should get press and backstage passes. They will also be responsible for scheduling and approving interviews and photo shoots before and/or after appearances. Tour publicists try to keep all of the media, as well as the tour's sponsors, happy. Often, the publicist will arrange private parties and special interviews, and present merchandising gifts to media people.

The tour publicist keeps in constant contact with the artist's management firm and recording label. In this way, management is aware of how the tour is going and can let the tour publicist know if there are any additional duties that must be handled.

The days often seem to be endless in this job. However, for individuals who enjoy traveling, love to be around entertainers, and are qualified to handle publicity, the job of a tour publicist is an ideal vocation.

Employment Opportunities

Tour publicists can either work as freelance independents or be on staff in a number of different entertainment situations. Touring rock-and-roll and country acts are the best possibilities. Other employment opportunities include:

- Recording artists
- Recording companies
- Entertainment managers or management firms
- Entertainment-oriented publicity firms
- Entertainment-oriented public relations firms

Earnings

Tour publicists are usually paid more than home-based publicists because they must travel for long periods of time with the artist on tour. Annual earnings for tour publicists working with established acts are between $40,000 and $90,000 or more. Those working with lesser-known acts will earn considerably less, sometimes starting at $20,000 annually.

Experienced tour publicists with proven track records can demand and receive $1,800 or more per week for specific tours. Factors affecting earnings include the type of employer and the specific act that will be publicized, as well as the experience, professional reputation, and responsibilities of the publicist.

Tour publicists employed by a recording company or by a publicity or public relations firm are usually paid a weekly salary plus a stipend to cover personal expenses on the road. All travel expenses are covered by either the act or its management firm. Individuals working as independent tour publicists may either receive a weekly or monthly fee plus expenses. There are some tour publicists who are paid by the tour.

Advancement Opportunities

Tour publicists can take a number of different paths to advance their careers. As individuals prove themselves, they may be assigned more prestigious acts and tours. They might also be offered the position of tour coordinator or tour manager. Many tour publicists employed by recording companies or by publicity or public relations firms strike out on their own and become independent tour publicists or tour coordinators.

Education and Training

Tour publicists, like others working in publicity, should have a minimum of a bachelor's degree. Good choices for majors include public relations, communications, journalism, English, music merchandising, music business, and liberal arts.

Seminars, workshops, and classes relating to publicity, writing, entertainment, and the music industry will also be useful.

Experience and Qualifications

Tour publicists have usually had some experience handling publicity. Most are familiar with the workings of the entertainment business.

Individuals in this field must have the ability to work under a great deal of stress and pressure. While all publicity jobs can be stressful, the tour publicist is often working in unfamiliar surroundings. The road is often a difficult place to write press releases, come up with interesting angles, and develop new stories.

For Additional Information: Additional information regarding publicity careers can be obtained by contacting the Public Relations Society of America (PRSA). The Touring Entertainment Industry Association (TEIA) can also provide information on touring positions.

TIPS

- Consider breaking into the field on a small scale. Offer to handle tour publicity for an up-and-coming act on tour regionally.
- The more qualified you are, the more marketable you will be. Learn as much as you can from seminars, workshops, and classes about publicity and the entertainment business. Read books about entertainers who made it big.
- Read the trades. They often discuss plans for tours of various artists. Contact the management firm of the act and inquire about a tour publicist position.
- Openings for tour publicists may also be advertised in the trades.
- Place a small ad in one or more of the music and other entertainment trades advertising your specialty.
- Try to locate an internship in the publicity department of a record company or entertainment-oriented public relations or publicity firm. While you probably will not go on tour, you will obtain valuable experience as well as make important contacts.
- Send your resume and a short cover letter inquiring about tour publicist positions to record companies, management firms, and music- and entertainment-oriented publicity and public relations firms.
- If you can't find a job as a tour publicist, look for a home-based publicist position at an entertainment public relations firm or recording label. Once you get your foot in the door, discuss traveling with your supervisors. While many people working in a company might want a job touring, many are not in the position to travel for any length of time.

ADVANCE PERSON

• •

Job Description: Go on road and arrive before artist, entertainer, or act to prepare for concert, event, or production; make sure details are taken care of.

Earnings: $20,000–$38,000+

Recommended Education and Training: No formal educational requirements.

Skills and Personality Traits: Detail-oriented; responsible; freedom to travel.

Experience and Qualifications: Experience requirements vary.

Job Description and Responsibilities

Advance people are responsible for going on the road before a scheduled production, concert, or event takes place to make sure that all details are taken care of and everything is ready for the artist or group. Individuals in this position usually arrive and leave before an act and its entourage arrive. Advance people work closely with the artist's management team, tour coordinator, road manager, public relations representative, and/or press agent.

Advance people have a great many varied duties and responsibilities, depending on the specific job. They may be responsible for checking transportation options in cities where appearances are taking place, measuring mileage between performance cities, and checking routing. This information is relayed to the tour coordinator so that estimated timing and transportation can be arranged.

Advance people go to each city in which performances are planned and check to see that everything is in order so that the show can go on without a hitch. Individuals may physically bring flyers and posters with them to put up, or they may just check that those sent ahead have been posted. Advance people also may be responsible for delivering press passes issued by the public relations firm, publicist, or management team. They also deliver promotional material, records, CDs, etc., to promoters, media, and fan clubs in the appearance cities.

In some situations, the advance person will be expected to check acoustics of halls or arenas where performances will take place. Similarly, the individual may make diagrams of entrances, exits, etc., so that the road manager can arrange the most efficient way to move an act into and out of a concert venue.

Much of this job involves talking to others to make sure that they have taken care of their responsibilities. Individuals may be expected to talk to media, fan clubs, radio and television station personnel, hall or arena managers, and event promoters on behalf of the management team, to be certain that everything is ready, all details have been taken care of, and everything is coordinated.

Advance work is a good job for people who have an interest in the entertainment industry, enjoy traveling, and don't mind working alone a great deal of the time. They must have the ability to structure a day efficiently in order to get all required tasks accomplished. Although they usually leave before a performance, they get the satisfaction of knowing that they helped make each appearance successful.

Employment Opportunities

Positions are usually found in cities where major management and booking agencies are located, such as New York, Nashville, and Los Angeles. This does not mean that these are the only areas in which to find jobs in this field; it just means that they offer more opportunities. Individuals may work for a variety of different types of clients. These include:

- Touring recording groups
- Dance companies
- Orchestras
- Opera companies
- Theatrical road company productions
- Circuses
- Television shows that go on the road

Earnings

Earnings for advance people working on a fairly consistent basis range from approximately $20,000 to $38,000 or more annually. Weekly salaries start at $400 per week for people with little or no experience. Individuals also receive a per diem or reimbursement for travel expenses.

Advance people on staff with companies may be compensated in the same manner whether or not they are on the road. Other individuals may be paid one amount for time spent on the road and a reduced amount when not traveling.

Advancement Opportunities

There are a number of paths for career advancement in this field, depending on the direction the individual wants to pursue. Advance people may find more prestigious acts to work for, resulting in increased earnings. They may also go on to become road managers or tour coordinators.

Education and Training

There are no formal educational requirements or training necessary to become an advance person. There are advance people with high school diplomas and those who hold college degrees. Those who start their careers as advance people in hopes of moving into better road positions may want to consider college.

Experience and Qualifications

Experience requirements vary for this position. For many, this is an entry-level job. Others have held prior positions as roadies.

A major qualification and necessity for this job is a valid driver's license. Individuals must have the ability to work on their own, be detail-oriented, and enjoy traveling.

For Additional Information: Contact the Touring Entertainment Industry Association (TEIA) for more information about this type of career.

TIPS

- Get experience handling details by volunteering with school and local community theater, music, or dance groups.
- Other valuable experience might include working for a travel agent, a travel escort, roadie, etc.
- Make sure your resume mentions everything that could possibly be applicable to this type of career.

- Have business cards printed indicating what you do and give them to everybody in the entertainment industry.
- This job is easier to get if you have a lot of contacts in the industry. Tell everyone from musicians to actors to agents what you want to do.
- Place a small ad in the trades advertising your availability.
- Send your resume with a short cover letter inquiring about positions to major booking agencies, management firms, and performing arts companies. Request that your resume be kept on file. Follow up often.

CHAPTER 10

. . . .

Miscellaneous Careers in the Entertainment Industry

Careers in the entertainment industry cover a broad spectrum. This chapter covers a number of the careers that do not fit into the specific categories set up in this book. Jobs included in this chapter are:

Bodyguard   Reporter—Print
Professional Wrestling Referee   Entertainment Journalist—Print
Ring Announcer

BODYGUARD

. . . .

Job Description: Protect entertainers, sports figures, and other celebrities as well as their families and property.

Earnings: $35,000–$150,000+

Recommended Education and Training: Police training helpful; courses in martial arts, wrestling, boxing, and related areas.

Skills and Personality Traits: Firearms skills; martial arts skills; good judgment; responsible; interpersonal skills; organized; detail-oriented; excellent driving skills.

Experience and Qualifications: Experience in police work, security, or related areas of law enforcement; driver's license/handgun permit required.

Job Description and Responsibilities

The main function of a bodyguard working for a celebrity is to protect the star. Within the scope of the job, bodyguards may also be responsible for the security, safety, and protection of the star's family and property.

As a result of being in the public eye, entertainers, sports figures, and other celebrities have always been at risk of being harmed by overzealous or crazed fans. Every celebrity is a potential target. Over the past few years, there have been a tremendous number of problems relating to the safety and security of celebrities. In addition to the threat of physical injury, many have been the target of death threats and stalkings.

Bodyguards have varied responsibilities depending on the specific situation and celebrity. Some are expected to develop the entire security program necessary to protect their clients at all times. This may include implementing security systems, electronic surveillance equipment, and burglar alarms. The individual may also be responsible for hiring and supervising additional security personnel.

The sole responsibility of some bodyguards is protecting the celebrity when in public. Individuals may be required to drive the celebrity's car or just accompany him or her in a vehicle. In many situations, the bodyguard will be responsible for determining the best way to leave or enter a building as well as for choosing the safest route to travel. They are expected to escort the celebrity every time he or she is in public.

Bodyguards must be in total control of the environment they enter. They need to watch everyone and everything that is happening to make sure that the celebrity is safe. One of the security problems surrounding celebrities is that they are often forced into situations where they must be in large crowds. Another major problem is that it is fairly easy to locate celebrities. Their appearances are usually well-publicized. Bodyguards must constantly be aware of the incidents surrounding the celebrity.

In the event that the bodyguard sees an impending problem, the individual must be ready to act and keep the celebrity safe. In addition to carrying a gun, many bodyguards are trained in some form of martial arts, boxing, wrestling, etc. Their main goal is to protect the celebrity with the least amount of disturbance at any event, program, or activity.

Celebrities may often try to stay away from the public. This attitude, however, is not always in the best interests of a successful career. Many feel that having bodyguards will provide the extra amount of security needed to keep them and their families safe.

Employment Opportunities

Bodyguards can be employed by a private security company or may freelance on their own. While opportunities can be located throughout the country, the greatest number are located in New York City, Los Angeles, Beverly Hills, Hollywood, and Nashville. Bodyguards may be hired by the entertainer, a manager, or an agent. Individuals may be retained by the following:

- Television stars
- Motion picture stars
- Comedians
- Recording stars
- Singers or musicians
- Other entertainers
- Politicians
- Sports figures
- Dignitaries
- Authors

Earnings

Earnings for bodyguards can range greatly, depending on a number of factors. These include the responsibilities, experience, and expertise of the individual as well as the prestige and reputation of the celebrity. Annual earnings are also dependent on the amount of work per year individuals do and whether or not they are employed on staff or freelancing.

Bodyguards may be paid by the project, day, week, or month. Fees range from $100 to $1,000 or more per day. Depending on the clients bodyguards have, successful bodyguards can earn between $35,000 and $150,000-plus per year.

Advancement Opportunities

Bodyguards working in the entertainment industry can advance their careers by locating more prestigious clients to work with. This results in increased earnings. Individuals working for private security firms may also strike out and open their own company.

Education and Training

Training requirements vary for bodyguards. The more training individuals have, the more qualified they will be to handle any situation that may arise.

While it is not always required, one course of action for individuals pursuing a career in this field would be to go through police or other law enforcement training.

There are bodyguards who have not gone through this type of training and have backgrounds and/or training in boxing, wrestling, and/or martial arts. There are also schools located throughout the country geared specifically towards training bodyguards.

Experience and Qualifications

As a rule, the better-known the client is, the more experience is required in this field. Experience is essential for bodyguards working with major superstars. Many obtained it in police work or related areas of law enforcement or crime prevention. Others started out handling security for lesser-known celebrities who have made it big.

Some security firms and clients prefer that the bodyguards working with them are bonded. Bodyguards need to know how to use guns and must have a permit to carry firearms. They should also be skilled in the martial arts. Excellent driving skills are also mandatory. In many states, bodyguards must be licensed.

Bodyguards are generally, but not always, people of large physical stature and in good condition. They must be very responsible, organized, detail-oriented individuals with good judgment. They need to be able to travel with celebrities who are on the road.

For Additional Information: There is no one organization providing information on bodyguards for celebrities. Additional information regarding licensing of bodyguards can be obtained by contacting the specific state's department of licensing. Other information may be available from schools specializing in training bodyguards.

TIPS

- Get as much experience as you can in the security field.
- Generally, when celebrities are looking for a bodyguard, they want to hire the most qualified person or persons. Get the best training you can. Continue taking classes and seminars in security, martial arts, and the like.
- A good way to break into this field is to start out handling the security of lesser-known celebrities.
- Get experience by offering to work with musical acts that go on the road. Similar experience can be obtained working with up-and-coming athletes.
- If you want to freelance in this field, you will either need contacts in the industry or the ability to make them.
- Print business cards with your name, phone number, and specialty. Go to places where entertainers, sports figures, and celebrities will be and hand them out.
- Consider placing advertisements in the trade magazines. You probably will have to run an ad a number of times to attract attention.
- Attend a school that trains bodyguards. Many of these have placement services or know of opportunities.
- Schools can be located in the yellow pages in major cities. Many schools offering training in this field also advertise in weight lifting magazines such as *Powerlifter*.
- Contact agents and managers of entertainers, recording acts, sports figures, and other celebrities. Send a short cover letter and a background sheet about yourself.
- You might also contact private security companies specializing in entertainers and celebrities to see if they have openings. These are generally located in New York City, Los Angeles, and Hollywood.

PROFESSIONAL WRESTLING REFEREE

Job Description: Control wrestling match; call counts and breaks between opponents; work with the wrestlers to provide the audience with a show.

Earnings: $250 per show–$500,000+ annually.

Recommended Education and Training: Training in officiating through other referees and wrestlers.

Skills and Personality Traits: Good showmanship; ability to take punches, blows, and falls; good physical condition.

Experience and Qualifications: Experience officiating matches; small in stature.

Job Description and Responsibilities

Professional wrestling has exploded onto the entertainment scene. While some look at professional wrestling as a sport, it is a far cry from amateur wrestling, and it is viewed by most people for its entertainment value.

Professional wrestling shows are hosted in arenas throughout the country and the world. They are also aired on network television, independent stations, cable, and pay-per-view.

Wrestling matches consist of opponents who chase, hold, confront, and wrestle each other, and an individual who controls the match. The person who officiates is called the referee.

Professional wrestling referees have a number of duties. Individuals inform the timekeeper when to begin and conclude each match. From the start of the match to its finish, the referee will be responsible for officiating in the ring. It is imperative that the individual have a complete knowledge of all the different "counts" that may be used by the participants during a match.

One of the important functions of wrestling referees is giving counts during the match to the wrestlers when there are illegal holds. A count is the number of seconds wrestlers have before they must release the other wrestler from an illegal hold. Counts are also used to determine the conclusion of matches. Another important duty of the referee is calling "breaks" between the wrestlers during the match.

Part of the entertainment value of a wrestling show is watching the antics of the wrestlers. To make the show more exciting, a good referee will become part of the action. The individual may, for example, let the wrestlers chase him out of the ring. A participant may bump into the referee and cause him or her to fall. Professional wrestling referees must be part of the show in order to catch the attention of an audience.

Depending on the league in which the individual works, referees may be expected to travel throughout the country and abroad to officiate.

Employment Opportunities

Professional wrestling referees may work full- or part-time. Some individuals work just a couple of days each month while others work over 250 days per year. Individuals usually start their careers in lower-level wrestling leagues. As they acquire experience, they can move up.

Referees can officiate at live or televised matches for males or females of any size. Wrestling leagues include:

- World Wrestling Federation (WWF)
- World Championship Wrestling (WCW)
- World Championship International World Class Wrestling (WCIWCW)

Earnings

Earnings for professional wrestling referees start at approximately $250 per show. Those who are successful can have very lucrative careers earning up to $500,000 annually. Factors influencing earnings include the experience and popularity of, and the demand for, the referee. Other variables include the type of bout and the level of the league in which the individual is officiating, as well as whether the show is being televised.

Individuals officiating at televised shows put on by major federations such as the WWF will earn the highest salaries.

Advancement Opportunities

Professional wrestling referees can advance their careers in a number of ways. Individuals may climb the career ladder by locating positions officiating for better wrestling leagues, or they may referee nationally televised shows. The top rung of the career ladder in this field is officiating shows for the WWF.

Advancement opportunities are based, to a great extent, on the drive and determination of the individual. Those who take chances in the ring and who are good showpeople will attract the attention of fans and promoters.

Education and Training

There are no formal educational requirements or training to become a professional wrestling referee. Individuals who want to work in this field must learn the skills from other referees and wrestlers.

To do this, aspiring wrestling referees must find skilled professionals willing to teach them. This can often be accomplished by working with referees from small wrestling leagues throughout the country, or by going to gyms where professional wrestlers train.

Professional wrestling referees must learn about the different counts, when to call breaks between opponents, and all rules and regulations utilized during matches. They must also learn how to fall and get knocked around by the wrestlers without becoming seriously injured. Showmanship techniques must also be acquired.

Experience and Qualifications

The higher the level of the wrestling league, the more experience will be required. Referees can obtain experience working with small, lesser-known leagues.

One of the most important qualifications a professional wrestling referee must have is good showmanship. Professional wrestling must be entertaining, and the referee is a part of the show. Referees with small builds are in demand. Promoters want the wrestlers to look as large as possible, so the smaller the referee, the better. Individuals must stay in good physical shape in order to run around the ring, be chased by the wrestlers, and the like.

It is imperative that the referee have a complete knowledge of the rules and regulations of professional wrestling.

For Additional Information: Individuals interested in learning more about becoming a professional wrestling referee should contact the WWF, SWC, or the UWF.

TIPS

- Find a gym where professional wrestlers train. Usually, referees train in the same locations. Talk to the wrestlers and referees to see if you can find someone who will become your mentor and teach you the required skills and techniques.
- You must pay your dues in this business. Start with low-level leagues and work your way up. It usually takes a talented professional wrestling referee around three years to learn the skills and techniques necessary to make it to the major wrestling leagues.
- Read wrestling magazines to keep up on happenings in the industry, locations of live shows, etc. These magazines also have the names and addresses of promoters and wrestling leagues.
- Contact each league (especially the small ones) until you find someone willing to teach you the skills of officiating.
- Attend professional wrestling shows and watch matches on television. This will help you learn the techniques and skills of professionals in the field.
- If you have any contacts in the industry, use them to get your foot in the door. If you don't, try to cultivate some. Consider asking the sportswriter of your local paper for help.

- Contact your state's athletic commission to see if there are any licensing requirements.
- Stay in shape, but be careful not to bulk up too much. Remember, the smaller you look, the bigger the wrestlers will appear.

RING ANNOUNCER

Job Description: Emcee boxing matches; announce pertinent information regarding bouts.

Earnings: $100–$4,000+ per show.

Recommended Education and Training: No formal educational requirements.

Skills and Personality Traits: Pleasant speaking voice; articulate; comfortable speaking in front of people.

Experience and Qualifications: Public speaking experience helpful.

Job Description and Responsibilities

The ring announcer at a boxing match is the master of ceremonies of the event. The main function of the individual is to announce all of the important information about the fight before a bout and after. Some announcers just state the information. Others have unique styles or phrasings that they use before a fight begins. The announcing is done in the center of the ring.

The ring announcer's job begins a few hours before the event. During this time, the individual collects information about each match including the names, weights, and hometowns of the fighters, and which corner they will be fighting out of.

Depending on the event, the ring announcer may introduce any celebrities in the audience, as well as the entertainer who sings the national anthem, the promoter(s), and the sanctioning boxing commissions. The individual will then announce information about the fighters in the particular match. This will include the names, weights, professional records, and hometowns of each opponent.

The ring announcer will also tell the audience the number of rounds the fight is scheduled to last. The individual will announce the fight judges, referee, and the physician on call for the fight.

The individual is responsible for gathering the scorecards from the judges at the end of the bout, announcing how each official judged the fight, reading the decision, and naming the winner. To do all of this, the announcer must know and understand boxing terminology. If the fighter was knocked out or the fight was stopped, the announcer must state the round and the exact time into the round that the fight ended.

Ring announcers usually handle all the bouts of the evening starting with the undercard and continuing through the main event.

Employment Opportunities

While there are people who do this as a full-time job, most freelance on a part-time basis. Individuals may work for one or many different promoters. Positions may be located throughout the country in any city hosting boxing shows. Some of the bigger ones include:

- New York City
- Las Vegas
- Atlantic City
- New Orleans
- Philadelphia

Earnings

Ring announcers usually receive a fee for each match they announce. Fees range from approximately $100 to $4,000 or more per show. Factors affecting fees include the ring announcer's experience, prestige, and popularity as well as the type of match. Ring announcers working at major events that are televised or shown on pay-per-view will usually earn the highest fees.

Advancement Opportunities

Advancement opportunities for ring announcers include securing jobs on a more consistent basis and announcing more prestigious events. Some announcers also go on to become boxing commentators on television.

Education and Training

There are no educational requirements necessary to become a ring announcer.

Experience and Qualifications

Ring announcers need to have experience speaking in front of groups of people prior to stepping into the ring. They should be articulate, well-groomed, and confident individuals.

It is helpful to understand and enjoy boxing. Having contacts in the industry—or the ability to make them—is necessary in order to obtain jobs.

Ring announcers working in states with athletic commissions that govern boxing often need to be licensed. Depending on the state, the individual may only have to fill in an application or may have to pass a written or oral exam.

For Additional Information: Individuals aspiring to become ring announcers should contact state athletic commissions as well as the various sanctioning bodies for more information. These bodies include the World Boxing Association (WBA), the World Boxing Commission (WBC), and the International Boxing Federation (IBF).

TIPS

- It is usually easier to break into the industry on a smaller scale. Try to find jobs with smaller promoters and obtain experience before trying to get jobs with major promoters.
- Get as much experience as possible speaking in front of groups of people.
- Visit boxing gyms in your area on a regular basis. Meet and get to know the fighters, managers, and trainers. They will teach you about boxing. You will also be making valuable contacts.
- Attend live boxing events in addition to watching televised bouts. In this way, you will learn about the various styles of the different announcers.
- Offer to act as the master of ceremonies for an amateur sporting or entertainment event.
- Send your resume, a short cover letter asking for an interview, and a demo tape of your voice to boxing promoters. If no one responds, call. If you still don't get an interview, write a follow-up letter and call again. Be persistent. Names and addresses of promoters can be located in the yellow pages of phone books, in many boxing magazines, or through the state athletic commission. Start with promoters that handle small, local events.

REPORTER—PRINT

Job Description: Write and edit stories, articles and columns; gather information through interviews and investigation.

Earnings: $13,000–$150,000+

Recommended Education and Training: Educational requirements vary from high school diploma to bachelor's degree.

Skills and Personality Traits: Excellent writing skills; communications skills; creativity; good interpersonal skills; computer literacy; ability to deal with deadlines; persistence.

Experience and Qualifications: Experience requirements vary from job to job.

Job Description and Responsibilities

The main function of reporters working in print media is to write factual, informative, and interesting articles for newspapers, magazines, and other print markets.

Responsibilities of reporters depend on the specific job. Some are expected only to investigate and write stories. Others may have additional responsibilities including taking photographs; writing captions and headlines; and editing wire service copy, press releases, etc.

Reporters are generally assigned stories or topics. Individuals gather information by conducting interviews, investigating leads, and reviewing preexisting documents and other information. Reporters may interview people in person or by telephone.

After reporters obtain the correct facts, they must develop an angle to the story. The angle or focus that they use often means the difference between a good story and a great one. Once an angle is decided upon, the reporter must write and rewrite the article until it is polished to perfection. The story is then given to an editor for review.

The reporter must have the ability to gather facts, develop angles, and write articles in a timely fashion in order to meet deadlines. There are morning, noon, and evening papers.

Reporters may work various hours depending on their assigned shifts. They often work overtime to finish a story or to meet with people for interviews or investigative purposes. Depending on the specific publication, individuals are responsible to either their section editor or editor in chief.

Employment Opportunities

Reporters may work in general areas or may specialize in particular fields such as entertainment, sports, news, family, fashion, current events, health, politics, police beats, education, foreign affairs, theater, music, consumer affairs, education, business, and investigative reports.

Individuals can work full- or part-time in a variety of settings. These include:

- Daily newspapers
- Weekly newspapers
- Magazines (general)
- Magazines (specific subject)
- News magazines
- Trade journals

Earnings

Earnings for full-time reporters in print media can vary from approximately $13,000 to $150,000 or more annually. Variables include the type of publication and its geographic location, circulation, and prestige. Other factors include the reporter's experience, responsibilities, education, and reputation in the field.

Reporters with little or no experience working on small-town weeklies will have salaries ranging from approximately $13,000 to $22,000. Individuals with more experience employed by larger dailies, weeklies, trade journals, or magazines can have earnings between $21,000 and $40,000. Very experienced reporters working on major metropolitan newspapers and nationally-known magazines can have annual earnings of $85,000. Well-known columnists can earn $150,000-plus.

Advancement Opportunities

Reporters in print media can advance their careers in a number of ways. Individuals with experience may be assigned more interesting or important stories. Others may locate similar positions with larger or more prestigious newspapers, magazines, or journals.

Some reporters become either section editors or editors for an entire publication. There are also a great many print reporters and journalists who move into the broadcast field.

Education and Training

Educational requirements vary for reporters in print media. There are many small-town weeklies that may only require a high school diploma. Associate degree programs in community and junior colleges offer majors in journalism.

For individuals interested in advancement, a minimum of a bachelor's degree is recommended. Good majors to choose include journalism, communications, English, and liberal arts. Courses and workshops in writing, journalism, reporting, editing, photography, and communications will all be valuable.

Experience and Qualifications

Experience requirements vary for reporters depending on the specific job. Positions at small-town weeklies are often entry-level and provide good experience. Other opportunities can be obtained by working on high school and college newspapers and literary magazines, and by writing columns for local newspapers. Internships also offer valuable experience. Generally, the larger and more prestigious a publication, the more experience is required.

Successful reporters are excellent writers with an ability to write quickly, clearly, creatively, and factually. They must have the ability to see unique ways of writing the same story that others are handling for competitive papers.

For Additional Information: Individuals interested in learning more about careers in print journalism can contact the American Publishers Association Foundation (APAF), the Community College Journalism Association (CCJA), the Newspaper

Guild (NG), the Accrediting Council on Education in Journalism and Mass Communications (ACEJMC), the Dow Jones Newspaper Fund, and the National Newspaper Association (NNA).

TIPS

- Positions in this field are advertised in the newspaper classified or display sections under such headings as "Writer," "Reporter," "Journalist," "Columnist," and "Correspondent."
- Get experience by becoming involved with your high school or college newspaper. If you are out of school, offer to write a column, sports news, or entertainment reviews for a local newspaper.
- Another way to obtain experience as well as get your foot in the door is by becoming a "stringer." A stringer is a freelance writer who develops or writes a story on speculation in hopes that a newspaper or magazine will buy it. On occasion, stringers are also assigned stories so that the publication does not have to send a reporter to the scene.
- Internships provide valuable experience. You can often locate one through your local newspaper, colleges, universities, larger newspapers or magazines, and trade associations.
- Put together a portfolio of your best writing samples. Bring copies of samples to interviews or send copies with your resume when applying for a job.
- It is easier to obtain a position with a small-town weekly or a suburban newspaper. Apply for a position with a larger newspaper or magazine after you have some experience under your belt.

ENTERTAINMENT JOURNALIST—PRINT

Job Description: Develop and write articles, columns, and/or feature stories about entertainment events, people, and news; attend entertainment events; review concerts, plays, movies, TV shows, recordings, theatrical productions, etc., for newspapers, magazines, and other print media.

Earnings: $11,000–$1 million-plus

Recommended Education and Training: Bachelor's degree in journalism, communications, English, or liberal arts recommended.

Skills and Personality Traits: Excellent writing skills; good command of the English language; creativity; objectivity.

Experience and Qualifications: Journalism experience helpful, but not always required.

Job Description and Responsibilities

Entertainment journalists and critics working in print media write about entertainment events, performances, happenings, and people. The critics attend entertainment events and review them.

Specific responsibilities of entertainment journalists or reporters will vary depending on the size, structure, and type of publication for which the individual works. As a rule, the smaller the publication, the more general the journalist's duties. Responsibilities become more specialized for those working in larger or more prestigious publications. Individuals may also specialize in writing about a particular branch of entertainment such as music, theater, television, film, or dance.

Entertainment journalists may either be assigned stories, receive tips, or develop story ideas on their own. These individuals will be expected to write interesting, factual, and creative articles with unique angles. The difference between a story that no one remembers and the one that no one can forget is often the angle that the journalist used when developing and writing it.

Entertainment journalists, like others in the reporting field, must gather relevant information through interviews, tips, and leads. They are responsible for thoroughly checking information for accuracy. While this is important in other forms of reporting, accuracy in entertainment news is essential. There is such a great interest in the entertainment industry and in those involved in it that news travels far and wide. Inaccurate information must quickly be uncovered and corrected. Entertainment journalists who make errors on a consistent basis will not be tolerated by most publications.

Responsibilities may also include reviewing or critiquing concerts, plays, movies, TV shows, musical recordings, etc., for the publication.

Entertainment journalists may write stories about national or international entertainment news. Individuals working for newspapers might also be asked to write stories or features about entertainment events that will be coming to that particular area. To accomplish this, the journalist must review press kits, press releases, and other information that is made available to the media prior to the event. He or she might also call or meet people involved in the event for interviews. These individuals may include entertainers, managers, promoters, press agents, and public relations people. Excited fans might also be part of the interview process.

Entertainment journalists are expected to attend press conferences, opening parties, cocktail parties, and entertainment events as part of the job. Depending on the event, they may need to attend concerts, plays, ballets, operas, films, etc.

In some cases, the entertainment journalist may be expected to take photographs. In others, a photographer may work with the journalist.

One of the best things about a career in entertainment journalism is that individuals can live virtually anywhere in the country and still write about entertainment. While the big entertainment news is usually centered in cities such as New York and Los Angeles, people with an ability to network, research, and relate entertainment news to the local scene in an interesting and innovative manner may succeed anywhere.

Employment Opportunities

Entertainment journalists and critics in print media can work in a number of different employment settings. There is a fairly high turnover in this field as a result of people moving up the career ladder, searching for better jobs, and changing geographic locations. Opportunities in this field include:

- Weekly newspapers
- Daily newspapers
- Trade journals
- General interest magazines
- Entertainment-oriented magazines and newspapers

Earnings

Entertainment journalists working in print media can have annual earnings beginning at approximately $11,000 and ranging to $1 million-plus.

Determining factors include the experience, responsibilities, and professional reputation of the individual as well as the size, type, and geographic location of the specific publication.

Individuals working on a full-time basis for small-town weeklies will probably earn between $11,000 and $15,000. Salaries rise in relation to the size and circulation of the publication. Experienced journalists working for dailies in metropolitan areas will earn between $25,000 and $60,000. Entertainment journalists and critics may earn over $1 million dollars annually.

Advancement Opportunities

The most common way for entertainment journalists and critics working in print media to climb the career ladder is to find similar positions at larger, more prestigious publications. Some people in this field seek advancement opportunities by specializing in a particular type of entertainment such as music, theater, or films. Individuals may also advance their careers by moving into broadcast journalism as a critic or entertainment journalist.

Education and Training

A minimum of a bachelor's degree in journalism, communications, English, or liberal arts is recommended for those interested in a career in this field. While smaller publications may not have an educational requirement, in order to move up a degree will be necessary for larger, more competitive publications.

Courses related to music, dance, film, theater, and other performing arts will be helpful in understanding more about these media.

Seminars, courses, and workshops in all varieties of writing and journalism will be useful in honing skills.

Experience and Qualifications

While there are some entry-level positions in this field requiring little or no experience, to compete in the work force individuals should have writing experience.

Working on a school or college newspaper is a beginning. Summer or part-time jobs in newspapers or magazines will also be helpful. Internships are another method of obtaining much-needed experience.

Individuals should be excellent writers with a great interest in entertainment. Objectivity is necessary when reviewing or critiquing performances. The ability to cultivate contacts in the entertainment industry is a big plus.

For Additional Information: To find out more about a career as an entertainment journalist, reviewer, or critic, contact the Music Critics Association (MCA), the New York Drama Critics Circle (NYDCC), the Outer Critics Circle (OCC), the American Theatre Critics Association (ATCA), and the National Critics Institute (NCI).

Other organizations and trade associations that may provide information include the American Newspaper Publishers Association Foundation (ANPAF), the Community College Journalism Association (CCJA), the Newspaper Guild (NG), the Accrediting Council on Education in Journalism and Mass Communications (ACEJMC), the Association for Education in Journalism and Mass Communications (AEJMC), and the National Newspaper Association (NNA).

TIPS

- Become involved with your school's newspaper or literary magazine. Request assignments reviewing both entertainment events at school and those in the community. Write articles about entertainment-oriented subjects. Get as much experience as you can.
- Contact your local newspaper and see if they are interested in a weekly column on entertainment. While this may not pay very well, it will give you an entry into entertainment journalism.
- You might also contact one or more newspapers or magazines in your area to see if they would be interested in using you as a freelance critic.
- Positions in this field are advertised in the newspaper classified section under such headings as "Writer," "Journalist," "Entertainment Writer," "Critic," "Reviewer," "Music," "Theater," "Dance," and "Performing Arts."
- Locate an internship in the entertainment department of a newspaper or an entertainment-oriented magazine.
- Put together a portfolio of your best writing samples. Send copies along with your resume and a short cover letter to the entertainment editors of publications you are interested in working for.
- You might have to work in a different department of a newspaper or magazine in order to get your foot in the door. Once you have a job in journalism and obtain professional experience, it is often easier to find the job you want.

APPENDIX I
Trade Associations, Unions, and Other Organizations
· ·

The following is a list of trade associations, unions, and organizations mentioned in the "For Additional Information" section of each job entry. There are also a number of other associations listed that might be useful in obtaining information on the jobs discussed in this book.

Many of the organizations have branch offices located throughout the country. Organization headquarters will usually provide the phone number and address of the closest local branch.

Academy of Country Music (ACM)
6255 Sunset Boulevard, Suite 923
Hollywood, CA 90028
(213) 462-2351

Academy of Television Arts and Sciences (ATAS)
5220 Lankershim Boulevard
North Hollywood, CA 91601
(818) 754-2800

Accrediting Council on Education in Journalism and Mass Communications (ACEJMC)
School of Journalism
University of Kansas
Lawrence, KS 66045
(913) 864-3973

Actors' Equity Association-Equity (AEA)
165 West 46th Street
New York, NY 10036
(212) 869-8530

Actors Studio (AS)
423 West 44th Street
New York, NY 10036
(212) 757-0870

Actors Working for an Actors Guild (AWAG)
12842 Hortense Street
Studio City, CA 91604
(818) 506-6672

Alliance of Resident Theatres/New York (ART/NY)
131 Varick Street
Room 904
New York, NY 10013
(212) 989-5257

American Advertising Federation (AAF)
1101 Vermont Avenue NW
Suite 500
Washington, DC 20005
(202) 898-0089

American Alliance for Theatre and Education (AATE)
State University
Theatre Department
Tempe, AZ 85287
(602) 965-6064

American Association of Community Theatre (AACT)
c/o L. Ross Rowland
8209 North Costa Mesa Drive
Muncie, IN 47303
(312) 288-0144

American Ballet Competition (ABC)
Box 328
Philadelphia, PA 19105
(215) 829-9800

American Composers Alliance
170 West 74th Street
New York, NY 10023
(212) 362-8900

American Dance Festival (ADF)
Box 6097, College Station
Durham, NC 27708
(919) 684-6402

American Dance Guild (ADG)
31 West 21st Street
New York, NY 10010
(212) 627-3790

American Federation of Musicians (AFM)
1501 Broadway
Suite 600
New York, NY 10036
(212) 869-1330

American Federation of Television and Radio Artists (AFTRA)
260 Madison Avenue
New York, NY 10016
(212) 532-0800

American Film Institute (AFI)
John F. Kennedy Center for the
 Performing Arts
Washington, DC 20566
(202) 828-4000

American Guild of Authors and Composers (AGAC)
(see The Songwriters Guild)

American Guild of Music (AGM)
5354 Washington Street
Downers Grove, IL 60515
(312) 968-0173

American Guild of Musical Artists (AGMA)
1727 Broadway
New York, NY 10019
(212) 265-3687

American Guild of Variety Artists (AGVA)
184 Fifth Avenue
New York, NY 10010
(212) 675-1003

American Institute of Certified Public Accountants (AICPA)
1211 Avenue of the Americas
New York, NY 10036
(212) 575-6200

American Library Association (ALA)
50 East Huron Street
Chicago, IL 60611
(312) 944-6780

American Marketing Association (AMA)
250 South Wacker Drive
Suite 200
Chicago, IL 60606
(312) 648-0536

American Meteorological Society (AMS)
45 Beacon Street
Boston, MA 02108
(617) 227-2425

American Music Center (AMC)
30 West 26th Street
Suite 1001
New York, NY 10010
(212) 366-5260

American Music Conference (AMC)
5140 Avenida Encinas
Carlsbad, CA 92008
(619) 431-9124

**American Music Festival
Association (AMFA)**
2430 West Broadway
Anaheim, CA 92804
(714) 826-1374

**American Music Scholarship
Association (AMSA)**
1826 Carew Tower
Cincinnati, OH 45263
(513) 421-5342

**American Newspaper Publishers
Association Foundation (ANPAF)**
(see The Newspaper Association of
America Foundation)

American Place Theatre (APT)
111 West 46th Street
New York, NY 10036
(212) 840-2960

American Publicist Guild (APG)
13415 Ventura Boulevard
Sherman Oaks, CA 91423
(213) 995-3329

**American Society of
Cinematographers (ASC)**
1782 North Orange Drive
Hollywood, CA 90028
(213) 969-4333

**American Society of Composers and
Publishers (ASCAP)**
1 Lincoln Plaza
New York, NY 10023
(212) 595-3050

**American Society of Journalists and
Authors, Inc. (ASJA)**
1501 Broadway
New York, NY 10036
(212) 997-0947

**American Society of Music
Arrangers (ASMA)**
P.O. Box 11
Hollywood, CA 90078
(213) 658-5997

**American Society of Music
Copyists (ASMC)**
Box 2557
Times Square Station
New York, NY 10108
(212) 586-2140

**American Sportscasters Association
(ASA)**
5 Beekman Street
Suite 814
New York, NY 10038
(212) 227-8080

**American Symphony Orchestra
League (ASOL)**
777 14th Street, NW
Washington, DC 20005
(202) 628-0099

**American Theatre Arts For Youth
(ATAFY)**
1429 Walnut Street
Philadelphia, PA 19102
(215) 563-3501

**American Theatre Critics
Association (ATCA)**
c/o Clara Hieronymus
The Tennessean
2200 Hemingway Drive
Nashville, TN 37215
(615) 665-0595

**American Women in Radio and
Television (AWRT)**
1101 Connecticut Avenue, NW
Suite 700
Washington, DC 20036
(202) 429-5102

American Writers Theatre Foundation (AWTF)
145 West 46th Street
New York, NY 10036
(212) 869-9770

Associated Actors and Artists of America (AAAA)
165 West 46th Street
New York, NY 10036
(212) 869-0358

Associated Councils for the Arts
1285 Avenue of the Americas
New York, NY 10019
(212) 245-4510

Association for Education in Journalism and Mass Communications (AEJMC)
College of Journalism
1621 College Street
University of South Carolina
Columbia, SC 29208
(803) 777-2005

Association of Entertainers (AE)
P.O. Box 1393
Washington, DC 20013
(202) 546-1919

Association of Theatrical Press Agents and Managers (ATPAM), AFL-CIO
165 West 46th Street
New York, NY 10036
(212) 719-3666

Authors Guild (AG)
330 West 42nd Street
New York, NY 10036
(212) 563-5904

Ballet Theatre Foundation (BTF)
890 Broadway
New York, NY 10003
(212) 477-3030

Broadcast Education Association (BEA)
1771 N Street NW
Washington, DC 20036
(202) 429-5355

Broadcast Music, Inc. (BMI)
320 West 57th Street
New York, NY 10019
(212) 586-2000

Broadcast Promotion and Marketing Executives, Inc. (BPME)
6255 Sunset Boulevard
Suite 624
Los Angeles, CA 90028
(213) 465-3777

Broadcaster's Promotion Association (BPA)
402 East Orange Streeet
Lancaster, PA 17602
(717) 397-5727

Casting Society of America (CSA)
311 West 43rd Street
Suite 700
New York, NY 10012
(212) 473-3400

Central Opera Service (COS)
(now part of Opera America)
777 14th Street NW
Suite 520
Washington, DC 20005
(202) 347-9262

Choreographers Guild (CG)
256 South Robertson
Beverly Hills, CA 90211
(213) 275-2533

Choreographers Theatre (CT)
94 Chambers Street
New York, NY 10007
(212) 227-9067

Community College Journalism Association (CCJA)
County College of Morris
Route 10 and Center Grove Road
Randolf, NJ 07869
(201) 361-5000

Concert Artists Guild (CAG)
850 Seventh Avenue
Room 1003
New York, NY 10019
(212) 333-5200

Conference of Personal Managers (National)
210 East 51st Street
New York, NY 10022
(212) 421-2670

Corporation for Public Broadcasting (CPB)
910 E Street NW
Washington, DC 20004
(202) 879-9600

Cosmetologists Association
1811 Monroe
Dearborn, MI 48124
(313) 563-0360

Costume Designers Guild (CDG)
13949 Ventura Boulevard
Sherman Oaks, CA 91423
(818) 905-1557

Country Dance and Song Society of America (CDSSA)
17 New South Street
Northampton, MA 01060
(413) 584-9913

Country Music Association (CMA)
P.O. Box 22299
One Music Circle South
Nashville, TN 37203
(615) 244-2840

Dance Critics Association (DCA)
P.O. Box 1882
Old Chelsea Station
New York, NY 10011

Dance Films Association (DFA)
1133 Broadway
Room 507
New York, NY 10010
(212) 727-0764

Dance Magazine Foundation (DMF)
33 West 60th Street
New York, NY 10023
(212) 245-9050

Directors Guild of America (DGA)
7920 Sunset Boulevard
Hollywood, CA 90046
(213) 289-2000

Directors Guild of America (DGA)
110 West 57th Street
New York, NY 10019
(212) 581-0370

Dow Jones Newspaper Fund
P.O. Box 300
Princeton, NJ 08543
(609) 452-2820

Dramatists Guild (DG)
234 West 44th Street
New York, NY 10036
(212) 398-9366

Friars Club (FC)
57 East 55th Street
New York, NY 10022
(212) 751-7272

Gospel Music Association (GMA)
P.O. Box 23201
Nashville, TN 37202
(615) 242-0303

Gospel Music Workshop of America (GMWA)
3908 West Warren Street
Detroit, MI 48208
(313) 898-2340

Hollywood Comedy Club (HCC)
c/o Jimmy Val Gray
649 North Rossmore Avenue
Los Angeles, CA 90004
(213) 467-4772

**Institute for Advanced Studies in
the Theatre Arts (IASTA)**
310 West 56th Street
New York, NY 10019
(212) 581-3133

Institute of Outdoor Drama (IOD)
University of North Carolina
CB 3240 Nations Bank Plaza
Chapel Hill, NC 27599
(919) 962-1328

**Institute of the American Musical
(IAM)**
121 North Detroit Street
Los Angeles, CA 90036
(213) 934-1221

**International Alliance of Theatrical
Stage Employees and Moving
Picture Machine Operators of the
U.S. and Canada (IATSE)**
1515 Broadway
Suite 601
New York, NY 10036
(212) 730-1770

**International Alliance of Theatrical
Stage Employees and Moving
Picture Machine Operators of the
U.S. and Canada (IATSE)**
14724 Ventura Boulevard
PH Suite
Sherman Oaks, CA 91403
(818) 905-8999

**International Alliance of Theatrical
Stage Employees (IATSE)**
Local 33 IATSE
1720 West Magnolia Boulevard
Burbank, CA 91506
(818) 841-9233

**International Association of
Auditorium Managers (IAAM)**
4425 West Airport Freeway
Irving, TX 75062
(214) 255-8020

**International Association of
Independent Producers (IAIP)**
P.O. Box 2801
Washington, DC 20013
(202) 775-1113

**International Boxing Federation
(IBF)**
134 Evergreen Place
East Orange, NJ 07018
(201) 414-0300

**International Brotherhood of
Electrical Workers (IBEW)**
1125 15th Street NW
Washington, DC 20005
(202) 833-7000

**International Conference of
Symphony and Opera Musicians
(ICSOM)**
6607 Waterman
St. Louis, MO 63130
(314) 863-0633

**International Theatre Institute of
the United States (ITI/US)**
220 West 42nd Street
Suite 1710
New York, NY 10036
(212) 944-1490

**International Theatrical Agencies
Association (ITAA)**
3900 Lemon
Dallas, TX 75219
(214) 582-8112

**League of American Theatres and
Producers (LATP)**
226 West 47th Street
New York, NY 10036
(212) 764-1122

League of Off-Broadway Theatres and Producers (LOBTP)
c/o George Elmer Productions, Ltd.
130 West 42nd Street
Suite 1300
New York, NY 10036
(212) 730-7130

League Of Resident Theaters (LORT)
c/o Harry Weintraub
1501 Broadway
Suite 2401
New York, NY 10036
(212) 944-1501

Makeup and Hairstylist Local 798
31 West 21st Street
New York, NY 10010
(212) 627-0660

Makeup and Hairstylist Local 706
11519 Chandler Boulevard
North Hollywood, CA 91601
(818) 984-1700

Meet The Composer (MTC)
2112 Broadway
Suite 505
New York, NY 10023
(212) 787-3601

Metropolitan Opera Association (MOA)
Lincoln Center
New York, NY 10023
(212) 799-3100

Metropolitan Opera Guild (MOG)
70 Lincoln Center Plaza
New York, NY 10023
(212) 769-7000

Modeling Association of America International (MAAI)
2110 Central Park South
Suite 14-C
New York, NY 10019
(212) 753-1555

Motion Picture Association of America, Inc.
1600 Eye Street NW
Washington, DC 20006
(202) 293-1966

Motion Picture Costumers
Local 705, IATSE, MPMO
1427 North La Brea Avenue
Hollywood, CA 90028
(213) 851-0220

Music Critics Association (MCA)
7 Pine Court
Westfield, NJ 07090
(908) 233-8468

Music Educators National Conference (MENC)
1902 Association Drive
Reston, VA 22091
(703) 860-4000

Music Publishers Association (MPA)
205 East 42nd Street
New York, NY 10017
(212) 582-1122

Nashville Entertainment Association (NEA)
P.O. Box 121948
Nashville, TN 37212
(615) 327-4308

Nashville Songwriters Association, International (NSAI)
15 Music Square West
Nashville, TN 37203
(615) 256-3354

National Academy of Popular Music (NAPM)
885 Second Avenue
New York, NY 10017
(212) 593-1685

National Academy of Recording Arts and Sciences (NARAS)
303 N Glen Oaks Boulevard
Burbank, CA 91502
(213) 849-1313

National Academy of Songwriters (NAS)
6381 Hollywood Boulevard
Suite 780
Hollywood, CA 90028
(213) 463-7178

National Academy of Television Arts and Sciences (NATAS)
111 West 57th Street
New York, NY 10019
(212) 586-8424

National Association of Accountants (NAA)
10 Paragon Drive
Montvale, NJ 07645
(201) 573-9000

National Association of Broadcast Employees and Technicians (NABET)
7101 Wisconsin Avenue, Suite 800
Bethesda, MD 20814
(301) 657-8420

National Association of Broadcasters (NAB)
1771 N Street NW
Washington, DC 20036
(202) 429-5300

National Association of Composers, U.S.A. (NACUSA)
Box 49652
Barrington Station
Los Angeles, CA 90049
(213) 541-8213

National Association of Schools of Theatre (NAST)
11250 Roger Bacon Drive, No. 5
Reston, VA 22090
(703) 437-0700

National Association of Television Program Executives (NATPE)
2425 Olympic Boulevard
Suite 550E
Los Angeles, CA 90404
(310) 453-4440

National Cable Television Association, Inc. (NCTA)
1724 Massachusetts Avenue NW
Washington, DC 20036
(202) 775-3550

National Critics Institute (NCI)
c/o Ernest Schier
Eugene O'Neill Theater Center
234 West 44th Street
New York, NY 10036
(212) 382-2790

National Dance Association (NDA)
1900 Association Drive
Reston, VA 22091
(703) 476-3436

National Dance Council of America (NDCA)
P.O. Box 2432
Vienna, VA 22183
(703) 281-1581

National Dance Institute (NDI)
594 Broadway
New York, NY 10012
(212) 226-0083

National Federation of Music Clubs (NFMC)
1336 N Delaware Street
Indianapolis, IN 46202
(317) 683-4003

National Federation of Press Women (NFPW)
1105 Main Street
Box 99
Blue Springs, MO 64013
(816) 229-1666

**National Hairdressers and
Cosmetologists Association
(NHCA)**
3510 Olive Street
St. Louis, MO 63103
(314) 534-7980

National Mime Association (NMA)
(now called National Movement
Theatre Association)

**National Movement Theatre
Association (NMTA)**
Pontine Movement Theatre
Porstmouth, NH 03801
(603) 436-6660

**National Music Publishers
Association (NMPA)**
205 East 42nd Street
New York, NY 10017
(212) 370-5330

**National Newspaper Association
(NNA)**
1627 K Street NW
Suite 400
Washington, DC 20006
(202) 466-7200

National Opera Association (NOA)
c/o Robert Murray
212 Texas Street
Shrevesport, LA 71101

**National Orchestral Association
(NOA)**
474 Riverside Drive
Room 455
New York, NY 10115
(212) 870-2009

**National Playwrights Conference
(NPC)**
234 West 44th Street
Suite 901
New York, NY 10036
(212) 382-2790

National Press Club (NPC)
National Press Building
529 14th Street NW
Room 1386
Washington, DC 20045
(202) 662-7500

**National Press Photographers
Association (NPPA)**
3200 Croasdaile Drive
Suite 306
Durham, NC 27705
(919) 383-7246

**National Society of Public
Accountants (NSPA)**
1010 North Fairfax Street
Alexandria, VA 22314
(703) 549-6400

**National Songwriters Association
International (NSAI)**
803 18th Avenue S
Nashville, TN 37203
(615) 321-5004

**National Sportscasters and
Sportswriters Association (NSSA)**
Box 559
Salisbury, NC 28144
(703) 633-4275

**National Symphony Orchestra
Association (NSOA)**
JFK Center for the Performing Arts
Washington, DC 20566
(202) 785-8100

National Theatre Conference (NTC)
c/o Barry Witham
University of Washington
School of Drama
DX-20
Seattle, WA 98195
(206) 543-5140

National Theatre Institute (NTI)
305 Great Neck Road
Waterford, CT 06385
(203) 443-7139

New Dramatists (ND)
424 West 44th Street
New York, NY 10036
(212) 757-6960

Newspaper Association of America
Foundation (NAAF)
11600 Sunrise Valley Drive
Reston, VA 20041
(703) 648-1000

New York Drama Critics Circle
(NYDCC)
c/o Michael Kuchware
Associated Press
50 Rockefeller Plaza
New York, NY 10020
(212) 621-1841

Opera America
777 14th Street, NW
Suite 520
Washington, DC 20005
(202) 347-9262

Organization of Professional Acting
Coaches and Teachers (OPACT)
3968 Eureka Drive
Studio City, CA 91604
(213) 877-4988

Outer Critics Circle (OCC)
c/o Marjorie Gunner
101 West 57th Street
New York, NY 10019
(212) 765-8557

Producers Group (PG)
630 9th Avenue
Suite 808
New York, NY 10016
(212) 581-4483

Producers Guild of America (PGA)
400 South Beverly Drive
Beverly Hills, CA 90012
(213) 557-0807

Public Broadcasting Service (PBS)
1320 Braddock Place
Alexandria, VA 22314
(703) 739-5000

Public Relations Society of
America (PRSA)
33 Irving Place
New York, NY 10003
(212) 995-2230

Public Relations Student Society of
America (PRSSA)
33 Irving Place
New York, NY 10003
(212) 995-2230

Radio Advertising Bureau (RAB)
304 Park Avenue South
New York, NY 10010
(212) 387-2100

Radio-Television News Directors
Association (RTNDA)
1000 Connecticut Avenue NW
Suite 615
Washington, DC 20006
(202) 659-6510

Recording Industry Association of
America (RIAA)
1020 19th Street NW
Suite 200
Washington, DC 20036
(202) 775-0101

Recording Institute of America
(RIA)
15 Columbus Circle
New York, NY 10023
(212) 582-0400

Screen Actors Guild (SAG)
7065 Hollywood Blvd.
Hollywood, CA 90028
(213) 465-4600

Screen Composers of America (SCA)
2451 Nichols Canyon
Los Angeles, CA 90046
(213) 876-6040

Screen Extras Guild (SEG)
3629 Cahuenga Blvd. W
Los Angeles, CA 90068
(213) 851-4301

SESAC, Inc.
10 Columbus Circle
New York, NY 10019
(212) 586-3450

Set Designers & Model Makers
Local 847, IATSE
14724 Ventura Boulevard, PH-B
Sherman Oaks, CA 91403
(818) 784-6555

Shriners
P.O. Box 31356
Tampa, FL 33631
(813) 281-0300

Society of American Fight Directors (SAFD)
1834 Camp Avenue
Rockford, IL 61103
(815) 962-6579

Society of Professional Audio Recording Studios (SPARS)
4300 Tenth Avenue North
Lake Worth, FL 33461
(305) 641-6648

Society of Professional Journalists (SPJ)
16 South Jackson
Greencastle, IN 46135
(317) 653-3333

Society of Stage Directors and Choreographers (SSDC)
1501 Broadway, 31st Floor
New York, NY 10036
(212) 391-1070

Special Libraries Association (SLA)
1700 18th Street, NW
Washington, DC 20009
(202) 234-4700

The American Mime Theatre (TAMT)
24 Bond Street
New York, NY 10012
(212) 777-1710

The Newspaper Guild (TNG)
8611 Second Avenue
Silver Springs, MD 20912
(301) 585-2990

The Songwriters Guild
276 Fifth Avenue
New York, NY 10001
(212) 686-6820

Theatre Authority (TA)
16 East 42nd Street
Suite 202
New York, NY 10017
(212) 682-4215

Theatre Committee for Eugene O'Neill (TCEO)
c/o Eugene O'Neill Theater Center
234 West 44th Street
New York, NY 10036
(212) 382-2790

Theatre Guild (TG)
226 West 47th Street
New York, NY 10036
(212) 869-5470

Touring Entertainment Industry Association (TEIA)
1203 Lake Street
Fort Worth, TX 76102
(817) 338-9444

United Scenic Artists (USA)
575 Eighth Avenue
New York, NY 10018
(212) 736-4498

University Resident Theatre Association (URTA)
1560 Broadway
Suite 801
New York, NY 10036
(212) 221-1130

Up With People (UWP)
3103 North Campbell Avenue
Tucson, AZ 85719
(602) 327-7351

U.S. Institute for Theatre Technology (USITT)
10 West 19th Street, Suite 5A
New York, NY 10010
(212) 924-9088

Women In Communications, Inc. (WICI)
2101 Wilson Boulevard
Suite 417
Arlington, VA 22201
(703) 528-4299

World Boxing Commission (WBC)
Genova 33-DESP 503
Mexico D.F. 06600 Mexico
(905) 525-3787

World Boxing Organization (WBO)
c/o Nick P. Erasiotis
412 Colorado Avenue
Aurora, IL 60506
(312) 897-4765

World Championship Wrestling
C.N.N. Plaza 105366
Atlanta, GA 30348
(404) 827-2066

World Modeling Association (WMA)
4401 San Pedro Drive NE
No. 810
Albuquerque, NM 87109
(505) 883-2823

World Wrestling Federation (WWF)
1055 Summers
P.O. Box 3857
Stamford, CT 06905
(203) 352-8600

Writers Guild of America East (WGA)
555 West 57th Street
New York, NY 10019
(212) 245-6180

Writers Guild of America West (WGA)
8955 Beverly Blvd.
West Hollywood, CA 90048
(213) 550-1000

APPENDIX II
Network and Cable Television Stations
· ·

The following is a list of network and cable television station addresses. This list only includes the major networks, independents, and the larger cable stations. Your local television guide can give you additional information on other stations in your area.

ABC Television
47 West 66th Street
New York, NY 10023

A & E Entertainment Network
235 East 45th Street
New York, NY 10017

BET (Black Entertainment Television)
1232 31st Street NW
Washington, DC 20007

CBS Television
51 West 52nd Street
New York, NY 10019

CMT (Country Music Television)
2806 Opryland Drive
Nashville, TN 37214

CNBC
2200 Fletcher Avenue
Fort Lee, NJ 07024

CNN
One CNN Center
P.O. Box 1053665
Atlanta, GA 30348

Disney Channel
3800 West Alameda Avenue
Burbank, CA 91505

ESPN
ESPN Plaza
Bristol, CT 06010

Fox Television
205 East 67th Street
New York, NY 10021

HBO
1100 Avenue of the Americas
New York, NY 10036

Madison Square Garden (MSG)
4 Penn Plaza
New York, NY 10001

MTV (Music Television)
1515 Broadway
New York, NY 10036

NBC
30 Rockefeller Plaza
New York, NY 10020

Nickelodeon
1515 Broadway
New York, NY 10036

Public Broadcasting Service (PBS)
1320 Braddock Place
Alexandra, VA 22314

Showtime
1633 Broadway
New York, NY 10019

Sports Channel
100 Crossways Park West
Woodbury, NY 11797

TBS
1050 Techwood Drive NW
Atlanta, GA 38318

TNT
One CNN Center
Box 105366
Atlanta, GA 30438

APPENDIX III
Entertainment Trades
· · · · · · · · · · · · · · · · · · ·

The following is a list of the names and addresses of the major entertainment trade publications.

Back Stage
330 West 42nd Street
New York, NY 10036

Billboard
Billboard Publications
1515 Broadway
New York, NY 10036

Cashbox
6363 Sunset Boulevard
Hollywood, CA 90028

Daily Variety
1400 North Cahuenga Boulevard
Hollywood, CA 90028

Hollywood Reporter
6715 Sunset Boulevard
Hollywood, CA 90028

Radio and Records
1930 Century Park West
Los Angeles, CA 90067

The Friday Morning Quarterback
Cherry Hill Plaza
1415 East Marlton Pike
Cherry Hill, NJ 08034

Variety
154 West 46th Street
New York, NY 10036